"Robert Wilder doesn't just need a drink, he deserves one, for writing the funniest, most irreverent book about parenting in recent memory. [This is] an affectionate, wickedly observant, unexpectedly tender account of one man's sleepless journey through the brave new world of diapers, toy trains, and very smelly snowman suits."
—Tom Perrotta, bestselling author of *The Abstinence Teacher*

"Funnier, snappier, and more creative in its parenting wisdom than I'd have been myself . . . This collection has enough heart and wit to win over most readers. . . . Even if your husband or father or brother isn't much of a reader, *Daddy Needs a Drink* would be sure to make him laugh come Father's Day." —*Cleveland Plain Dealer*

"I know, as a dad, I reached for [this book] without even consciously making the decision, like a moth drawn inexorably to the flame."
—*Tampa Tribune*

"Hilarious . . . By turns wild, raunchy, and funny, Wilder's parenting observations are like Erma Bombeck on steroids."
—*New Mexico Magazine*

"Witty and extremely humorous . . . Wilder writes about the experience as if you were there . . . simply hysterical. I tried reading it to my wife but was unable to finish through the tears of laughter. . . . Rarely have I read a laugh-out-loud book like this. I certainly recommend it to all men who've been through the parenting experience or are about to be."
—*Wichita Falls (TX) Times Record News*

"His take on parenthood is refreshingly candid enough to make this a read that's more fun than reaching for the wine rack."
—*Charleston (SC) Post and Courier*

"*Daddy Needs a Drink* cuts through the sentimentalism of parenthood and smacks into the chaos that children bring to an adult's life. It's hilarious, loving and refreshing."
—Parentworld.com

"Truly hilarious . . . [Rob is] a sharp observer. He has one eye focused on detail, the other on irony." —*Westport (CT) News*

Also by Robert Wilder

Daddy Needs a Drink

Robert Wilder

Tales
from the
Teachers'
Lounge

What I Learned in School the Second Time
Around—One Man's Irreverent Look at
Being a Teacher

Delta Trade Paperbacks

TALES FROM THE TEACHERS' LOUNGE
A Delta Book

PUBLISHING HISTORY
Delacorte Press hardcover edition published September 2007
Delta Trade Paperback edition / September 2008

Published by
Bantam Dell
A Division of Random House, Inc.
New York, New York

Book design by Carol Malcolm Russo

Library of Congress Catalog Card Number: 2007077437

ISBN 978-0-385-33928-5

Printed in the United States of America
Published simultaneously in Canada

www.bantamdell.com

BVG 10 9 8 7 6 5 4 3

a. For my father, Ben Franklin Wilder

b. In memory of my mother, Joan Helen Wittmer Wilder

c. For my students (past, present, and future)

d. For all those who choose to teach other people's children

e. All of the above

Contents

Part IV: **School Daze**

Part I:

The

Apprentice

Born with a Grimace

When people ask me how I became a teacher, I tell them my career literally crashed into me. I was twenty-six and had been in New Mexico for barely two years, and married for less than twelve months. Everything seemed fresh to me—my beautiful wife, Lala, the pale blue southwestern sky, even the crusty enchilada casserole I served waiting tables in the evenings. After leaving a hectic advertising job in New York City, my life seemed as simple as an inmate's wardrobe choices. Then, one day, I was visiting a friend who worked part time at a local hippie school. While we were talking, a boy tore around a corner and ran straight into my groinage. I doubled over while he hit the deck headfirst. Just as I'd always done with my younger brothers, I picked the kid up, brushed him off, and sent him on his way. I didn't ask him how he was feeling about our collision, or if he

needed to apologize to my bruised junk to create a sense of clo-
sure. We did no art therapy, aromatherapy, or *Real Boys* sharing
out. The head of the school had been watching from her window
and liked my simple, direct approach, which my friend translated later into *We desperately need a goddamn man around here.*
Even though I was waiting tables at night, I thought being a
teacher might be fun. I imagined a lot of picking up, brushing off,
and sending kids off to play in the fields of the bored. Obviously,
as any teacher sober or otherwise would tell you, I didn't know
shit.

And, as I learned later, if you teach in a private school, you
don't have to. Private schools don't require a certain number of
degrees or multitiered levels of certification the way the public
schools do, which was perfect for an uncertified guy like me. I
was assigned to be an assistant first-grade teacher in this alter-
native school on the southeast side of town. Classes were held in a
series of ramshackle adobe buildings with low ceilings adjacent
to a moldy greenhouse and a hardscrabble playground. Like any
hippie school worth its patchouli, we offered circle time and a
rabbit named Loveheart, and instead of saying grace, we sang
about the earth being a harbor, a garden, and a holy place, which
covered the mariners, horticulturists, and zealots among us.
Even though the school was founded on pursuing kindness and
peace, many of our students had felony-with-training-wheels
behavior patterns that had barred them from attending the local
public elementaries. Since this was my first teaching gig after a
short career in the backbiting business some call advertising, I
was eager to help these little critters learn to read and write and
do the kind of simple math even the actors from *Saved by the Bell*
could master. I imagined myself sitting next to a girl in pigtails,
helping her sound out *Dick and Jane* books. In this hippie haven, I

never saw the Janes, though, and dealt mostly with the dicks. While Carly*, the head teacher, was leading counting games using rods made from recycled organic materials, I was escorting Jack, a local ambulance chaser's son, to the bathroom to flush the giant turd he'd left for his classmates to view, and then rinse out the liquid soap he had kindly poured into all our drinking cups. Other days, I would try to coax a walrus-toothed kid named Elijah Muhammad into joining our circle instead of scowling at us from his scrotum-like throne on our only beanbag chair. This little baseborn Bartleby, however, preferred to do nothing most days but construct elaborate forts in thornbushes, swear under his incisor, and pendulate exclusively on the middle swing outside.

The freakiest student we had by far was a nine-year-old girl named Ray who was born to a crack-addict mother and immediately adopted by a man whose love for elaborate drapes and exotic sea salts made it apparent that he was probably playing for the wrong team. Today we would bandy about famous names for Ray's tangled and moist web of issues—Tourette's, Asperger's, Kanner's—but back then everyone just called this oddity with the short and uneven bangs "that girl."

At one of our first circle times that year, all the six- and seven-year-olds were gathered near the turquoise-tiled fireplace sharing their fear of fascism and wishes for renewable energy resources, but I couldn't help watching Ray because of her smorgasbord of twitches and tics. It was as if a violent video game had been implanted into her brain and her face was the exploding screen. Her eyes were never both open at the same time, and the side of her mouth always held a small balloon of air—ready to spit,

---

* Other than my close family and friends, I've changed the names and identities of people mentioned in this book.

whine, or bubble in some spasmodic sound effect. Maybe the other students were accustomed to Ray and kids like her, or they had their own inner twisted shit to contend with, but they basically ignored Ray until she jumped up and ran to the outside door screaming, "Watch out for the danger! Watch out for the danger!" Shaking her fist at the small glass window, she stamped her feet and then butted her head against the wood like a ram learning to count the hard way. Carly quietly asked me to handle it. I had absolutely no training dealing with crazies other than my three brothers, their sketchy friends, and the high-maintenance (read: bitchy) customers at the hotel restaurant where I worked at night. I didn't know what to do other than open the door and let this girl follow her batty-ass bliss. Once she caught a glimpse of daylight, Ray bolted out of there like a rabbit violated with a cattle prod. She scooted down the open stretch of dirt road in front of the school legs and arms akimbo—like the scarecrow's love child in *The Wizard of Oz*. Since I was chasing her, I guess that made me Margaret Hamilton sans broom, which, given my naturally squinty eyes and the way I wore my hair at the time, is a pretty fair comparison.

"Who's in danger, Ray?" I asked when I caught up with her and my breath. She'd stopped at the edge of a steep arroyo, the bank thickly lined with juniper and chamisa bushes.

"The deer," she said plainly, but pointed to the sky, then twirled around three times.

"Flying deer?"

"No, the mama and her babies." Ray's intonation seemed to suggest we had both been here before and I knew this family deerly. Her eyes spun around her head like she had bought them from a costume shop.

"Right," I said, rolling my own eyes.

Then she slipped down the elastic waistband of her pants and farted. "I have gases," she said, and shrugged.

"I can see that." I hung my head at my pathetic life. "Smell it too."

It became pretty clear that the bulk of my time would be spent escorting Ray, keeping her from running away to join an invisible family of elk or infringing on the other kids' low safety thresholds by screaming strange non sequiturs in their ears. Her little outbursts caused more than one girl to wet herself and aggravated the problems with Carly's already depleted immune system. Carly was the kind of mellow educator who prided herself on her ability to stay calm under all circumstances, and Ray's explosions put a dent in her goals and a bloody ulcer in her gut. As for me, each day with Ray started to feel more and more like the few disturbing times I'd dropped acid in college; here I was again, half a decade later, trying desperately not to let Ray become the Cheshire cat in my Go Ask Alice in Wonderland nightmare.

Even though Ray was at least two years older than the rest, she wasn't even close to first-grade level. She couldn't count past three, spell words other than her name, or articulate anything clearly except for this one phrase taken from *The Great Mouse Detective*, a video that her father admitted she'd watched more than a hundred times. Like a comedian who bases his or her act on general annoyance (read: Jeff Foxworthy), Ray found her catchphrase funnier every time she repeated it.

"Good morning, Ray." Carly would be on her knees, arms open wide, welcoming her student into our quiet and serene class environment.

"BYE-BYE, BASIL!" Ray would shout, doubling over in spittle-infused laughter.

"Would you like to color a petroglyph or push heirloom sand in the Zen garden?"

"BYE-BYE, BASIL!" She'd be flat on the floor by this time, gagging on her own giggles.

"Ray," Carly would whisper through clenched teeth, "it helps people when you react to what they are saying because . . ." She leaned closer, hoping to make an intimate connection to her lost sheep.

"BYE-BYE, BASIL!"

Carly would turn and call, "Rob?" which was my cue to drag the little one-hit hyena outside.

I don't know if it was Stockholm syndrome of the special ed variety, but all that time together established an oddly close relationship between my little Rain Girl and me. Even though I was completely exhausted and covered in various fluids and flakes of animal excrement by the end of the school day, we had still survived our own buddy movie, albeit a warped one. What made the situation even more like *Dumb and Dumber* was that shortly after I started teaching there, the hotel where I moonlighted demanded that I get my hair cut. I had prided myself on my long, rebellious Jesus mane and thought I'd done a good job slicking it back off my face with Vaseline, but the manager said I looked like I was sporting the helmet hairstyle of one of the Golden Girls. He put it plainly: I had to cut it or get another job. Pissed off, I stormed into Supercuts, closed my eyes, and had it all chopped off by a trainee who didn't know the sharp side from the dull on a pair of clippers. When I faced my new head in the mirror, I gasped. With my short bangs and uneven sides, I looked like an older, male version of Ray. On our decompression walks, with my new asylum hairdo, I'd often be mistaken for her father or older brother by the *On Golden Pond* neighbors strolling along that dirt road.

When a stranger initially pegs you as a relative of someone you're not sure you even like, you feel a bit unnerved by being grouped so intimately together. If people do it all the time, you grow weary of explaining, especially given the complicated bond I shared with Ray, so I just gave in and nodded along with the gross misconceptions. I was now this crazy little girl's bitch, plain and simple.

About a month into my work at the school, I was huddled with two other teachers, Holly and Agnes, on the playground, all three of us sneaking coffee in Dixie cups since caffeine had been outlawed by a New Age board who rolled their own tampons. We were discussing how that little fucker Loveheart was crapping all over the place and some of the slower kids were snacking on the pellets, mistaking them for raisins. Ray galloped over with her hands cupped together in front of her. We hid the shots of java behind our backs as if she cared or would have even noticed. She stood before me like a little Oliver Twisted wanting more gruel from me, but instead of begging, she was making an offering.

"Here, Rob." She had practiced saying my name clearly, which made me feel rather proud. She pushed her hand cocoon forward so it was about an inch from my chest. I expected to see a shiny rock or a stinkbug, maybe, an insect whose name alone never failed to make her laugh, but when she unhinged her hands, all three adults recoiled in horror.

"Oh my God!" Holly, the younger teacher, dropped her forbidden coffee from behind her back as though her water had just broken. Agnes, who'd been at the school for over ten years, calmly stepped back.

Resting in Ray's white palm was a perfectly formed human turd. She had somehow managed to neatly shit into her own hand just for little ol' me.

Holly spoke to Ray sternly in rapid-fire commands: "Forthe-loveofJesusRay, you go put that in the toilet and flush it twice, then you wash your hands in hot water with soap twice also, and if you ever, *ever* . . ." Holly escorted my charge into the sagging building without touching her. I prayed that Jack hadn't left his Yule log in the toilet like he did every other day.

"I think she loves you," Agnes said, and winked.

"What every teacher must dream of," I said, running to the bushes to throw up.

The gifting happened on a Friday, and I felt dizzy that evening during my entire shift at the hotel. I dreamed all night of serving elaborate five-course meals, each dish offering a different type of exotic animal dung. On Saturday, I thought I would be a good husband and visit my wife at Trader Jack's flea market, next to the Santa Fe Opera. We had been married for about a year, and Lala had just launched her art business at what locals called "the flea" because it was a cheap place to tout her wares. After I hung out with Lala at her booth, I strolled the aisles, passing the toothless guy who sold unsterilized probes, hooks, scalers, and mirrors so you could do your own thrifty dental work at home. Next to him were the Rasta beekeepers in a narrow space adjacent to a travel-ing band of albino Gypsies whose children and dogs were impos-sible to tell apart. In those days, before the flea was taken back by the tribe who owns the land, before the FBI raided the stolen pre-Columbian art, before loaded firearms were outlawed, it was a fun place to hang out. Kind of like a carnival sideshow where you could buy stuff directly from the Bearded Lady, the Pinhead, and a gun-toting, pissed-off Tiny Tim.

On the last aisle there stood a bleak booth with a handmade banner that read "Learn About the Method!" Under the sign, a guy in a wool cap kicked the dirt, his hands shoved deep into his pockets. On a folding table, stacks of sun-bleached papers languished next to small plastic bags so cloudy I couldn't see what was in them. I felt hung over even though I'd had nothing to drink the night before. All this weird shit was happening to me, and I wasn't exactly sure what to do about it. I had left a lucrative job in advertising in New York because I thought Santa Fe would offer the kind of personal freedom I couldn't get in the tight gridlock of the East and thought I might have found a new and noble calling: teaching. Instead of freedom for myself and inspiration for others, however, I was a guy with a prison haircut who collected turds during the day and lousy tips at night. So much for my fancy education and fresh life plan.

The guy in the booth didn't look at me directly or bother to introduce himself. He just started talking as if I had been standing there all day. "It all originated, some say, in Mesopotamia. The Great Goddess created people out of clay and infused them with life. If you think about it, it contains all the life-giving properties."

I glanced over my shoulder but, nope, I was the only one there. The guy had thin white scars along the lines where people usually get their deepest wrinkles.

"Some people called them witches, but the Egyptian pharaohs became divine that way, right?" He pointed to a bulletin board behind him, which hosted more papers with faded red circles and charts as unintelligible as the fuzzy time-travel math they did on that cheesy television show *Quantum Leap*.

I couldn't take it any longer. "What the hell are you talking about?"

"The method."

"What method?"

"That's the thing." He dropped his gaze to his old work boots, which seemed to be unearthing something from its clay tomb.

"Most people aren't comfortable talking about it, but Chinese sages and African tribes believed it had life giving properties. . . ."

I crept closer and held a plastic bag by its corner. What was inside looked like the head of a condom, only larger and crafted from the kind of thick rubber used to make toilet plungers.

"What's this?" I waved the bag at him.

"A menstrual cup."

"Holy Jesus!" I dropped the specimen and wiped my hands frantically on my jeans. "A what?"

"To collect the fluid." Maybe it was the perturbed look on my face or the fact that I was walking backward, but he started speaking quickly and waving his hands in the air. "I've seen cleft palates on babies cured by applying menstrual blood topically."

"You've seen that?" Next to the bag I'd dropped was another filled with tampons so dirty they looked like ancient firecrackers.

"People apply it on their faces and they hardly wrinkle. Mothers use it on their babies to keep their skin looking young."

I couldn't contain my disgust and started to gag.

"Some people ingest it—small amounts, mind you, but it makes sense if you think about it." He nodded thoughtfully. "All that embryonic life force, you know? Wait a sec." He ducked into the cab of his truck and pulled out a videotape sealed in a besmeared Ziploc bag. "Here."

He said "here" the exact same way Ray had the day before, so I turned around and scurried back to Lala like a frightened child to vomit in the Porta Potti behind her booth. When Lala asked me what was wrong, I just shuddered. How could I articulate a life where unbalanced children hand you shit in school and drifters want to give you bloody facials in the back of their pickups?

On Monday, I was still in a daze following Ray around as she went from her imaginary deer klatch to the trio of swings on the playground. She seemed pretty happy that morning; the venison weren't in as grave danger as the week before, and while her tics were noticeable, they were minimal in comparison to other poppin' and flinchin' times we'd shared. I started her off with an underdog push and then let her pump herself into a joyful lather. She sang a song that only she could understand, but that was fine by me. I didn't need to know the lyrics to hum autistically along. After a few minutes, Elijah Muhammad emerged like a troll from his thorny thicket and was waiting by Ray's side even though there was a swing available. Ray was parked on his favorite patch of rubber, and I was about to counsel Elijah to tuck in his tooth and test-drive the model on the left when I heard screaming behind me. Jack was holding a stick over his head like a midget samurai, ready to bring it down on his little sister's back again. Leaving monkey tails in the toilet must have lost its appeal for the little miscreant.

I ran over, yanked the stick out of his hand, and sent him to the head hippie's office. Rubbing his sister's back, I nudged her toward Agnes, who was half asleep monitoring the sandbox. When I turned back, everything seemed to be in slow motion.

"My swing!" Elijah demanded, whipping his arm out and clotheslining Ray across her chest. The swing spun, Ray screamed, and I ran like the Six Million Dollar Man, slow and bulky but with a most heroic mission. Here was the girl with the most issues in school on her happiest day, the student who cared enough to offer me feces from her own ass. I locked my arms around Elijah like an iron maiden, wary of his lethal walrus tooth, and carried him away. He squirmed in my arms and swore like Richard Pryor on fire. Looking back, I saw that from a safe distance Holly was consoling Ray, who had collapsed into a hysterical heap under the swings.

When I reached the director's office, she was busy scolding a slumping Jack. The sight of a teacher carrying a squirming and swearing kid into her office gave the head hippie pause. She excused Jack, who grinned happily and tore out of there before his captor could change her mind.

"Well, Elijah, what happened that would make Rob carry you in like that?" the director asked, her arms tucked loosely in front of her chest.

Elijah muttered like the gangster Rocky in a Bugs Bunny cartoon, grunting epithets from the "Why, I Oughta . . ." School of Thinly Veiled Threats.

I explained the scenario. Seeing no sign of remorse on the boy's torqued face, she said, "Better call the parents."

Ray was too upset to finish the day, so her dad left his life cabaret and picked her up. Elijah's parents came in, and we sat across from each other at one of the work areas in the classroom. A plastic tub of clay had been left in the middle of the table, and we all stared at it in silence as if that formless mass held some key to what was about to unfold. The father was tall and lean and wore rimless glasses and a ponytail gathered behind a nearly hairless head. The mother was frighteningly pale, with hair so black it was almost blue; she reminded me of Elvira without the benefits of a Wonderbra.

"I'm Elijah's dad." He offered me his hand, and I took it. When I stood up, I saw that someone had formed a cock and balls from the clay and tucked it into the corner of the tub. I pushed the basin to the far side of the table.

"Oh, what do you do?" I asked.

"I'm an organic domestic environmental energy consultant."

"What's that?"

"I'm working on ways to use our own human effluent to insulate and heat our homes."

"Figures," I said.

"I'm Elijah's mom, and I'm a Rolfer, but I also do past-life regression therapy." She tucked a wisp behind her ear. "Rolfing is—"

"Don't bother." I held my hand up. "I'm good."

The director entered and explained that we were meeting to discuss the incident on the playground, and she asked me to speak first. I calmly relayed the stiff-arm by their son and how I'd handled it. I left out the walrus tooth, their bad taste in haircuts, and the boy's potty mouth, though given the dad's profession, that made much more sense to me now.

The mother closed her eyes and placed her hands palms up on the table while the father seemed to be clenching his teeth. "I feel I need to give you some background," she whispered as if she was about to channel my dead mother. "I had a difficult pregnancy with Elijah, and when he was being birthed into this spinning planet, he got stuck in my birth canal."

I mustered what some might construe as a faintly compassionate look. The father's face tightened.

She exhaled. "When he was finally delivered, he was born with a grimace."

"A what?" I thought I'd misheard some odd medical term for the porcelain bottle opener jammed in his mouth.

"A grimace. That's why he can seem angry at times. That grimace has followed him all the way from my birth canal into this earthly world." She allowed some air to leak from her lips.

I glanced sideways at the director, but she didn't do anything.

How does one argue with a blanket excuse that would cover the shoplifting, carjackings, and illegal animal loving that Elijah was bound to commit in the future?

"Can I speak?" The father pushed his glasses up on his nose. "I need to say that I don't think physical restraint is ever the proper way to deal with a child."

"Your son knocked a girl off a moving swing," I countered. "I didn't want him to hurt her or anyone else, so I put my arms around him. I wasn't trying to hurt the kid."

Papa de Poo-Poo leaned in. "He had red marks on his torso," he said accusingly.

I shot him my own version of the infamous grimace. "From trying to punch and kick me."

The mother started to weep into her transparent hands while the director peered anxiously like a referee who has just lost all control of the game. The dad rose to his feet and I followed suit, trying not to glance at the adobe frank and beans in my periphery.

"If you ever touch my son again . . . ," he threatened, cocking his head.

"I'd do the same thing if that boy ever—" "That boy" was probably not the best way to refer to their miracle baby, whom they'd named after two prophets.

"Okay, everyone calm down, calm down," the director said with a weak smile.

"He was born with a grimace! Born with a grimace!" the Rolfer-who-rocks-the-cradle wailed, pulling at her cheeks so you could see the blood vessels under her milky eyes.

The hippie headmistress stood up. "I think we should all take a break."

During the pause that followed, I realized this confrontation had nothing to do with their boy; it was about Ray, and fighting them would not make her way any easier from the birth canal and through this earthly world filled with amorphous antelopes and visions that most of us could never imagine even with the best chemical enhancement. I reached over and squished the clay genitals into an unrecognizable mass, then took a deep cleansing breath. "That's a good idea," I said. "There are drinking cups in the bathroom." As I pointed them toward the dank water closet, I prayed that Jack had done his dirty diligence that day and the couple soon would be swallowing liquid soap while viewing Jack's infamous root growing inside the toilet.

"Bye-bye, Basil," I whispered as I watched them go in.

Blue Eye
Brown Eye
Black Eye

Even after my hallucinatory hippie school experience, I still (for some unknown reason) wanted to stay in the education game. I landed a job teaching seventh grade at Prep, a local independent day school that had no bunnies or beanbag chairs as far as I could tell. My first year there, I had a colleague in the English department named Thad. He was young and athletic and full of the kind of boarding-school bullshit that belonged in some Molly Ringwald movie, not in a small day school in New Mexico. Thad was the kind of guy who firmly clasped your right hand in his while his other hand gave you a squeeze on your right shoulder to let you know that he was a bit more earnest and dedicated than other teachers, including yourself. His lingering stare said that he listened more closely and cared just slightly more deeply than

the chalk-covered masses who stood in front of other people's
children for a living. He never let his hair grow longer than the
prep school shag and favored pressed blue button-down shirts
over sharply creased khakis held up by whale-patterned web
belts. Soccer in the fall, skiing in the winter, lacrosse in the
spring—a three-sport man. So when he asked me to sub for his
eighth-grade English class, I thought nothing of it. I was young
too, though not as young as he, and even though my parents had
never sent me away to get homophobically hazed at Choate or
Exeter, I sometimes acted and spoke as if I had trodden among
those lush green fields back East. I admit it—at times in my life
I've had fleeting bouts of boarding-school envy. More so, I
wanted to be a good colleague, someone people said nice things
about around the faculty lunch table. "Oh, that Rob," they'd say
over their brown plastic trays, "he's a real trouper. A natural
teacher. So giving." When I asked Thad how I should prepare in
anticipation of his class—read some Plato or Aristotle, perhaps,
view one of his detailed lesson plans, buy some Top-Siders—he
just clapped me on the back and forced a laugh on loan from the
millionaire on *Gilligan's Island*. "Don't worry," he whispered
with a reassuring wink. "They know what to do. I've got them well
trained."

I entered Room 16, and the classroom was surprisingly dark.
Venetian blinds blacked out the morning sun in the room's only
two windows. The tables and chairs had been jammed in the corners, creating thickets of office furniture around a central clear-
ing of worn carpet. I recognized the thick odor of middle school
in the unmoving air—hot and wet and musky, the way I often
imagine a beaver lodge to smell during rutting season. My arrival
had let in a wedge of light that sliced onto a tangled pack of girls

in the corner. They reminded me a bit of the prisoners in *The Deer Hunter*, squinty eyed spooks crazy playing with imaginary threads on the tips of their fingers.

"Hey, Mr. Wilder," a voice called, growing closer. Before I could step back and brace myself against the blackboard, Dennis, a kid I'd heard was trouble, emerged within inches of my face. At faculty meetings and formal gatherings of the admissions committee, we always speak of the "whole child" (we really do, I swear). Around those conference tables, we discuss how Sally Student is doing in precalc and World I, what's going on with her mom's latest in a knotted string of not-so-single men, and even how she's faring socially with the goth kids who cluster behind the scoreboard during lunch. As in any business, the unofficial version of the story is retold by the water cooler (in this case the teachers' lounge), where that same whole child often gets boiled down to one defining attribute. "Oh, that Dennis kid, he's *poison*" is what I'd heard. I couldn't even recall from whom.

"Are you subbing for Thad?" Dennis asked me, our faces still too intimate for my liking. I thought the close-talking trait emerged later, during adulthood, when it was clear that people were avoiding you at the office Christmas party. "Hey. Are you subbing for Thad?" He said his teacher's Christian name again even though in middle school, students were to address their teachers by *Mr.*, *Mrs.*, or *Ms.*, followed by their last names. Thad thought he could transcend the blurry boundary issues young kids have by a blend of trust, respect, and an extreme case of narcissism. The administration let him get away with his kids being so informal too. I'm not sure if it was because he was the poster boy of East Coast boarding academies, something this home-grown western day school aspired to be, or because the admin wanted to avoid the handclasps and deep-eyed stares that such meetings with Thad would undoubtedly produce.

"Yes, I am subbing for him," I declared, trying to evoke confidence stemming from experience that I did not yet have. I might have even made a fist and raised it into the air like I was the captain of the crew team and we'd just won the Head of the Charles.

"Should we get back to our places from yesterday?" Dennis' lips were severely chapped and sore, and he licked them incessantly.

"Sure." I shrugged. Seemed right. Ride Thad's work for fifty minutes. Don't screw anything up.

Dennis curved his hands around his messy adolescent mouth in a way that was not unfamiliar to coxswains, captains of the pep squad, and seasoned bullies. "Come on, guys, back to your positions!"

With groans and sighs, weepy girls tore themselves away from each other like they were family members being separated at Auschwitz. Pretty soon the class was evenly divided; only the kids on the left side of the room by the teacher's desk and empty bookshelves were all standing. The ones on the right side were sitting, squatting, crouching, or knuckle dragging like that slobbering scrotum of a creature Gollum in *The Lord of the Rings*.

"Okay, go," Dennis said, and the left flank charged the right, wagging fingers, shaking fists, and screaming PG-13 profanities.

"Cower, you vermin," a thin girl with straight bangs yelled.

"Pick up that trash," a boy shouted, pointing toward an overflowing garbage can. He summoned the specter of his absent teacher—*Thad said!*—and the submissive one obeyed. Bossy the Clown didn't let up until his charge, a chubby boy with bad skin, emptied the contents into the larger trash can outside the door.

I heard another voice call "Tie my shoe, you animal," but could not place its origin. From the shards of light stealing through the gaps where the blinds had been bent, I could see that except for maybe one kid, the left side was really into their parts in this odd role-playing game: faces squeezed tight, jaws clenched. If this was only performance, I was witness to the best display of Method acting our school had ever seen. The right side's reaction was mixed—some kids shook with fear, while others showed a wide spectrum of teenage emotions from despair to boredom to just downright annoyance. I saw a kid really cowering, bent over in a way he had obviously learned from watching someone else, an actor in an educational video, maybe. The image triggered the realization that Thad was having them do the Blue Eyes/Brown Eyes experiment. I had seen the social experiment once or twice before, but only an abbreviated showing in a large group with an audience. I'd read about it a bit in college too. Jane Elliott, an elementary school teacher in Iowa, had created the experiment in 1968 to teach her all-white fourth-grade classroom about racism. According to Elliott, this exercise helps us to discover that if you can create racism, then you can destroy it. From where I was standing in this pubescent petri dish, the only thing Thad's creation of racism was destroying was any last shred of order or decency these damaged kids possessed. I was reminded more often of Frankenstein's monster than Malcolm X.

As the volume in the classroom grew, reverberating off the low ceiling, I wondered why the hell Thad hadn't told me what he was doing. At first I thought maybe he'd been afraid that I wouldn't agree to sub for him, but then I realized he was not a guy who'd admit that openly to failure, even if he had set the school on fire with a flamethrower in a drunken fit. One of the kneelers stood up like a finger on an otherwise closed fist. Immediately, Dennis ran to me and whipped his arm back toward the boy.

"Mr. Wilder, Steven over there . . ." He paused, licking his lips again. I could hear the cracking as his tongue stroked the scabby skin. "Can I call you Rob?"

"No."

"Thad says—"

"I don't care what Thad says. Mr. Wilder to you."

"Okay. Mr. Wilder, Steven won't cower. He has to cower, it's part of the assignment. None of the blue eyes can be taller than the brown eyes. It's an integral part of the experiment." I surveyed all the kids kneeling or sitting or, even worse, squatting, something I've never been able to do without serious knee or groin pain. Didn't seem like a whole lot of fun to me, even though at another school I'm sure it's a burned-out teacher's fantasy to have students inflict harm upon each other instead of the dope with the grade book.

"What would you like me to do?" I asked.

"Tell him to obey me." He crossed his arms over his flat chest.

"Really?"

"That's what Thad would say. He told us that if this was gonna teach us anything, we all had to play our part."

"Okay. I'll take care of it," I said, just to get him out of my face.

"You'll tell him to do whatever I say?" He tried to mask his overflowing hopefulness that he, probably like his father before him, could actually be a Master of the Universe.

"I said I'd take care of it."

All I wanted to do was walk by that boy out the door and into my car. Thad had totally fucked me. Leaving wasn't an option, however. At our last middle school meeting, we had discussed unsupervised classrooms. According to a study with a forgettable title, that's where all the terrible teen things happen—where students are subjected to all forms of abusive behavior, including sexism, bullying, bad pickup lines, and, ironically, racism.

As I approached the defiant one, I understood that Thad really expected these kids to govern themselves under these extreme circumstances even though they were still too young to get a learner's permit for a Vespa. It's frightening for me when I see how rarely teachers of literature or history learn from the books they assign to kids. I vowed to make sure that Thad received a copy of *Lord of the Flies* soaked in pig's blood for our next Secret Santa exchange.

The defiant one was peering wistfully out the small window embedded in the classroom door. He was a head taller than Dennis, quieter, gentler in the movement of his still-growing limbs and appendages.

"Hey," I said calmly with a light sprinkling of sarcasm. "Aren't you supposed to be sitting or something?"

"This is stupid," he said, still not facing me. "I'm getting a headache."

In retrospect, I should have sent him to the library or the nearest escape vehicle. Maybe a long walk to the rest room or a video arcade in another state. Back then, however, I so desperately wanted to be a good teacher, which I thought meant sticking to the lesson plan, making a go of it, filling every second of that fifty-minute period, that I asked this younger version of myself if he couldn't just sit down and try to ignore Attila the Teen's rants for the rest of the class. "Try to think of something else" was my suggestion, which came closer to my grandmother Mildred's school of emotional complexity than a middle school teacher's sage advice at an independent day school.

"Like what?" he asked earnestly.

"I dunno." I quickly scanned the room for inspiration. Someone had done a posterboard project on bloody genocide in the Philippines. "Someplace warm. A beach, perhaps." I patted him on the back in a way that was less phony than Thad's public displays of chummy affection. I was helping him get through this, I told myself, trying to sound convincing in my interior monologue.

Most of the blue eyes had resigned themselves to their fate by playing along, bowing to their captors, picking up pieces of rubbish invisible to the unoppressed eye. One nerdy girl with glasses wearing an anime jacket mimicked a geisha in her walk and demeanor, bowing, clasping hands, and taking baby steps to and from her imposed destinations. The more the blue eyes obeyed, the more Dennis and the brownies pushed them. I glanced at my watch repeatedly, trying to speed toward the ending time of 10:55 A.M. As part of that same unsupervised classroom talk, the admin had warned us against letting our classes out early. But what could have been worse than one group of kids demeaning another set? The only difference was that this abuse was sanctioned by a teacher and school, under the guise that they were all learning something. I knew what Dennis was learning, and it didn't sit right with me.

The defiant one popped to his feet and went after Dennis like a hitter who had just been beaned by a pitcher in the minor leagues. Dennis turned to fetch me, the big boss man, and almost skewered my eye with his index finger.

"He's doing it again," Dennis sang in an angry falsetto, his head lolling from side to side. "Tell him to sit down!"

"Asshole spat on me," the defiant one leaked through gritted teeth.

I turned to Dennis. "You spat on him?"

"Thad said we could do or say anything except touch them. I didn't touch him. Thad said there would be a lot of gray areas, just like in real life."

"You actually spat on him?" I thought of saliva passing over those diseased lips onto the face of another.

"What do you think the slave owners did to the slaves?" Dennis asked with a breed of melodrama rare for even his age. "Far worse than spit. Look at Martin Luther King Jr."

"Come on, now. Really." I couldn't believe what I was hearing. The bully invoking MLK. That was like me (or any other teacher) designing the spring line for Gucci.

Dennis ranted on: "We saw photos of lynchings and other, um, unspeakable acts."

"Unspeakable acts?"

"It was in the movie," someone whispered from behind me.

"How are we supposed to know what racism is like if we don't fully do it?" Dennis pleaded. I could tell he was on the verge of weeping. I didn't know these kids, didn't know this experiment, didn't know how to deal with issues that included aimed and intentional bodily fluids, and there were still ten minutes left in the period.

If it happened today in the era of Homeland Security–sanctioned post-9/11 Columbine-type lockdowns, I know what I would do. I would utilize my training and employ the Blood-borne Pathogen Exposure Control Plan, which includes all types of bodily fluids, even spittle. Without hesitation, I could clear the room, telling all the students to go wash their hands and around their exposed orifices *Silkwood* style while I took Dennis to the health counselor for a battery of tests including flu, mono, foot-

and-mouth disease, plague, hantavirus, and HIV. The institution that had sanctioned this mess could goddamn well clean it up.

But my Blue Eyes/Brown Eyes day happened before my ECP (Exposure Control Plan) training, so instead I cowered in front of twenty frozen children as Dennis' refrain echoed deeply in my ears: "How are we supposed to learn if you don't do something?"

I never slugged Thad for setting me up like that or lectured him on how potentially damaging the Blue Eyes/Brown Eyes experiment was to everyone involved. Maybe it was good workplace manners or just plain cowardice, probably the latter, but after that I avoided him the way you do used-car salesmen or someone who really wants to get his freak on with your stepsister. It didn't take long for Thad to find our prosaic school a little too confining for his colossal mind, so he lit out for Paris, a place far more enlightened than our scrubby little land of entrapment. Even though many of his students were heartbroken, institutional memory is as fleeting as the life of a snowflake, and the next year hardly anyone mentioned his name again.

Two years after he left, I was walking to lunch and saw a group of people huddled at a picnic table usually favored by middle-schoolers who like to practice their scrimshaw and profanity in the same place. I made the mistake of looking over to see Thad leading a Socratic discussion with a few former students and a panting faculty member who still harbored the kind of crush usually reserved for high school quarterbacks and daytime television stars. The expatriate educator caught my stare, excused himself from the table, and strode over to where I was standing. He still wore the same boarding-school uniform of creased shirt, khaki pants, and boat shoes, though I was sure he wasn't back in New Mexico for the sailing.

"Hey there, guy," he said, clasping my hand and clapping my back. He told me all about Paris and the international school where he taught the brightest students in the world in the most cosmopolitan city in the world. I waited for him to add that he'd recently been voted the best teacher in the world by the globe's population of six billion, but instead he asked, "So, what do you have to say for yourself?"

I thought about all the things I could tell this man—how his messed-up experiment had shown me that teenagers are not guinea pigs even if they smell like them, and that a real teacher would never actually believe he could "train" his students. The best teachers I know help students to make discoveries on their own, not force them to think or act in a prescribed way. Teachers should be more like midwives and less like drill instructors. Hell, we dress like them already.

I thought maybe I should thank Thad because, in a sense, my subbing for him that day had forced me to realize I'd been too passive from the beginning with him. I should have asked what to expect and then, when I saw the mess his class was in, changed the lesson to something I felt more comfortable teaching, such as writing or how not to mention your obsession with being a Pokémon trainer on a first date with a live human.

I said none of those things because I knew a guy like Thad would never hear me. Teachers can be awful listeners if they don't watch out; just ask my patient wife, Lala. Instead, I joined my fellow faculty for a lukewarm lunch and never looked back. Thad had confirmed my belief that the only experiments I wanted to deal with came from the cafeteria kitchen, not the classroom.

Summer Jobarchy

It was one of the hottest summers on record, and my three-cylinder Daihatsu Charade had no air-conditioning. Even with the addition of a clip-on fan I plugged into the cigarette lighter and a bucket of ice water to dip my hand into, I was burning up. The fan just blew hot air into my contacts, drying them out, and the ice melted before I even left the driveway. I was a young teacher, early in my career, and I wasn't going to let such a trivial thing as heatstroke stop me from a paying summer gig.

I was driving fifteen hundred miles to Yellow Springs, Ohio, to teach writing at the Antioch College institute. My wife and daughter were off gallivanting in Italy and France with Lala's sister Emily and her husband, whose financial firm was one of the sponsors of the United States cycling team. They were all staying in a massive villa in Tuscany and would later jet over to Paris to watch the finish of the Tour de France from the polished balcony of the Ritz. I had been invited to go along too but had already accepted the job at Antioch and needed the income since my pay from Prep didn't cover our yearly expenses. When I started the saddest pleasure called teaching, I knew my summers would never be fully free. My Spanish teacher in junior high school had manned a tollbooth during the summer, choking on fumes and chasing after dropped nickels. My colleagues at Prep patrolled art galleries, catered fancy opera dinners, and waited tables in these off months, sometimes serving current students and their families. No one has ever tracked the correlation between gratuity and grade, but teachers aren't paid enough to be saints, if you know what I mean.

As I steered my Charade behind eighteen-wheelers to be pulled along in their draft and cooled in their shadow, I thought of Lala in a hired, air-conditioned Mercedes touring the vineyards and museums with a charming guide named Guido. While I shoveled truck-stop chili into my mouth and then shot it out my ass, Lala was feasting on handpicked olives and pasta freshly made by Guido's grandmother. My Motel 6 bed in St. Louis was lumpy and stained; her frequently fluffed mattress was filled with down from Italian geese who'd never suffered in the sun. Needless to say, while my wife and daughter were enjoying summer break, my summer was already breaking me down.

Antioch College is considered by some to be the most radical institution of higher learning still standing in the United States. While I was there, the students were always protesting something—the recent firing of a professor or the fact that they didn't serve bisexual chicken in the dining hall. On my first day, I toured the campus with one of my students, Max, whose hobbies included disturbing the peace and obstruction of justice. He hurried me past classrooms and dorms to the student center, which, unlike other phony poser colleges, was actually run by the students themselves.

"You'll love this place," he said, and I expected something akin to my own undergrad experience at Wesleyan, cozy nooks where students could gather to discuss musicians who were so talented they never had to play a note, but what I saw at Antioch was closer to Beirut than Beethoven. Every wall in the activity center was covered with years of graffiti, and students venting anger for injustices done to animal, vegetable, and mineral had smashed all the nonacademic amenities like televisions and pool tables. Nothing worked. Everything reeked. Max must have noticed the quizzical look on my face because he smiled and said, "I know, isn't it great?"

He led me down hallways that housed offices for the myriad student clubs that had received funding for that school year. Each door was splattered with slogans hating this and embracing that. Even the profanity was proprietary. Max was happy to translate for me, and I received a Berlitz course on rabbit revolution in Cuba and something called Mountain Justice, which sounded like the way my friend Tom had been disciplined by his dad back in Georgia. At the end of the hallway, one door looked as though Jack Nicholson had taken an axe and had his way with it.

"What happened here?" I asked Max as he stroked his wispy Che Guevara beard.

"Oh, that. The womyn's club got into a fight with the women's club. Happens all the time."

Because Yellow Springs is a pleasant little town, one of the few in Ohio that doesn't have strip malls or fast-food restaurants that offer to smother chili on every menu item, housing is at a premium. Since my family had abandoned me to single housing status, the college had stuck me under a stairwell of a larger home. The place was pretty grim; no television, radio, or even a fan to toss the thick air around. The phone they'd given me didn't allow for calls over a mile away, and my back started to ache after the first hour from all the stooping I had to do. It was hard to sleep in the heat, and truth be told, I was lonely. Only after I tried befriending a family of spiders under the stairwell did I finally fall asleep. About 2:00 A.M., there was a sharp knock on my door. Dressed only in my boxer briefs, I grabbed my outdated glasses, which made me look like Leonard Nimoy in his twilight years.

Outside my door stood Max and a straight-looking kid named Carl who reminded me of Willie Aames from *Eight Is Enough*, before Aames hoovered drugs and got more tattoos than Tommy Lee. Carl was dangling a half case of cheap beer in a torn carton.

"This is our teacher," Max said, pointing to me in all my glory.

"Cool." Carl stepped into my place and sat down on my spiders. I could tell both he and Max were high on something. Their eyes rolled around like lottery balls in their pasty skulls.

"Let's talk writing," Max said, looking around for a chalkboard or chair, but I had neither.

"Guys," I pleaded, "it's two o'clock in the morning."

"Cool." Carl nodded.

"What do you think of R——?" Max asked, naming a writer I had studied in graduate school.

"Well"—I shrugged—"his early work is obviously important."

"I hate that fucker," Max said, searching for something to hit. I stepped back, just to be safe. "He's dead now, you know."

"I don't give a fuck. He's got no heart. Has he ever seen a woman let down her hair? I mean, really seen a woman really let down her hair?"

"Yeah," Carl said, agreeing with whatever the hell it was Max was babbling about.

"I'm not sure exactly what you mean." I stared at my shitty phone, wondering if the police station was within my calling area.

"You ever get that feeling when you are writing, you know the feeling, where the egg cracks open and leaks vital seminal ambiguity in to the open sore of wonderment?"

"Cool." Carl nodded, then chugged a warm beer.

I said, "I don't know how to talk to you guys," but they weren't exactly tuned in to my frequency.

"Sure you do. You're the teacher."

I had to get rid of these two, but I had no drugs to throw outside the house for them to chase after. As Max rattled on about writing as a multispatial interpretive dance, I reached into a box of books and handed him a copy of *Jesus' Son* by Denis Johnson. This collection of short stories centered around a drug-abusing wanderer aptly named Fuckhead who, at times, thought he was God.

"You should read this," I said, tapping on the cover of the paperback. "It might connect with what you're feeling."

Max eyed the back of the book. "This ain't no Christian shit, is it? 'Cause those Christians are real fuckfaces."

"Not even close."

"Great. We'll read it soon." He nodded at Carl, who had his finger stuck inside his beer can.

"I think you guys should go off and read it now." I opened the door wide so that even their tunnel vision could see this mystical sign.

"Now?" Max cocked his head like a confused ape.

"Now."

"Cool," Carl said, fumbling to take a sip of beer with his finger still jammed in the can's orifice.

The book must have made some impact on them, because before the start of class the next morning, Max was waiting outside the classroom door. He looked like ass—eyes black and blue, shirt wrinkled, multicultural stains staging a protest on his nonunion pants. "Listen, Rob, I need you to do me a favor," he said, talking way too close to my face. His breath smelled like a mix of patchouli, gin, and bat guano.

I stepped away again. "I'm a teacher. I don't have any money."

"No, no, nothing like that. I just want you to call me Fuckhead. In class."

"I don't know. I'm new here," I said, backpedaling. "Haven't even met the students. I'm not sure that would be appropriate."

"Everything is appropriate at Antioch. It'll be cool. Really."

I agreed just to stop his breath from melting my skin.

"Oh, and one more thing," he said. "If Carl also asks you to call him Fuckhead, tell him I got dibs."

Because Antioch's goal is to empower students and allow them ultimate freedom, trivial things like time and soap tend to be overlooked for loftier pursuits such as random acts of anarchy and late-night chanting. My first day was a scene from the movie *Freaks* meets *Dead Poets Society*. Kids of all different not-so-sensibilities entered that room. A boy covered in dried mud held hands with a Brit-lit girl dressed like Sherlock Holmes. A few kids were over ninety minutes late to our three-hour seminar. Each student's individuality was so distracting, I wondered how we would ever jell as a class. I had prepared a rigorous syllabus and nightly writing assignments that wouldn't work if people weren't on time and ready to go. I decided honesty was the best policy and explained my concern about punctuality.

"Ten o'clock in the summer is kind of a cruel time," one of the students informed me. "I'm just getting to sleep around then."

"I think time is such an inconvenient concept," a waif of a girl called Butterfly said. Her real name was Janey but she had killed it, she said, just to watch it die. I still have my roster from that class and none of the printed names (Bill, Suzy, Sam) are what the students wanted to be called. Some kids even changed their names on a daily basis depending on the weather, their menstrual cycle, or the market price of Fair Trade coffee beans. One girl wanted her name erased forever and hated any form of written communication because it was so approximate and inexact. Her stories were typed in lowercase and void of punctuation in order to "stop the hierarchical nature of capitalization and paragraphs." Early on, she tried to pitch me the idea of handing in blank sheets, but I cleverly argued that doing so would be a waste of paper and, in turn, trees.

She didn't care. "I never really liked trees," she said, frowning. "I'm much more of a shrub person, actually."

I explained to the class when they complained about our ungodly meeting hour that there were mandatory lectures in the afternoon, so we couldn't switch our class to a later time.

"Mandatory?" Mud Boy asked the group.

"It means you have to do it," Butterfly said.

"Bummer."

"What do other teachers do about issues like these?" I asked, hoping for some radical new ideas in higher education.

Max waved his hand in the air, even though I told the students such formality was unnecessary in this setting. I knew what he was doing. I sighed. "Yes, Fuckhead."

Smiling, he clasped his hands in front of him like an excommunicated preacher. "There are two types of teachers at Antioch.

Some have to become total hardasses and almost fail you for being late or skipping a class."

"Yeah, I had a visiting prof last year who made you sit meditation at seven A.M. for every minute you were late or absent," Sherlock Holmes said, puffing on her pipe. She shook her deerstalker hat. "No one ever missed that class."

The group hung their heads at the idea of such strict discipline killing the lifeblood of the freedom to attend or not to attend.

"What about the other type?"

"They just give up and teach to whoever shows," Max said. His classmates nodded; they all wanted me to be of that ill ilk.

I didn't desire a contentious relationship with students who knew where I was staying and were capable of applying amateur tattoos. I also wanted them to learn something since we all had to be there. I'd passed up a sprawling villa in Italy and free-flowing Bordeaux in France for this. I spoke to the supervisor of the program, and she became my enforcer, hassling the ones who came in late or missed a class, so my students arrived mostly on time and mostly exhausted. Their writing, when completed, was actually quite good—wild and imaginative and racy. I stayed up late at night with a bolted door, marking up manuscripts with a flashlight in my mouth.

Lala called me the day after the Tour finished. I asked her how things were going, and she said she was tired. She had attended a series of dinners after Lance Armstrong's victory when all she wanted to do was take a hot bath in the claw-foot tub in her room at the Ritz.

"Who watched Poppy?" I asked, dearly missing my daughter.

Lala told me the Ritz had an international nanny who played games and sang songs to my girl in three languages. Poppy referred to her as Marie Poppins.

Lala is quite shy by nature, and for most of the fancy events she'd kept mum. "I couldn't compete with Robin Williams or Michael J. Fox telling stories," she said.

"You didn't say anything?"

"Well, for one of the dinners, I was seated next to the postmaster general and his wife, who were really nice, normal people. During a break in the conversation, I asked him why postal workers shoot so many people."

"You did what?" I sat up, bumping my head on the stairwell.

"Well, I always wanted to know."

"How did everyone react?"

"Emily freaked out and said *'Lala!'* so loud I could've died. Then the postmaster whispered that the job was stressful because of the monotony."

I stared at all the manuscripts piled under my dim light. "I know what he means."

"I have to let you go soon. Room service will be rolling in here at any minute. Poppy says *bonjour*, by the way. Quickly, tell me, how's the teaching?"

"Well," I started, trying to think of something as newsworthy as Hollywood celebrities in tight cycling pants or sleeping in 1,000-thread-count sheets. "There's a kid who comes to class covered in mud."

Early in the second week, half the class was missing, including Fuckhead and Carl, whom, after much discussion, Max allowed me to call Fuckhead 2, or F2 for short. Carl said F2 was cool because it sounded like the nickname for Terminator 2, who, according to Max, "represented the breaking of the postapocalyptic fetal heart."

Fearing a mutiny, I flirted with the idea of meditating at 7:00 A.M., but luckily, the missing students weren't being truants, they were just in jail.

"Yeah, they all went to protest the Republican National Convention over the weekend and their puppets got them arrested," Sherlock said, using her pipe as a pointer.

"Puppets?"

"The FBI considered the puppet-making materials dangerous weapon parts."

"Now they're just in jail, all naked and shit," Mud Boy said.

"Naked?" I was so confused.

Butterfly sighed. "For a teacher, you don't know much."

I nodded, rubbing my temples. "Tell me about it, twisted sister."

She explained to me that at Antioch, the students train each other in how to professionally disobey. During a protest, no one carries identification, and they wear thin clothes like tearaway jerseys in the NFL. Once they get arrested, they immediately strip like Paris Hilton in front of a video camera.

"You can't get arraigned in front of a judge if your dick is hanging out," Mud Boy said, grabbing his dusty frank and beans.

I guessed not. "Don't the cops just dress them?"

"You have a daughter, right?" Butterfly asked me.

"Yeah."

"Think about trying to dress her when she doesn't want to. Now imagine pulling that same trip on a three-hundred-pound bull dyke named Yolanda."

I had no idea what to say after that.

"Tell him about the Vaseline," Mud Boy said to Sherlock, patting her hand.

"Each protestor has Vaseline behind their ears, so right before they're to be fingerprinted, they rub their fingers behind their ears so the fingerprint is smeared. About a dozen Antioch students are in jail but they can't identify a single one." She nodded proudly at the idea of all her radical Watsons stewing in the joint.

"So what happens now?"

Sherlock shrugged. "We start class."

The story up for discussion that day had been written by Butterfly. When the students read their pieces aloud, it allowed me to study them more closely. Butterfly was a fragile girl with pale skin and long, thin hair the color of ink. My dad would have said that she was in desperate need of sun, a dark beer, and a porterhouse the size of Webster's dictionary. Her story was about a girl who lived alone in an apartment void of luxuries like television and any emotion above apathy. Her story, although overly dour and sentimental, echoed my own aching late at night under the stairwell. I was riveted to her words as she read them, and she seemed to pick up on my interest because her elocution became more and more dramatic. She stuttered a bit, and her eyes rolled up in her head in true Method-acting form. Was she as moved as I was? Was this a genuine student-teacher connection?

"She's having a seizure," Sherlock Holmes deduced, then backed away from the scene of the crime.

Here, faced with a real emergency, all the wild anarchists and mud dwellers became children again, frozen with fear. All their Vaseline training was doing them no good in front of something as apolitical as epilepsy.

I vaulted to her chair and searched for something to wedge between her teeth. A pen? I thought of all the ink stains I'd endured over the years and thought "lawsuit" if she swallowed the blood of a nonorganic writing utensil. Then I heard a whisper squeak from her mouth, sounding a lot like the Tin Man's first lockjawed words to Dorothy.

"Kiss me," the voice coming out of Butterfly's clenched teeth said.

"What?" I must have misheard. There's no kissing in English class. "What do I need to do?" I asked the trembling twenty-year-old.

"Kiss me. On my forehead." The class stared as I pressed my lips together and attached them to what I would later learn is called the "third eye." She started to calm down after a few more tremors. This cure didn't seem scientific to me, but at Antioch, biology and chemistry were definitely the lonely and forgotten disciplines. I always tell people that the relationship between teacher and student is never clear. There's nothing in the policy manual about loaning kids money for lunch (read: cigarettes) or what to do when you see your student sprawled over the hood of a Camaro making out in the Oooo parking lot at 9:00 A.M. I tried to tell myself that what I did with Butterfly was noble even though it felt creepy. I kept thinking of an ironic line from *Jesus' Son* where Fuckhead's fucked-up friend tells a hitchhiker that they "save lives." I guess that's what teachers try to do, in a sense.

At the end of that day, after a lecture by another summer faculty fellow, I dragged my ass across campus, wanting to get home to my hovel, where I could crouch like a troll and wait, on the chance that Lala and Poppy would call from back home in New Mexico. When I approached the student center, I saw two distinct mobs mixing together. On the steps were some protesters, upset by the student newspaper's decision to print the names of the puppet detainees and thereby identify them for the "FBI spies on campus." The other, more festive group consisted of a bunch of alums left over from a weekend fund-raiser doing keg stands and dancing as though the Grateful Dead still roamed the arenas promoting free love and body odor for all. This is what anarchy breeds, I thought, acute awareness and reckless behavior bumping uglies. The groups commingled deeper—the partiers pouring the demonstrators beer from a keg while the protesters educated the wasted on the subtleties of their cause. This mixing would soon become the closest thing I witnessed to Max's egg cracking open and leaking vital seminal ambiguity into the open sore of wonderment.

A girl who was not from my class left the circle and came over to where I was standing under a giant shade tree. She must have recognized the look of deep befuddlement on my tired mug. She was thin and tan and wore the hempish uniform of the posthippie aftermath. Her white teeth, however, showed she came from a place where dentistry was still practiced by people with actual diplomas.

"Wanna get lifted?" she asked.

"Lifted?" I imagined some sort of keg stand hosted by a family of acrobats. She laughed lightly and produced a joint from one pocket, a lighter from the other. I closed my eyes and thought of my teaching there at Antioch, from the first time Max had knocked on my door to the rich work the students were producing in the class after a little prodding and encouragement. The image of Butterfly calming down after her unnerving seizure filled my head when the girl asked, "So what do you do here, anyway?"

"I save lives," I said.

Part II:

Flashbacks

Sub Par

When I was in high school in Connecticut, my geometry teacher died. Mr. Potson was a meek, soft-spoken guy who favored button-down shirts with short sleeves and slacks the color of a rusty gate. He had a very round head with what seemed to be a small marsupial parked upon his sweaty scalp. Potson wasn't exactly a memorable teacher while he was still alive, except for his habit of letting us out early every few days. During his initial lectures on the radius and circumference of a circle, he'd take a deep breath, wipe his brow, and say, "Class, that's enough for today," and we'd get out fifteen or twenty minutes before the bell. No one bothered to call the nurse or feel alarmed about the welts erupting on our teacher's neck or when he slammed his head against the chalkboard after fainting. We just packed up our books and ran out of there before he could regain consciousness.

I'm sure his fellow teachers or administrators came in after we bolted; we just never looked back to check. We were teenagers

My best friend, Todd, sat in the desk next to me during geometry. Neither one of us had any idea that Mr. Potson was suffering from spells. Todd was especially clueless (and light-headed) from trying to shed pounds for the upcoming wrestling season. He wanted to drop a few weight classes and body-slam the scrawny kids who were thrown in garbage cans or given bleeding wedgies at rival schools. Todd ran up and down stairs, swore off solid foods, and sat in the steam room dressed like Nanook of the North. Like Courtney Love at a custody hearing, he could hardly keep his head up.

After one particularly dramatic episode where Potson staggered a bit and spat a string of bile on the desk of a pimply girl named Lisa, we never saw him again. Ours was a large high school where there was no peacetime contact between students and the administration, so we never really expected any information about our math teacher's disappearance. When a student died, they broadcasted his or her gauzy yearbook picture on the television screen in the cafeteria with Led Zeppelin's "Stairway to Heaven" playing lightly in the background. Potson just evaporated, and for all we knew, he was manning the tollbooths near Sherwood Island beach on Long Island Sound for extra cash, just like the other pathetic teachers did when they vanished for the summer.

A chorus line of substitutes cant-canted their way across our class, including other teachers still sympathetic enough to volunteer for a dead colleague. None of them knew geometry well enough to spell it. The drama teacher came in and tried to get us to imagine math in its ethereal form by burning incense and using guided meditation exercises. When she closed her eyes, people in the class flipped her off, mooned her, or ran out the door. One grizzled PE teacher openly admitted he couldn't even balance his goddamn checkbook, so we might as well try to teach ourselves. This meant that Todd covered his head with his parka and nodded off while I squinted at the mysterious shapes and lines in my thick textbook. I was a pretty horny kid, so all I saw were tits and dicks after about ten minutes of staring. Whatever expectations or degree of formality we had in that class wore off after the initial few subs finished their brief stints. I remember a shaky and stoic Vietnam vet who played us Allman Brothers albums, followed by a woman who was so unhealthy she could hardly talk after one of Todd's wrestling buddies swiped her inhaler. Some kids stopped coming altogether, while others treated the room as a lounge to play tongue hockey with girlfriends or work on their racist epithets. Then, two weeks before our new permanent teacher would arrive and clean house, in walked trouble.

"Oh shit," Todd mumbled, and shot his eyes toward the door. The mother of our good friend Mark Steen was waiting nervously in the hall with the gnome-like assistant principal. Mrs. Steen was not a MILF or yummy mummy by any stretch of the imagination. Her permed hair fanned around her head like an orangutan's, and she had a full set of braces. She was the only adult we knew who had them, and they were so primitive that it looked like someone had parked a car in her mouth. Having that kind of dental work translated her otherwise earnest speech into a spitting (and broken) public address system.

"We are so fucking dead," Todd said from under his hood, and he was right. Kids at our school lived to torture subs, and by the time Mrs. Steen entered geometry, the students in our class had become pros at such punishing pursuits. Todd and I were stuck in the middle. Mark was one of our closest friends, but trying to save his mom from these goons would be a task even Charles Bronson would turn down.

"Hello, clash," Mrs. Steen said after the squat administrator slithered away. She directed her gooey smile right at Todd and me. We had been to her house many times before and she was far friendlier than our own parents, offering us iced tea in real glassware and actually listening to our fascinating debate on whether Gary Coleman was really a midget or a dwarf.

"Clash?" one of the older guys asked her. I could tell by the gray in his hair that he had been left back a few times.

"Exchuse me?" Mrs. Steen smiled.

"You said *clash*. What the hell is a *clash*? Are you into, like, punk rock or something?"

The class thought that remark was the pinnacle of high comedy. Even though Todd whispered, "Dude, don't," I had to do something for the sons of dorky moms everywhere. "I think she said *class*," I said quietly, hoping not to draw attention and get jumped after the period was over.

"Yesh, I didsh," Mrs. Steen answered eagerly. Spit leaked from the edges of her chapped lips. "You are the clash and I'm the teachcquer."

I covered my face with my textbook while everyone else laughed uproariously and pointed. Mrs. Steen just blinked repeatedly like an exotic nocturnal mammal with a light shining in its face. Todd groaned and then farted from a serious lack of nutrition.

The hard thing about Mark's mom was that she had all the characteristics of a classic sub. She was earnest, clueless, and awkward in both dress and demeanor. All she had to do was stumble into the room in her lime-green pantsuit dragging overstuffed canvas bags, her hands fluttering like spastic butterflies, and the teenage laugh track started. Mark later told us that she believed our hysteria stemmed from the grief we felt about having a teacher die. That's why she never did anything to stop us. She didn't understand that we felt no misery or despair about Mr. Potson because, sad to say, we didn't care. We didn't even know we should care. We were teenagers. We focused on more important matters, like the invention of button-fly jeans and whether you had to put your finger inside a girl for it to count as third base.

Then the pranks began. Stolen erasers followed by chalk jammed in the erasers followed by more calculated gags like inserting all the drawers in her desk and file cabinet upside down so when she pulled them out, crap flew everywhere. Todd was laughing so hard at the sight of Mark's mom scrambling around on the floor like a crazy spider crab that he shit his pants. After an embarrassing exit, he was forced to wear his wrestling singlet to all his afternoon classes.

Most of these capers were executed before I entered the classroom, so I didn't feel culpable, even though Todd and I probably wouldn't have prevented them. The crowning prank was held on a Friday. Mrs. Steen had told us to read over some chapter, and she would use the overhead projector to explain the concepts to us. That was like telling John Hinckley that the president would be taking an unguarded stroll naked with Jodie Foster down Pennsylvania Avenue. After Mrs. Steen retrieved her overhead sheets from her bag, grabbed the appropriate pens, and plugged in the projector, she went to the Da-Lite screen bolted above the chalkboard. Looking back, I should have thrown myself across the room like a member of the Secret Service, shouting "Nooooo!" but on that day I couldn't keep my eyes off her recently singed hair. What was that color? Orange? Brown? Burnt rust?

Mrs. Steen stretched on her tiptoes and pulled the screen down by its thin metal handle. Pounds of talcum powder flurried down, covering her from crazy hair to crooked toe. She said nothing. Instead, she stood before us like a blinking scarecrow stuck in a snowdrift. When she parted her lips, her tinny grin glared at us from inside the pale backdrop. It was like a scene out of *Carrie's White Christmas,* only Mrs. Steen didn't have the power to set our cruel asses on fire.

Todd and I arrived early on Monday with the idea that we might try to say something to the guys who were pulling the pranks. These boys were older than we were; some were repeating the class, while others moved on a very slow math track. By the scabs on their dragging knuckles I guessed they were not only older but far tougher as well. They weren't the brightest lights on the street and were known more for passing out at parties than for passing classes. When we arrived, the rabble were gathered in a circle, soaking tampons in a bowl of hot water. Their furry hands were submerged like cavemen in a Palmolive commercial, happily mashing the pulp.

"Um, what are you going to do with that?" I asked, my voice cracking like a true pussy's.

"Dis," one of them grunted. He flung a wad against the chalkboard, where it stuck like shit from a prehistoric bird. Another gob thwacked against the board, followed by another. The line of mash was leading right toward the door. Mrs. Steen would definitely be the next target.

"Don't you think maybe we've done enough?" I squeaked.

"Don't you *wah* think *wah* we've done enough *wah*?" one of them mimicked me in a high falsetto. They didn't care that our teacher had died; well, neither did I, actually. But they didn't care that the class didn't know how many sides a triangle had, and it was almost November. Well, I didn't either, but one thing I did care about was that Mark was my friend and the bull's-eye was painted right on his mom's bony back door.

"Todd, help me out here," I called, but he was already back at his desk, nodding off like a junkie. "Do something," I pleaded. "You're a wrestler. Um, go wrestle them."

"Dude, I can't. I gotta sleep. The only thing I've eaten in, like, twelve hours is an orange. If I don't lose four and a half more pounds, I'm gonna have to hit the Ex-Lax diet, and that shit hurts. Literally."

I turned back to the gang with one final plea: "It's Mark's mom, guys."

They all threw me mad-dog looks like I was stealing their drugs and said, "She's not anyone's mom in here. She's a fucking sub." Cocked over their shoulders, their hands all held globs of masticated Tampax. I could hear Mrs. Steen's corrective footwear click-clacking down the hall, growing closer and closer to the geometry of torture. I flipped up the hood on my sweatshirt, closed my eyes, and kept my head down.

I could hear the sounds of the pulp hitting the board and walls. When I peered up from under my coward's shell, I saw that Mrs. Steen had escaped relatively unscathed. A white wad dripped down her trouser leg, but the rest of her pink pantsuit was clean. Her face, though, was another story. Her skin turned red, and she lost the cool she'd been keeping for days. Dead teacher or no dead teacher, she let us have it. The funny thing was, no one could understand a word she was screeching.

"Yoush godaqmnrd kisdch," she screamed, her fists clenched in anger. Viscous spit flew from the machine installed in her mouth, slathering the front row of students, who quickly slid their chairs back to a drier patch of linoleum. At first, everyone looked around to see how to react. Fury had transformed this otherwise calm woman we'd thought we knew into some sort of strange alien being that was apparently expressing anger, but in what language?

"I donschnt knowsh whynt I comel insh harq," she ranted on, staining her top with the clam chowder bubbling from her mouth.

One by one, we all started to laugh until the room was engulfed with the overwhelming sounds of youthful merriment and joyousness. Anyone passing by our class that day would have remarked, "That teacher sure knows how to make mathematics fun."

Now that I'm a teacher, I have different issues with substitutes. Since most of my students have been reared in smallish schools in multicultural Santa Fe, they are far more civilized than my peers were in high school. Instead of taping "I suck hard" to my friend Jennifer's back during class when she covers in my absence, they take it out on me as soon as I return. The class will have compiled a list of complaints about my temporary replacement ranging from the innocuous ("She didn't inspire us") to the more personal ("She had those sick whitish strings in the corners of her mouth"). They trash the subs from bumpy head to fungal toe, comparing their smell to clever descriptions of diseased genitals found on nasty Internet porn sites. But overall, I can't complain, since the real crazy subs are reserved for my daughter, Poppy.

Every Thursday at one-thirty, as part of the community service component of Santa Fe Prep, I take five teenagers to Poppy's public school class to teach writing. That's a lie, actually. My school's community service program neatly camouflages my selfish desire to see my daughter each week with barrettes in her hair, clothed in her "suggested dress" outfit, sitting behind her elfin little desk. I don't think I'm fooling anybody, especially Poppy, and her classmates do happen to learn something from my weekly exercises. I just know from watching moody teenagers interact with their parents that Poppy's days as a sweet young kid are numbered, and I want to spend as much time with Little Miss Demeanor before she blossoms into a full-grown felon.

Poppy's teacher is a young and energetic redhead named Kate. She's happy to have us come and teach, and each week I bring strong coffee to revive her from her exhaustion after dealing with nutty nine-year-olds all day. One Thursday, Kate informed me that her father was retiring from his job as the head of another school, and as part of the educational mafia, she would have to miss our next visit. While the kids were writing stories about the secret life of kitties, she told me she was having a hard time finding a sub.

"I had to hire a guy I haven't even met," she said. "I mean, he's approved by the district and all, but I'm a bit concerned."

"You worry too much. I'm sure he'll be fine. Besides, we'll be right here," I said, and pointed to my students, who were actively ignoring Poppy and her classmates.

"I hope you're right," Kate said. Since she was new, I didn't want to scare her by telling her about the last sub I'd found. According to my students, he was clever and edgy and could really relate to them. According to the police, he had two felony gun convictions.

When we arrived the next Thursday, the kids were just returning from music class and, as always, they were excited to see us. Poppy raced to me, throwing her arms around my waist. She's a pretty even-keeled kid and has always loved school, but on this day she seemed like an ADHD kid who forgot to snort her Ritalin.

"Dada, guess what?" she asked me, rocking in her saddle shoes.

"You just got married."

"No. Mr. Z.—you know, the sub? He plays guitar and we made up songs and he's really funny."

I crossed my arms and shot her a look.

"Not as funny as you, though." Funniness is a big deal in our lives. My youngest brother, Crazy Eddie the Disney actor, currently holds the title as wackiest person on the planet. I'm a distant second, and it looked as though this sub was battling my other brother Tom for third place.

A cartoonish voice squeaked from behind Kate's desk in the corner. A balding man in shirtsleeves wearing an ID badge stood petting a green puppet that could have been a dragon or a snake. It was hard to tell from all the wear and tear. "Okay, kids, let's settle down now. Hee-hee!" the puppet said. My teenagers quickly gathered behind me to shield themselves.

"Oh, you haven't met Mr. Wiggles," this Mr. Z. said. He had sweat stains under his arms the size of small pizzas and his tongue kept circling his mouth like an imprisoned centipede. "Come over and say hello." My students hid while Poppy's class squealed with delight at both the sight of the puppet and our unease at the situation. Poppy enjoyed the awkward moment the most, throwing her head back so I could spot the two fillings in her teeth. She loved seeing her father play the dupe.

"I'm not going near that dude, no way," my student Jonathan said. Since this service project was all my idea, I always took the bullet whenever things got tricky. If one of Poppy's classmates had a nosebleed or vomited chocolate milk on the computer screen, I cleaned it up with Kate's help. When the principal complained about one of my students breaking their dress code by wearing her "Jesus Is My Homeboy" T-shirt, I tried to explain the holy humor.

I waded between the desks, each one littered with stuffed animals and dying plants from a failed photosynthesis project. "Hello, Mr. Wiggles," I said, tentatively touching the puppet's fur, which was both wet and undulating. The nasty rag then purred like a horny Tribble and emitted a sour odor. I recoiled in disgust.

"Isn't he great, Dad?" Poppy asked.

"Just swell." My palm felt sticky. "Go wash your hands, Pop."

"Why?"

"Colds are going around." I pointed to the doorway. "Now, hit the sink. And use lots of soap!" I called after her.

With a paste-eating grin on his face, the sub kept stroking his puppet while I began the exercise for that day. I handed my students a bag of bandannas, and they started blindfolding each member of the class. Half of my students would lead the younger kids around the school while the other half would set up a writing activity that would ask the kids for sensory descriptions of their sightless journey. I chose the girls in my group to lead the young ones since the boys would have made this activity more like an episode of *Jackass*, hooking up Poppy and her pals to car batteries and forcing them to snort wasabi stolen from the cafeteria.

"Whee-hee! That sounds great, kids!" Mr. Wiggles squealed, and yanked his mouth wide open in excitement. He hammed it up, moving from side to side, trying to get every kid to view his lice-ridden mug.

"Right," I said. "Okay, everybody, get in single file." The girls led the blind conga line into the hall, gently steering the kids away from glass trophy cases and protruding nails left over from the last student art show.

"I hope no one eats it," Jonathan said, chuckling.

"That would be cool," his buddy Scott answered.

"I hope no one gets hurt! Hee-hee. That would be AWWWWW-FULLLL," Mr. Wiggles added, twisting his head upside down. I turned around, hoping to find at least one child left behind, but it was only the two boys, me, and a half-finished diorama on King Tut's vital organs.

"Dude," Jonathan whispered, which meant *That fucking puppet is still talking*.

"Dude," Scott said, as in *Do something now, Rob. You are the teacher*.

How was I supposed to tell a complete stranger to put his creepy puppet away? I once attended a fancy pool party in the hills of Santa Fe, and the host was walking around in a thong bathing suit offering his guests cocktails. When he approached my group and asked if he could do anything for us, my friend Don told him, "Sure. You could put some clothes on, for Christ's sake." That always struck me as a tad mean even though the guy had an ass like two quivering mounds of headcheese.

Mr. Z. just waited there, caressing Mr. Wiggles. I half expected the puppet to spit up seminal fluid from all that rubbing. Maybe if I questioned Mr. Z. directly, he'd put the tube of fur away in a hazmat bag.

"How much subbing do you do?" I asked, then quickly added, "Mr. Z.," so there'd be no confusion as to who should answer.

"Oh, all the time. I do all the schools." Like Rain Man, he listed every elementary in town in alphabetical order. "I guess you could call me a professional sub."

I guess I could call you a professional wack job was what I wanted to say, but I employed more diplomacy. "I'd love to be a sub sometimes, you know," I said. "Come in for a day. No responsibilities. Just hang out with the kids."

"We do love it, don't we, Mr. Wiggles?" He looked lovingly down upon his creation, eyes a-twitchin'.

"Sure do! Hee-hee."

Then the two misters, Z. and Wiggles, kissed.

Jonathan shuddered. "Dude!"

"Dude." Scott shook his head.

Mr. Z. noticed the reaction in the previously stoic teens. "Mr. Wiggles wants to know your names."

"Well," Jonathan answered, pushing up his designer eyewear, "I have to go to the bathroom." He knew stranger danger when he saw it.

"I'll go with you." Scott tore out of the room like his nads were on fire.

I could hear the two boys laughing in the hallway, asking each other, "What the hell was *that*?" as they searched the corridors for the blind leading the blind. But now, without anyone under thirty-five in the room, surely this guy would ditch the rag.

"What did you do before you were a sub?" I asked.

"I was a sock," Mr. Wiggles said flatly.

"That's it," I said, and left the room. The community I'd signed up to service didn't include Pee-Wee Herman in a dark theater. When I caught up with the class, they were weaving between the stacks in the library like blind lemmings about to plummet off a jagged cliff. I pulled my daughter from the line and led her toward the librarian's office. Poppy still had her blindfold on and grinned widely, thinking this was all part of the assignment.

I whispered in her ear. "Poppy?"

"Is that you, Dada?" She fumbled around waving her hands in the air like little Helen Keller.

"It is. I just remembered that I need to take you out of school early today. After we finish the writing assignment, you'll leave with me." I rubbed her back in assurance.

"Why?"

I knew Mr. Z. and Wiggles were a tough act to top, but there was no way my daughter was spending another unsupervised minute with that creepy combo.

"How does ice cream followed by some time at Quiggy's Playland sound?" Quiggy's was a low-rent Chuck E. Cheese's, but it was miles away from the school and void of men with their hands up the asses of moist moppets.

"Great!"

Even with our escape plan, I couldn't shake the residue of Mr. Wiggles still lingering on my hand (and crawling through my mind). "One more thing, Poppy."

"What's that?"

"On our way out, we need to drop by the nurse's office for some sanitizing gel." I considered a tetanus shot, but our pediatrician was the thorough sort and would ask too many questions.

She put her hands on her hips and cocked her head. "You're so funny, Dada."

"I know," I sighed, wiping my palms on the back of my pants. "I'm freaking hilarious."

Dramarama

One of the most challenging aspects of day-to-day teaching is classroom management. In graduate school, a professor of education can easily illustrate how, by using a green pen instead of a red one to grade essays, you can reduce stress in the average thirteen-year-old by 27 percent. In your teacher training, you can quickly learn to use software that can help you take attendance, create nonlinear outlines, and catch and punish those evil cheaters when they lift paragraphs from www.SchoolSucks.com. However, successfully managing a class full of hormonal teenagers can come only from experience and, for better or worse, my training began when I was still hormonal myself back in high school.

During my senior year, I was the president of the Staples Players, our high school's drama program. As far as secondary school theater groups go, we had a decent reputation. Sure, there were your run of the mill nerds who wore fangs in their prom photos and kids questioning their sexuality at night in the cat-walks, but we did a fair number of legitimate plays and musicals, a few of which won awards named after long-forgotten actors and dramatists. Our alums ranged in talent and notoriety from Hollywood legends like Michael Douglas and Christopher Lloyd to that famous crowd-pleaser Marilyn Chambers, who gave us a slew of new ideas about what might go on behind the door to our greenroom. As president of the Players, not only did I have to stop the tech crew from giving each other hand jobs behind the backdrop of *Cabaret* during the weekend performance, but I also unwittingly fell into a student-teaching role during the school day. I wasn't remotely qualified for this position, nor did I fore-see teaching as a possible career choice; it was more that after twenty years of daily performances, our drama teacher, Al Pia, wasn't always ready to go on before an audience full of mawkish teenagers.

Al Pia was an old-school drama teacher who had studied Constantin Stanislavsky and Uta Hagen and utilized those meth-ods in bit parts in B movies with titles like *The Toxic Avenger* and *The First Turn On!!* Mr. Pia even had famous friends like Telly Savalas and Gil Cates, the guy who produces that annual marathon borefest, the Academy Awards. While Telly never showed up to ask us "Who loves ya, baby?"—which is good, be-cause I would have drawn a blank—we did have to perform Gil Cates' musical version of *The Comedy of Errors*, entitled *Dromio, Dromio*. I've tried to block out any memory of the pathetic pro-duction, which I recall had really bad songs that rhymed *errors* with *fellas*, a lot of running, and fake noses that melted under the hot stage lights. Come to think of it, that description pretty much sums up the Academy Awards if you replace the noses with breasts.

During the fall, I took Advanced Acting with a trio of rabid stoners who got thrown out of PE and a bunch of other theater kids, including a boy named Seth who was obsessed with *Man of La Mancha* because his uncle was Richard Kiley, the Tony Award–winning lead. Seth drove everyone so crazy with his *La Mancha* crap that Pia swore he'd stage *Oh! Calcutta!* before the one with "that goddamn Don Quixote and the whore, whatshername."

Advanced Acting was held in a small classroom next to the lobby of the theater and, as he was many days, Mr. Pia was late. Like a true brownnose, I told everyone not to leave and ran up to the cluttered drama office, which was located above the ticket booth. I gently knocked and opened the door to find Pia fully asleep in his blue pajamas on a couch stolen from the set of *The Dick Van Dyke Show*. We had often seen the blue cuffs of Pia's sleepwear peeking out from under his polyester trousers, but I for one had never been witness to the undergarment in full repose. Now that I'm a teacher I have more sympathy for an educator napping in his office (and underwear), but for a student, that's a pretty fucking creepy sight to behold.

"Oh, hello, Bob," Mr. Pia said in his droll theater voice. He's one of the few people in my life who have called me the B-word and lived to tell the tale.

"Time for class, Mr. Pia," I said, trying to sound chirpy.

"You take the baton today, Bob." He gave me a confident nod, then turned to face the wall. What was left of his hair stared back at me. "You can handle it."

Mr. Pia had always been good to me, so I couldn't really argue with him. I was a mediocre performer who thought Method acting could explain my sweaty palms and constant erection, yet he was still encouraging. Even after I graduated, he continued to load on the flattery to my younger brother Eddie, who, after hearing countless stories about this boy named Bob, questioned how close I actually got to those infamous pajamas.

As I ran down the stairs that day, I thought of the laissez-faire way Mr. Pia conducted class, and figured I could just mimic what he did. We'd set up an ordinary improvisation scene, and I'd let the students do most of the work. I could sit back like a director, starting and ending each scene with a hint of a British accent. How hard could it be?

When I reentered the class, the drama freaks were putting their jazz hands up each other's shirts and practicing monologues from that morbidly dull play *The Children's Hour.* "Okay, people," I said, employing a term I'd never use again in my life, even after I started teaching. "Mr. Pia isn't feeling very well today, so we'll have class without him. Are we mature enough to do that?" Maturity was a big deal to us in those days, something we didn't fully understand yet desperately wanted to possess. I remember a girl I really liked telling me I was far too immature to go out with her. This was the equivalent of saying I was hung like a fetal grape.

I explained to the class that we'd be doing a simple domestic improv with a husband coming home to his wife after work. I asked for volunteers, and my friend Melanie immediately raised her hand. She felt bad that I had to stand in for Pia, but she also desperately wanted me to keep her secret about having had sex in eighth grade with my buddy Paul. The other hand raised that day belonged to JT, one of the exiled stoners, who had a dark mane of hair and an extensive collection of black concert T-shirts. The word on the street was that he'd put Ben-Gay in all the jockstraps and got tossed from PE after the second case of what Jerry Lee Lewis would call great balls of fire. He had never volunteered in class before. He usually sat in the back with his brain-dead cronies, laughing while the rest of us pretended to be the symbolic animals and trees that resided deeply in our inner souls.

Melanie took her place behind a table in front of the room and started wringing her hands in anticipation of her husband's late arrival. JT stood off to stage left with his back to the audience. I rapped on the desk in front of me. This was JT's cue to enter. He didn't budge.

"Ding-dong," I chimed.

"He said *dong*," one of the giggling stoners whispered behind me.

"Begin scene." I clapped my hands, but there was no response from my husband. "Action!" I yelled.

Nada.

"John," I said, calling him by his real name, "you can enter now."

He lifted his head like a sleeping lion and turned around. His face was cherry red, as if he'd been holding in a colossal bong hit.

"Sit down, honey." Melanie patted the metal chair next to her. "Tell me about your day."

John just stood there glaring at her with curtains of hair framing his face.

"Sit down, honey," Melanie said with a cutout smile stapled to her face, her eyes all the while fixed on me. "How was your day?"

JT started screaming: "LIONS in the STREET and ROAMING, dogs in heat, rabid, FOAMING." Fists clenched, he paced back and forth, THC-laced spittle flying all over Melanie. "A BEAST caged in the heart of a CITY, the BODY of his MOTHER ROTTING in the SUMMER GROUND, he fled the town."

"Okay, end scene." I stood up. From all the hours I'd spent

with my ear pressed against the door to my older brother's room, I knew those words belonged not to Ibsen or Chekhov but to that other famous drama boy Jim Morrison. Even though JT's flunkies were on the floor in hysterics behind me, our husband wasn't laughing. He had obviously been dying to perform his one-man show years before Val Kilmer greased up his package and slipped into those leather pants for a panting Oliver Stone. I told Melanie to pause while I asked JT to step outside.

"You can't do that," I said to him, a bit uncomfortable with my role as disciplinarian. The last teacher who'd reprimanded him had found a lagoon of urine in the top drawer of her desk.

"What?" His eyes were the color of menstrual fluid.

"You know. Scream the words of the Lizard King when we're supposed to be doing a domestic improv." The s stuck to the roof of my mouth when I said domestic and I sounded a bit like a stage door Nellie boy. Next I'd be lisping "Five minutes, Miss Bacall!" in a halter top and culottes.

"Why not?" JT asked.

The truth was I didn't know why not. Improv was supposed to be a place that could handle any type of crazy shit, but truth be told, he was freaking out all the freaks. There would be many unclear times like this in my future teaching career, situations where I couldn't say exactly why, but in my spleen I knew the shit going down was deeply wrong.

"You just can't. That's why," I said, sounding like a nun leading a sex ed class.

He dropped his head and peered up at me from under his dark fringe of hair. "When I was back there in seminary school—" he bellowed.

"Seminary school? You went to seminary school? Wow, didn't know that."

"There was a person there who put forth the proposition that you can petition the Lord with prayer."

I nodded with lips pressed together. "That's the opening to *Soft Parade*, isn't it?"

"Petition the Lord with prayer." He paused and swallowed a huge chunk of air. His lungs wheezed and rattled like an old ventilator. "Petition the Lord with prayer." He inhaled again and filled his cheeks. "YOU CANNOT *PETITION* the *LORD* with *PRAYER!*" he wailed right into my fucking face.

When I reentered the class, everything seemed much calmer and drier. The other stoners had exited through the window and were going to join JT in the lobby, where he was yelling "The monk bought lunch!" over and over. Seth stood waiting in the wings, ready to go as our new husband. Far as I knew, his musical tastes leaned closer to Moss Hart than Morrison. I rapped on my desk. On cue, Seth twisted and pulled an invisible doorknob.

"Finally," I whispered to the person next to me. "Some decent Method acting."

"How was your day, dear?" Melanie asked, looking more at ease.

"DULCINEA! DULCINEA!" Seth sang with arms opened wide, then dropped to one knee. "I see heaven when I see thee, DULCINEA, and thy name is like a prayer an angel whispers . . . DULCINEA . . . DULCINEA!"

I knew Seth was trying to gain our sympathies to petition Pia to release his *Mancha* moratorium, but I was too tired and dizzy from my contact high to fight. I could even use a little music, I figured, after dealing with such a savage beastie boy.

"What should I do?" Melanie asked me, breaking down the third wall.

"Just go with it," I said, waving a limp hand. "You're a hooker."

"I always knew you told," she said, and stormed out in tears. The class gave her a standing ovation.

Fast-forward twelve years. Somehow I end up becoming a teacher, not of theater, yet high drama often plays a leading role in daily classroom management. The crazy part about trying to create a safe, calm environment where all students can learn is that once you have set the scene, the characters and plot constantly shift. What works in one class won't necessarily fly in the next, and the cast of characters and their relationships change quicker than a Mexican *telenovela* on fast-forward. In one of my seventh-grade English classes my first year at Prep, I had two male students who developed a strangely symbiotic relationship. Charlie was an eccentric white kid who favored Eastern European hats and language peppered with Mandarin Chinese. If the combination of English and Spanish is now commonly referred to as Spanglish, then Charlie spoke Manglish. His parents owned a world bookstore just outside of Santa Fe, and on the first day of class he asked me if I'd read *Ulysses*, and when I admitted I hadn't, his muddled-professor-to-be face told me I was already a grave disappointment to him. He was one of those kids who had been raised mostly around adults. His cultural touchstones were not Magic: The Gathering card games or Power Rangers cartoons but Borges and action heroes of the Che Guevara sort. After unsuccessful attempts to make friends by showing peers his collection of dusty first editions, he would often trap me into having discussions about topics inappropriate for middle school. That year, *Pulp Fiction* had just been released, and my friend Patrick, who worked for Miramax, sent me a sweatshirt from the production. I wore it on a community cleanup day, and Charlie, who had been reciting Chinese poetry to a rake, spotted the orange logo and ran over.

"Mr. Wilder, did you see *Pulp Fiction*?" he asked, panting rather heavily for my taste.

"Yup," I answered curtly, knowing where this would lead.

"What did you think?"

"I think it was rated R and you shouldn't see it."

"I already did." He blinked, staring at me in the sun. "Twice. What did you think when Jules Winnfield accidentally shot that kid in the car?"

"I think we shouldn't have this discussion."

Charlie paused and searched his brain for something else we could talk about. He didn't want to go back to his only friend, a very unresponsive lawn tool. "Read *Ulysses* yet?"

Charlie's partner in crying was a surprising choice. The kid's name was Christopher and he had a quick mouth and high intelligence but the maturity of a sperm. Like Charlie, he didn't fit in with the crowd. Most kids in middle school have their slovenly moments, yet Christopher's hair was always unwashed or covered by a baseball cap stained with what appeared to be castor oil. His shirt was forever untucked, his laces never tied. In my father's day, he would have been a perfect candidate for military school or a severe bitch slap from Jack LaLanne. While Charlie's backpack neatly contained out-of-print novels or obscure chapbooks by Lithuanian prisoners, Christopher's was a jumble of papers, baseball cards, and textbooks with the covers chewed off. Because Charlie and Christopher were both outcasts, this commonality forced them together and they clung on desperately. However, given their distinct personalities, their relationship was always in a state of flux.

A middle school child doesn't have the most accurate perception of time. He or she is not unlike my four-year-old son, London, who, when you ask him the hour, will look at his broken Buzz Lightyear watch and say "Sixty-five" or "Last year." So in order to get class started punctually, instead of locking kids out of the classroom like my more militaristic colleagues, I began shouting bartenders' phrases from my doorway a few minutes before class. "You don't have to go home, but you can't stay there," I'd bellow, and like prairie dogs, the kids would look up, see me, lick their paws, and drop everything to find their backpacks and race into class. One day, we were working on two topics that without profanity can be pretty dull: subjects and verbs. In that class, I used a seating chart to stop girls from giggling and passing notes and boys from lighting each other's farts. I'd planted Charlie in the back row since concentration didn't seem to be an issue for a kid who read Homer in Greek, and I placed Christopher front and center where I could throttle him if necessary. Scrawling on the board, I'd started my lesson on how to locate a compound subject, and turned back to make sure the class was with me. The better students were taking notes and the middle pack was paying some attention, while about a third were looking out the window, drawing pictures of anime characters with ridiculously large breasts or still sweating from what my dad would call "playing too much grabass" on the quad.

Christopher was dressed in white, which seemed to be his favorite hue. I wondered why his parents would clothe a stain sponge like him in such virgin shades. He seemed fine, almost too much so. It looked as though he was holding his breath, trying not to move a muscle. I considered it a victory; maybe Charlie, whose nose was deep in the *Sentence Skills* textbook, had taught

his little buddy some form of Eastern meditation. I continued to
write:

**At the insane asylum, Rocky and Dennis screamed in
terror at the sight of Sally eating her own head lice.**

For my own amusement, I always inserted some obscure movie,
TV, or music reference into my sample sentences. Rocky Dennis
was the name of the lead character from the movie *Mask*, where
Eric Stoltz plays a boy with a massive facial skull deformity and
Cher plays a biker chick with a massive overacting handicap.

"Hey, Coach," Adam called to me, and as I turned (expecting
to give him extra credit for spotting Rocky Dennis), I saw a trickle
of blood drip out of Christopher's nose, a thin rose petal crawling
down his lip and curving around his mouth. I was slightly hypno-
tized by that sight of red against such a large white background.
Christopher didn't move to grab a Kleenex on my desk even
though that kid normally used more tissues than my grandmother ever did. I watched as the blood first bubbled and then
gushed from both nostrils, full force. Columns of blood showered
onto his shirt and the pale wood of his desk, and he did nothing
to stanch the flow. The whole scene looked like the opening of
a German graduate student's film on the effects of war—blood
on the white shirt, white pants, white desk, white kid. Oh, the
horror!

"That is so sick," some girl whispered, but the hypnotic effect
still had its hold on me as well as the rest of the class. We were
witnessing an unnatural occurrence straight out of the *X-Files*.
When the blood plopped onto the floor, I snapped out of it and
threw the bleeder a carton of tissues. Why a kid like Christopher,

who freaked out if someone's fly was down, didn't react to his own hemorrhage frustrated me. Now I'd have to clean up the mess, and my brilliant lesson on spicy action verbs was ruined. Like my days subbing for Mr. Pia, all would be lost if I didn't get the class under control.

"What the hell is wrong with you? Why didn't you run to the bathroom?" I spoke these words in the same way I would to a dog that had just crapped on my pillow. I didn't mean to sound cruel, but here was a kid who'd known his nose was going to explode but decided to ignore all the warning signs. When the same student touting the same drama frequently interrupts your class, you'd have to be in a coma not to lose your cool once in a while.

Christopher trembled, still trying to mop up the blood with a bouquet of tissues but creating a larger mess as the bloody Kleenex stained his pants and fell to the floor like murdered clouds. He violently twisted two tissues into cones and shoved them deep into his nostrils. He looked like something out of George Lucas' arrested imagination. After Christopher caught his breath through his mouth, he stood up. "Charlie!" he shouted. "Charlie did this to me." Then he pointed to his friend hiding in the back row, who, when accused, put down the OED and rose also. "Charlie hit me with his hand," Christopher cried. "On my nose."

"Now, that's not true, Christopher, and you know it," Charlie responded. "Mr. Wilder, we were playing shapeshifter—you know, the Native American spirit—and by accident my backpack hit him in the face. It was not on purpose, and I don't appreciate—"

"That's bullshit," Christopher yelled, twitching. "You hit me on purpose and you are a liar and look at me now." He ran his palms in front of his body the way hand models showcase new cleaning products on television. Only instead of freshly scrubbed and neatly manicured hands, his gory mitts looked as though they had just finished an extensive errand for Charles Manson.

As they like to do, the other kids in class started taking sides, hands shooting up in the air to add more fuel to a fire that was already blazing.

"I saw Charlie in the bathroom the entire time!"

"Christopher hit him first. I swear!"

"They're both lying! They're faking the whole thing to get out of PE!"

"They're gay! I'm, like, so serious! Really gay!"

Meanwhile, Christopher cried, shook his fist at Charlie, and changed the plugs in his nose. There was no easy solution to this stripling standoff. We don't have a nurse at our small school. The PE teacher is an EMT, but she also drives the bus, coaches two teams, sells snacks, and chairs the prom committee. Trying to locate her was like trying to get a urine sample from J. D. Salinger. I did what I had to do, what teachers must eventually learn to master when they cannot wrangle a spooked herd: I passed the buck. I sent the two of them to the head of the middle school, who was far better than I was at sorting out shit like this. It didn't feel fair or right, but I was shell-shocked. You'd think that my student-teaching days standing in for a horizontal Al Pia would have taught me something about the unpredictable nature of teenagers. In retrospect, what I should have done was send the whole class to the office since all we did for the rest of the period was study the pool of blood as it dried on Christopher's desk like it was some Postimpressionist painting at the Metropolitan Museum of Art.

The theatrics between those two boys didn't end even though they both had endowed chairs in the middle school head's office. One day Christopher came hopping in with only one shoe, claiming that Charlie had tossed the other one onto the roof. Charlie responded by saying that he'd thrown it on the roof to knock down his Mongolian hat, which Christopher had thrown up there first.

Other days, they'd amble in with their arms around each other like drunken Russian comrades, laughing at jokes in a language only the two of them understood. During another class, I caught Christopher flipping Charlie off every time I went to the board. I warned him a few times and then he started shielding his middle finger from me by using his left hand. The dumbass forgot that he was in the front row, sitting, and I was standing above him. I hate throwing kids out of the class and rarely do so now that I teach mostly juniors who are dying to leave, but I had to kick Christopher out that day since all the other boys and some of the girls started hoisting the middle finger. If someone had walked in, it would have seemed like I was teaching a lesson in profanity for the hearing-impaired.

Most of the kids in that period looked forward to the Charlie-versus-Christopher antics because they knew it meant diversion or digression from whatever we were studying that day. I'm sure they were baiting the odd couple before class with a litany of he said/he said rumors: that Christopher secretly hated the Chinese language, or that Charlie had said Christopher desperately needed a shower with steel wool, ammonia, and a fire hose. By the time they reach high school, kids learn to be subtler when trying to invite digression, usually by asking me about Poppy's horse, London's finger sucking, where I got my hair styled, or how to make a kick-ass green chile salsa. But then all the seventh-graders, or "sevvies," as we called them, had to do was to get Christopher wound up and you could stick a fork in my class because it was done.

Then, for a few days, everything changed. Charlie was traveling to Mexico on the back of a burro with his family and would miss a week of school. I liked Charlie but looked forward to a break from the daily schoolboy soap opera. Without Charlie to squabble with, maybe Christopher could actually write something down and we could all get a little more work done. On Monday, Christopher spent the period peering around the room as if an imaginary friend was calling his name. He'd pop his head up, pivot his neck, maybe whisper a few words to the kids seated next to him, but not one of them spoke back. He was like that pathetic Fozzie Bear from *The Muppet Show*, delivering lines and jokes that even puppets think suck royal ass.

The next day Christopher basically sulked all period, pressing his forehead against his desk, complaining that he was tired. I tried to get him into the lesson, opening his notebook and putting a pencil in his hand, but his hangdog look remained, even after multiple pats on the back by a teacher who has intimacy issues. I missed Charlie, if only for Christopher's sake. I think teachers always root for the underdog, especially if the underdog doesn't carry weapons. It's in our nature as underpaid professionals to try to save the junior versions of ourselves; otherwise we'd have real jobs that offer actual money, like those of sanitation engineers or waiters in restaurants that serve wine in stemmed glasses. I thought Christopher would sulk a few more days and then Charlie would return bearing Aztec relics and all would be fine. I was dead wrong. That's another thing about teachers. We foolishly believe that we know kids pretty well and think we can predict their behavior (and futures), but we learn day after day that even with all we know about chaos theory, teenagers defy such petty prophecy by the likes of us.

On the third day, Christopher bounced in like he had just swallowed a carton of NoDoz, but I knew he wasn't wasted. Something in him was off. We were working on vocabulary that period, and one of the featured words was *disrespect*. Slang terms come and go, and teaching keeps you abreast of every *wicked*, *chronic*, and *dawg* as they enter the vernacular. *Dis* was a big one that year. *Dis* could be a verb, as in "He just dissed your sorry ass," or a noun: "What a dis. He said your mom was so fat she wakes up in sections." Since kindness was something we attempted to teach during the middle school years, any form of dissing was not allowed on campus. However, since the origin of *dis* came from *disrespect*, Christopher felt he was allowed, after a burst of celebratory moaning, to freely explore the etymon.

"What is a synonym for *disrespect*?" I asked the class.

"*Dis!*" Christopher shouted, grinning so widely that I could see both upper and lower teeth.

"Okay," I pointed toward the back near Charlie's vacant chair. "What else?"

"*Insult?*" a girl answered.

"Good. Another?" I scanned the other faces for signs of a pulse.

"Dis! Dis! Dis! Dissssssssssssss!" Christopher slithered, rattling two clenched fists in front of him like a gunner in a dogfight.

"That's enough, Christopher. No more *dis*. Okay? I'm serious."

He stood up and placed his hand over his heart as if he was reciting the Pledge of Allegiance, something that goes in and out of style in schools like pants with flared bottoms. "I DISagree with your DIScipline," he said. "I am not your DISciple."

"Okay, very funny . . ."

"Mr. Wilder, you are showing your DIStemper and DISregard for my DISorderly conduct. That is most DISsatisfactory." He appealed to his peers to confirm that what he was doing was not only clever but also just shy of a real revolution. However, Charlie was far away and the class would never follow Christopher's unkempt lead.

Even with such a broad display of vocabulary, I regrettably lost my cool. "Shut up, Christopher," I shouted. "You may not speak again this class. If you utter one word, even one syllable, I will send you to the headmaster's office." Even though the headmaster was a nice enough bear of a guy who favored long answers to short questions, the kids blindly believed he was a disciplinarian who put most Third World dictators to shame. Over the years, students created crazy stories of screaming, detention, and straitjacketed expulsion, so my threat carried some mythical weight. Christopher stopped speaking but I could tell by the grinding of his teeth and sweaty hairline that he wasn't finished.

I continued on, feeling a mix of anger and shame as I chalked more vocabulary words on the board. When I turned around abruptly to try to catch Christopher in the act of flipping me off, I saw that even though he gripped his pencil too tightly, he was actually taking notes. Maybe showing him my full range of emotion had made him realize that I was serious about his education and that I truly cared. I wasn't like Mr. Lord, my science teacher in junior high, who never got up from behind his desk unless it was to puff on the pipe stashed in his office. Mr. Lord who told us that he'd still have his bacon and eggs in the morning even if we didn't learn a thing, or that it was no skin off his nose if we scorched our fingers playing Viet Cong with our Bunsen burners. Paused between *tenuous* and *domain*, I caught myself smiling at the thought that my anger might have struck something in this lost boy, something that would change his life forever. I took a deep breath. The class was finally in order.

The choking sound that emerged from Christopher's throat whipped me around from my meditative state. He had sealed his lips shut with a half dozen pieces of tape stolen from the black dispenser on my desk. Saliva bubbled along the edges of the cel lophane where Christopher's breath and words were being extinguished. Below his pulsating face stood a battalion of papers of varying sizes, folded so they stood like nameplates on his desk. The smallest was the size of a postage stamp and the largest was a full sheet of notebook paper folded in half, all containing a single syllable in dark black ink:

Dis Dis **Dis Dis Dis Dis Dis Dis Dis Dis Dis Dis Dis**

The class gathered around the gagged kid's desk, staring for ages at those folded sheets of notebook paper, ever increasing in volume in our collective minds. What was someone like me to do in front of the type of expression that belonged in a place with restraints, morning meds, and pre-masticated yams? As I started walking toward the door, Adam called, "Hey, Coach, where you going?"

I raked my fingers through my hair. "I've had enough. I'm sending myself to the office."

"Can you do that?"

"I can do anything I want," I said. "I'm the teacher."

Bully Bully

I. Origins

When prompted, most of my students can recollect the first bully they ever encountered. Sometimes without even flinching. They may not remember the main character's name in the Faulkner reading they were assigned the day before, but they are quick to recall the boy from ten years ago who called them slutbags on the monkey bars or hung them by their underwear on the showerhead in the boys' locker room. When I was in first grade at Sacred Heart Elementary, there was a boy named Leonard who wore his thick black hair in a dripping pompadour. He was twice as big as the rest of us, though I'm not sure if his freakish size was biological, dietary, or due to the fact that he'd been held back in kindergarten for picking pockets during naptime. So when I'm asked at trainings and in-services to recall my first bully, by all rights my mind should lock onto Leonard and his ham-sized fists, but I don't because in that class there was a far more intimidating presence, one who not only had years of torture experience but also had the seal of approval from the king bully of Old Testament fame himself.

Sister St. Ignatius had steel-gray eyes that matched the thin strip of hair just below her habit. Any little thing would set her off—from the Caputo twins eating sticks of grape ChapStick to some slow kid who didn't learn his letters fast enough for the Lord's liking. Sister ran a tight ship, and even our bodily functions were to conform to her strict schedule. We all lined up to use the bathroom—once in the morning and once in the afternoon—cued by the double click of a tin frog she kept in the hand not wielding a metal ruler. Some of my classmates frequently suffered accidents at their desks and sat trembling in their own filth until they heard the metalline frog's call. We were terrified of upsetting this huge sexless monster, any trace of gender or humanity hidden by the folds of the same black robes worn by witches at Halloween. We had seen her wrath on the opening days of school when a few boys made smart remarks during religious instruction. Sister slammed their knuckles so hard with her heavy ruler that their hands resembled osso buco more than an appendage that could help tie your Keds. Even the metal frog had sliced one kid's cheek open when he was horsing around in the bathroom line. As blood seeped from between his fingers, Sister told us that even though she hadn't meant to hurt the boy, God had, which was all that really mattered. This type of reasoning really confused me but excused her for any harm she would commit in the future. I feel the same way today when I hear politicians tell me to surrender my civil liberties because an Islamic terrorist might want to commandeer my Southwest Airlines flight to El Paso.

Even though I was a quiet and somewhat dreamy (read: slow) boy, I could see the logical conclusions to the meeting of two distinct forces. I knew when my mother bought the wrong milk at the store that my father would come home and use the Lord's name in ways that were quite different than how he employed the same words at mass. I also knew that having a dark cloud like Sister St. Ignatius in the same room as a lightning rod like Leonard was a really bad idea. The first incident between the two came early in the year. I remember sun streaming through the window and my being lost in a *Dick and Jane* book. When I say lost, I don't mean deeply absorbed in the complexities of plot and character; I mean I had no idea how to read, and Sister had dropped these books in front of us expecting to teach us through sanctified shock and awe. My parents weren't like many now who feel the need to get a jump on things by teaching their son or daughter how to spell and count in three languages before pre-K. That's what school was for, according to my parents. Especially the kind of school you had to pay money for. So I stared at the open pages and felt time drip by like melting wax down a holy candle. That first year at Sacred Heart may have been the longest of my life. In the corner, Leonard cracked some joke to his sidekick Errol, who snickered as a sidekick is meant to, and then the holy shit went down in biblical proportions. Sister St. Ignatius stomped over to the corner like Nunzilla in her flowing death robes, knocking over desks as if they were illegally parked cars on a Tokyo side street. Sister reached over and grabbed Leonard by his lime-green collar (our uniforms were hideous even by 1970s standards). She wasn't strong enough to yank him completely off the floor, but she could drag him across the slick wood until he fell in a rumpled lump at her feet. She grabbed that collar again and dragged him out of the room toward purgatory (the boiler room), but before she left, she gave the class a look whose origins had to have come from the horned man, not the haloed one.

After his expulsion from the classroom, you'd think Leonard would have learned to behave or at least become more discreet in order to avoid the wrath of a woman who would be a major horse thief in the apocalypse. He didn't. The next incident occurred the following week when I was getting on the bus for my hellish ninety-minute ride home. Those of us from Point Lookout were the farthest out on the easternmost tip of Long Island, so we were always the first on in the morning and the last off in the afternoon. Everyone at Sacred Heart took a bus because we were in the middle of Hempstead's urban fringe, which meant the neighborhood was like Compton before all the A&R guys homed in to find rappers to promote. From the steps of his bus Leonard waved and shouted, "Goodbye, Sister DEVIL Ignatius," thinking he was securely stowed on his ferry ride across the river Styx to the Meadowbrook Parkway. It must have been a Friday for him to feel so safe, counting on the holy car wash of confession to wash away all his sins over the weekend. Sister St. Ignatius reached to lift Leonard out of the mouth of the bus and in the process yanked a clump of hair from his slick scalp. Even though I was raised well after the atomic age, I knew that when you saw two forces of the universe clash, the best thing to do was duck and cover. I ran into the bus and hid my face in the shredded back of the seat in front of me. I would have prayed, but God seemed to have his hands full outside.

II. The Bullied

Fast-forward six years. My family had since moved from a small beach community on Long Island to the fleeting country sprawl of suburban Connecticut. After spending the fifth and sixth grades—sans uniform—at Greens Farms Elementary, I was beginning junior high at a place called Long Lots. While I was excited about a larger school with kids who wouldn't know I'd worn velvet bell-bottoms to the sixth-grade dance, I was more nervous than your average boy with a bad-skin-and-haircut combo. Long Lots was the first school since Sacred Heart that I would share with my older brother Rich, who had evolved from a nondescript kid into a low-grade juvenile delinquent who hung with a group of guys called the Grubs. I don't know if this middle school mob came up with the name themselves or were given the moniker because of bad hygiene, laundry detergent avoidance disorder, or the willingness to do things that would have landed them on *Fear Factor*, if it had aired in the late 1970s. My brother was a fringe initiate of the group, not as tough or athletic or good-looking as the other members, who'd gotten laid at fourteen in their parents' Gremlins. At the time Rich was called Spoon by anyone under thirty-five outside of our family because of some banal joke he told when we moved from Long Island. Lame comedy has always been the way Wilders try to make nice. Even now I'll bump into a high school friend and she'll ask me, "How's Spoon?" which causes my brain discomfort as it tries to hold two versions of my brother simultaneously: (a) a teenage ruffian with a fascination for homemade weaponry and (b) a muckety-muck executive flying all over the country to sell information storage and retrieval to major corporations. While Rich was still a novice at being tough after missing the necessary training while at Sacred Heart on Long Island, the other Grubs were close to pro. Like a bad after-school special, they ran the junior high. They could intimidate teachers by their sheer physical size, through their expert thievery of chalk, erasers, textbooks, and doorknobs, or by peeing in a desk, which is really nasty if it sits overnight in a heated room. The teenage throng could manipulate time by padlocking the doors of the school or—a more frequent occurrence—pulling fire alarms right before an exam. Unlike Sacred Heart, where the nuns did all the hazing, at Long Lots the Grubs were the Lords of Flatbush. Having a brother who was an assistant Grub made me a recognizable target. I was someone they could pick on and know I wouldn't rat them out. My brother once told me that I should appreciate the fact that his friends paid attention to me and were toughening me up, even if that so-called attention and training could land me in the hospital.

For the first week or so, I kept a low profile, lingering close to teachers like a pantywaist and walking in the other direction when I heard my brother's or his friends' voices echoing in the hallway. The Grubs traveled mostly in packs, so they were fairly easy to spot. Luckily, I wasn't alone. The summer before junior high I'd made friends with a kid named Jeff Vannart at the Jem amusement center, where we played foosball and Captain Fantastic pinball (when Elton John was actually cool) while listening to tough bands like Bad Company and Foreigner on the jukebox. One morning at Long Lots, Jeff and I had been released from class early for some errand, and we wandered the halls basically alone. Excited with our newfound freedom, since in junior high you actually switched classes, we took our eye off the ball. The Grubs turned the corner and, like idiots, we froze. We should have run. Sometimes—really, most times—it's a good idea to run

away in an uncomfortable situation. As a teacher, I preach otherwise when discussing morality in *The Great Gatsby* or heroic deci-
sions according to Joseph Campbell or Donald Trump. Yet I think
in today's America, running away is your best call. It gives you
time for the booze to wear off, a plan to emerge, an alibi to be secured. Any good politician knows that if you're caught later, it's
always harder to prove exactly what you did with the tranny
hooker at the meth lab in the No-Tell Motel.

"There's Spoon's brother," one of the Grubs yelled (that
probably made me Demitasse), and we were quickly engulfed in a
cloud of BO and the aroma of stale bong water. There wasn't much
for the Grubs to do except choose from their arsenal of conventional and innovative bullying, and Jeff and I knew that not only
was resistance futile, it actually backfired on your sorry ass.

I should say in full disclosure that my brother did not partake
in the following. He just smirked in the background under some
really heinous bangs (my father had a blind man's taste in hair-
cutters). One guy held me down by placing his scabby knees on
my chest and pinning my arms while another pried open my jaws,
which is not hard to do when the victim can't really breathe.
Another guy, carefully chosen for his pre-emphysemic lungs,
bent over and summoned up a hairy ball of phlegm from the
deepest recesses of his diseased and decaying innards. The thick,
gathering noises in his throat were not unlike those of a garbage
disposal grinding a full load of fatty pork cartilage. Because my
face was clamped *Clockwork Orange* style, I could not see Jeff, but
the same thing was happening to him somewhere nearby. The
Grubs were nothing if not fair in their own twisted way.

The mucus masticator leaned over, his cheek fat with what
passersby would have guessed to be a wad of Big League Chew. He
rolled the clump around in his mouth and then let it fall in a

prolonged viscous string into mine. Torturers, like retirees at a restaurant bathroom, love taking their time. I started to cough but could not close my mouth to repel the vile chowder. I gagged and tried not to taste, but nothing went my way that day. We all have to swallow shit sometime or another in our lives. Sometimes it's in a bad job with an overbearing boss; other times we do it because we foolishly love the one who gladly force-feeds us excrement. For me that day, it was because I happened to be related to a semi-notorious boy who was named after the utensil you use to stir your morning coffee. Some people might react to my phlegmatic force-feeding with the same horror as they would watching wolves attack a poor bunny rabbit on the Nature Channel. But any good naturalist will tell you that one species' cruelty is another's brotherly love.

III. The Bullying

If the bullied are given a chance to bully, they'll take it every time. Look at history. Look at *Benito Cereno* by Herman Melville. Look at *Hardball* or Bill O'Reilly. You know that fucker was given atomic bleeding wedgies or duct-taped to his locker as a kid. Hell, I'm no better. At Long Lots, just like my brother Spoon, I rose to the fringes of a group, only mine didn't have an official name and had more to do with early metrosexual grooming, silver S-chains, and overindulgence in Polo cologne. I left some former companions behind in my rise, but not many, since my friend pool was rather shallow to begin with. The one pal I did abandon was a boy named Stuart, who lived in the narrow strip of a working-class neighborhood in Westport, which I'm sure now doesn't exist since celebs like Phil Donahue and Don Imus moved in. Like my brother (and Bad Company), I was running with the pack by ninth grade, and one Saturday we were going from my house on Hillandale Lane to the Post Road to slurp oily pizza and shoplift numerous packs of Bubble Yum from the drugstore. The quickest way to get there was to cut through a series of backyards, a pleasure my own children will never enjoy living in the dusty and sprawling Southwest. For my friends and me, it cut our traveling time in half and often felt as though we were housebreakers casing the homes of people who owned sporting goods stores or were the copywriters on commercials for Tang instant breakfast drink.

My little gang crossed the small road bordering our old elementary school, and I saw Stuart and a friend just benignly sitting on the swings like two kids in *The Day After*. It was a milky, bleak Connecticut day. In ninth grade, I felt like Bill Murray in *Stripes*—a goofy guy with bad skin who had made it into the big leagues on nothing more than luck and a smart mouth. I didn't want to go back to my former life of loneliness and really bad fashion choices. Or maybe, like any other young boy in America, I wanted to be a tough guy like Harrison Ford or Kurt Russell, the only real action heroes in 1981. Either way, it was one of the few times in my life when I went a-lookin' for a fight, as they say out West.

I called Stuart a stupid name, seeing our forthcoming tangle as a movie fight where I would land a punch, knock him out, and slap my hands together like a blackjack dealer, ending with a witty line like "Well, I had to take out the trash, boys" or "Someone had to clean up this playground." What I got instead was some odd existentialist play where whatever I did, Stuart did back, only slightly better. I tried to hit him in the face but ended up just slapping his neck like he had an annoying mosquito problem.

He landed a blow on my chin with hands that were far more working class than mine, even though my dad was a slave driver when it came to weekend chores. When I put him in a headlock, Stuart reached around with his long arms and locked me into a tighter version. Fighting, I soon realized, (a) was exhausting, (b) hurt, and (c) lasted longer than the scene where Indiana Jones shot Osama bin Laden's dad in the bazaar. The painful charade was really like fighting with myself. My last effort to win and save face and end this thing was to try to knee him in the balls. I realize this was, and still is, a coward's way out, but since I was a coward on the way in, I figured I had nothing to lose. My knee hit the inside of his thigh, while his return landed dead on my unremarkable junk. I felt the familiar ice-melt burn of getting clocked in the nuts followed by my stomach dropping out by way of the length of my colon. I lost my breath and fell into another headlock, where I muttered the words "Had enough?" and my shadow self echoed, "You had enough?" We did this fancy-nancy dance a few more times before I just gave up. The bully's life was apparently not for me. I was destined for a different type of manipulation—one that used tests instead of fists, ink instead of spit, and promises of extra homework instead of physical threats.

IV. Cyberbully

With the invasion of the Internet, bullying has become high tech, and we know that technology scares the bejesus out of parents. Since most adults raising teenagers today did not grow up with computers, they react to what's happening in cyberspace the same way my father reacts when he reads an article on bareback gay sex parties in Manhattan. Schools feel the need to address the concerns of the folks who ferry their customers back and forth, so our administration decided to approach the topic head-on. Since part of my job is bringing speakers to campus, I was instructed to invite the FBI to discuss cybersafety with our students. Usually I am wary of inviting any law enforcement to campus unless I need help warding off gangs of faculty from rival schools or deciphering who wrote that obscenely creative profanity on the wall about me romancing farm animals. However, I did as I was told and ended up developing a phone friendship with a bona fide Special Agent and attending a proprietary (read: painfully dull) training at the FBI headquarters in Albuquerque. Even though the presentation was long and boring, I fancied the idea that I now had a powerful friend who was an actual Special Agent in the FBI. I imagined phoning her from a pay phone if I needed some dirt on the scumbag who was hassling my family. I wasn't sure exactly how that scenario could actually occur or what that scumbag would look like (maybe close to Steve Buscemi), but if it did, the FBI had my back. It felt like I was the new kid at school who'd befriended the bully for future protection, only my bully carried a gun and could tap phone lines.

After the FBI swooped into our school and spoke at painful length about credit card fraud to kids who didn't even have driver's licenses, the Parents' Association at our school decided that moms and dads also needed to be educated on the issues surrounding cybersafety. At first, the PA proposed bringing in the DA's office to come in and yell at the parents for an hour or so, then pass out glossy brochures in both English and Spanish. Luckily, the administration knew how that would go over, so they asked a local business that dealt with computer training to speak to the collective in a more reasonable manner. I showed up the night of the presentation to support the administration, help the parents, and brag to anyone who'd listen about my close friend in the FBI. The computer folks who were running the show were all dressed like food court workers in colored polo shirts with their goofy logo printed on the chest. This was my third meeting in as many days, and my goal was to listen, nod thoughtfully, help the neophytes turn on computers, and go home for a badly needed adult beverage. The admin told me that these computer geeks would present a fair and clear picture, answer questions and try not to incite a cyberriot. For some reason, I cyberbelieved them.

The presenter was a curly-haired woman who tried to keep things light by asking silly questions and getting us to repeatedly raise our hands like children desperate to pee. She advised parents that the best way to deal with any issue of adolescence was to speak to your kids, and she told us that *parent* was a verb as well as a noun. She relayed anecdotes about how parents had done their job despite the invention of the wheel, telephone, radio, automobile, television, and Betamax; the computer was just another thing to rip our kids away from after their eyes went glassy or they got painful erections. Maybe it was because she looked and acted like a washed-out Ronald McDonald, but I felt safe.

We strolled down to the networked classroom where a baker's dozen of us logged on to computers using the ID *cyber* and the password *yikes*, an odd choice given the objective of being calm and rational, but I played along. A few of the parents knew as much about computers as I do about equine insemination, but I happily showed them how to log on, ignore the stream of error messages popping onto the screen, and launch themselves head-first onto the information superhighway without a seat belt or helmet.

I don't know if our presenter took a fall on the blacktop on her way down, but the person leading parents in front of the glowing banks of computers seemed itching to start something akin to the hysteria surrounding the Salem witch trials. She started mimicking the tone and demeanor of the hectoring we were supposedly here to stop.

"Who are you?" she asked me as I scurried around, touching the parents and the keyboards at the same time.

"I'm a teacher."

"Good," she said, glancing toward her partner like Edward G. Robinson in a hostage situation. "We like teachers. Do you use a computer?"

"Well," I sighed, "to be honest, I got trained by the FBI in cybersafety."

She slapped on a smile and clamped her hands on her hips. Her expression reminded me of a bumper sticker I'd seen that day that read: *How would you like a big cup of shut the fuck up?* She was subtler, though. "Why don't you sit down? You might learn something."

Instead of easing us into the session by tracing how the Internet actually works or showing us fun ways to use pastels in e-mails, our task mistress plunged the parents straight into the heart of a most nasty beast. She had us go to MySpace.com, a Web site where all types of people post way too much information about themselves in mostly unpleasant and poorly worded ways. It's like being trapped in some bad singles bar where everyone is a close talker with heinous-smelling ass breath.

"What boxes should we check?" a teacher from a visiting school asked.

"Check that you are seeking all men and women looking for swingers. Oh, what the hell? Check everything!" Bossy yelled with abandon. This was like telling your teenager to skip that whole kissing thing and head straight to an S&M club in lower Manhattan.

"Oh my God!" someone yelled behind me, and the gasps started popping like dropped lightbulbs on a concrete floor. All these adults who had never used a computer before were staring at the types of deviance that did not play well inside a classroom, networked or not.

"This is sick!" A woman dragged her fingers across her scalp.

Another parent turned for help from our leader. "You mean my child could go here? Oh my Lord."

"Your child most likely HAS gone here," Bossy said. She cocked her head in a look that combined both concern for our children (she, of course, had none of her own) and deep pity for our ignorance.

I stepped back and viewed all the images on the screens—men in G-strings looking for older men with petite dogs, women in bikinis with spray-painted slogans that read "She has no limits" and "Feed this bitch." When people looked closer, they saw more F-bombs than Dick Cheney used when he accidentally shot his hunting buddy.

"Hey, I found my high school class!" a board member chirped happily, somehow managing to avoid the nastiness covering us all.

"You're on Classmates.com," Bossy said, disappointed in her pupil.

The man swiveled around on his chair. "Should I join? Gee, I haven't seen some of these people in thirty years." You could tell by his grin that he'd been reminiscing while his peers had been dry-heaving.

Bossy snapped: "Sure. If you want your inbox full of spam telling you how to enlarge body parts you never knew you had."

She shook her head. "Okay, people, look up here." She tapped a pen on a dry-erase board at the front of the class. Some parents still clicked rapidly, unable to tear themselves away from all the freaks lookin' for love.

In a maudlin tone, our instructor listed the many ways a student might bully another. It could start with a simple e-mail, she said, sent to a few kids saying your daughter was as fat as a house or looser than a ten-cent slot machine. "Cyberbullies can also create fake e-mail accounts using your child's name," she said, "and send hate messages to other students and, yes, even teachers." She shot me a sympathetic smile as if to say my inbox would be filling up any day now. The parents began murmuring, desperately trying to navigate all these twisting side roads on the information superhighway.

"People, here's the biggie!" the facilitator exclaimed, trying to get her chimps-on-typewriters back in line. She informed us that if a few angry nerds get some time, they could create a whole Web site devoted to slandering your little Jessie.

"Last year one of the Queen Bees did that to my daughter," one of the parents confessed. "They Photoshopped her head onto animal bodies as well as, ahem, other, nastier images."

"So true." Our leader nodded happily along with her convert. "And good luck trying to get a Web site down. After a lot of time and a whole lot of money, the cyberbullies just build another one."

As the facilitator was talking, the idea of nasty gossip via the phone or poorly spelled graffiti on the bathroom wall seemed as old and archaic as the Teletype. I knew what the parents were thinking—nothing could stop these armies of cyberbullies. Everyone in that room seemed to be resigned to the fact that somewhere someone was online sullying their child's good name. Our own Simon Legree had whipped everyone into such a frenzy that by the time we all logged off, I felt afraid for my own daughter's safety even though she was only nine and didn't own a radio, let alone a computer. Exhausted and defeated, we plodded like zombies back up to the auditorium.

I understand that kids offer too much information on MySpace and Facebook and that cyberbullying takes place in and out of schools, yet as we lurched back toward cold coffee, I wondered if this was the best way to educate parents about their own offspring. When I was a kid, I knew that giving out personal information over the phone would get me in hock with my dad, and that I needed to steer clear of bullies even if I was related to one. After this supposedly educational night, I imagined all these crazed, googly-eyed parents running home and yanking their kids from their beds to interrogate them about someone named Zophyr or find out who was the Queen Bee in the histrionic hive we call history class. On the way up, I heard one parent beg the instructor to come to her house and investigate her daughter, tracking where she went, whom she met, and what she and her friends said online. This seemed an expensive and roundabout way of getting to know your own child, but who was I to stand in the way of progress?

When we all reassembled in the auditorium, it was as if someone had sucked the air from the room, and given my extensive FBI training, I had my suspects. Some parents perched on the edge of their seats, waiting for the next half-naked piece of bad news to be shoved down their gullets. I had this sinking feeling that people were getting what they'd come for. The facilitators were grinning knowingly with the rush that comes from deflowering a string of forty- and fifty-year-old virgins, and the parents were like bad-news junkies, jonesing for the next horrible thing that could happen to their babies. The curly-haired woman in-

troduced her partner, a big, beefy man who had remained curi-
ously silent for the first part of the presentation. He sauntered up
as if he was Clint Eastwood seeking his revenge and he'd been
biding his time.

"I was a Marine for twenty years," he started, squinting at the
parental parishioners of pain. "And then, ladies and gentlemen, I
was a cop." He scanned the rows to see if anyone was going to dis-
pute this fact. "My happiest day in the force was finding a missing
kid." This line seemed all too familiar to me. Every cop show,
movie script, and comic book contained this line, and I could
guess the next one before he delivered it: "The saddest day was
when I had to knock on a door and tell parents I couldn't find
theirs." Before he could bring out the color photos of dead and dis-
membered victims of misplaced keystrokes, I slinked out of the
auditorium. I'd had enough of the FBI, CIA, and all the other forms
of bullying in America, cyber or otherwise. At home, I had a
behind-the-times family who was connected only to dessert and
the cableless television set, and I couldn't wait to log on.

White Boy Sings the Blues

I grew up in a town so white that our celebrity holy trinity consisted of Martha Stewart, Paul Newman, and Jason Robards. Westport had all the offerings of a cake eater's paradise: a yacht club, a golf club, and a polo club, none of whose grounds I ever set foot on except to let loose the boats, steal the carts, and tear up the greens by dragging boats behind golf carts. Even with my self-inflated radical teenage behavior, growing up in Izod heaven made me an absolute dumbshit when it came to ethnicities that didn't sail freely on the *Mayflower*. My nine-year-old daughter, Poppy, knows far more about Martin Luther King Jr. and civil rights than I did in my freshman year in college. Until I was twenty, I was a happy cracker idiot wearing my collar up, eating crustless cucumber sandwiches, and dreaming of never having to wear socks inside my loafers.

In high school, my interests weren't very wide. Besides soccer, drama, and trying to convince girls that they should use my pool for skinny-dipping, the only hobby I had was a secret affinity for music, the way I suppose most teenagers do. My hidden passion started with my dad's love of jazz, swing, and *The Most Happy Fella* soundtrack, which played too loudly on our RCA in the living room. As I grew older, my tastes mirrored the sounds coming out of my older brother's dank bedroom: classic rock like AC/DC, Led Zeppelin, and The Who, then less classic offerings from Bad Company and, rather unfortunately, the Stray Cats. I graduated from high school in 1984, not a great year in music, but still before Madonna could even spell *Kabbalah* and Michael Jackson became famous for his more childish pursuits.

I hauled my whiteness and bad taste in music less than an hour north to Wesleyan, a college all the guides referred to as Diversity University. My sophomore year, I gathered enough nerve to sign up for a course called the History of African American Music, taught by a music professor who had once played trombone for James Brown's touring band. This professor had a radical-looking beard, deep-set eyes, and black-rimmed Malcolm X glasses and spoke with a hipness I'd never heard shopping on Main Street in Westport. The few African Americans we had in my high school didn't live in our town, and we treated them more as exotic exchange students from a land with flashy footwear, hair products in unfamiliar packaging, and a national anthem performed by the Sugar Hill Gang.

The music class was held in a limestone-block-and-glass building erected in the 1970s that rose from the ground like a giant ice cube. I was surrounded by a storm of people of different races, genders, and sexual orientations. Lesbian dancers sat elbow to elbow with black militants and anarchists who hated apartheid.

In that dim room, I felt the same way I would later in Amsterdam
while viewing my first live nude bed show: titillated, frightened,
and severely unnecessary. Professor Cool, as I called him, moved
his body like a shadow dancer and said things like "Mother is only
half a word" and "Dig it, baby." He had us read Amiri Baraka, who
shocked me by breaking all the rules of conventional grammar by
spelling business *bizness* and suppose *s'pose*, and Charlie Mingus,
who had claimed to fuck twenty-three girls in one night even
though, from what I could tell from the cover photo, he was
grossly overweight. Needless to say, in Professor Cool's course, I
felt like I'd showed up at basketball tryouts with my ice skates on.

Realizing I had some serious cultural catching up to do, I'd
steal away late at night and head up to the listening library to
check out these new things called CDs. Strapping on cushy head-
phonoo the size of loaves of bread, I'd repeatedly listen to
Mingus' "Goodbye Pork Pie Hat" and the music of artists such as
Jelly Roll Morton and Billie Holiday. Lost in the beats and chords,
I imagined myself at the Cotton Club in Harlem with a scratchy
goatee on my chin and a beret on my head, smoking a bidi and
sipping scotch and milk. In my diasporic dream, I was so cool
that I snapped my fingers instead of offering the laissez-faire golf
clap so popular at summer concerts in my honky hometown. My
deep love of this music and my new hip attitude would disguise
my taste for baron of beef and Yorkshire pudding, as well as the
fact that I was once auctioned off as a slave for a day at a high
school fund-raiser. Even though the bid I received was by far the
lowest of the evening and made by my brother Tom out of pity, I
knew I should harbor deep shame.

In Professor Cool's class, I hid on the fringes with my eyes
wide, ears open, and mouth clamped shut. I would sometimes

quietly laugh along with the professor's joke about sticking it to the Man, not fully realizing that all my dad's friends were the Men and that I, in fact, was the Man-in-Becoming. After our time was up, while the rest of the class trotted off to O'Rourke's Diner to discuss signifying monkeys and code switching, I ran to the gym to slip on my jockstrap with a roomful of soccer players hosting athletic mullets on their heads.

At the end of the semester, we were supposed to do a final project of our own choosing as a culmination to the course. I hadn't given it much thought because Professor Cool hadn't really assigned us any graded work all term, and even after all that reading and listening, I still felt out of place. Sure, I liked to think I could eventually fuck like Charlie Mingus by using the methods so vividly described in his book. I'd even tried to speak like Baraka, peppering my language with profanity and academic-sounding words I didn't know the meaning of. No one took me seriously, though. When I told my older brother on the phone that "a white motherfucker like me don't s'pose his bizness will contain the vicissitudes of verticality," he just thought the drugs were better at my school than at his.

So when Professor Cool began class one day by asking each person what their project was on, I started to sweat. Each student's project sounded so smart and, using my new lingo, all racial and shit.

"I'm going to show how the Rolling Stones inappropriately appropriated black culture by stealing the blues and amassing capitalistic goods and services based on this most heinous hijacking," a Hispanic kid in a Bob Marley shirt said, drumming his ring-covered fingers on his desk.

The Asian girl next to him whispered, "Amen, brother."

"I'm going to research the Barbados slave songs that arose after the passing of the Slave Consolidation Act of 1826," another
hipster offered.

"Right on."

When Professor Cool called on me, I squeaked out, "I'm going
to sing the blues in Central Park." I don't know where either the
idea or the high voice came from, but there was a brief pause
where I almost believed I'd been accepted into this happening
collective. I saw my pale face inserted into the class photo like the
United Colors of Benetton ad campaign so popular at the time.
Then everyone laughed at me, the guy with the athletic mullet on
the left side eyeing the fire exit. The professor did too, then adjusted his glasses and joked, "You're gonna need some brothers
to go with you," winking at some black students from Malcolm X
House seated in the front row. Professor Cool stepped closer to
me and must have realized that I hadn't uttered one "amen" or
"solid" all semester. He didn't even know my white man's label.
Nodding, he said, "I'm gonna hold you to that. You don't follow
through, you fail."

I turned even whiter than I already was.

"Better get someone to film it," he said before moving on to
the next student, a bald girl in military fatigues. "This, my brothers and sisters," he said, raising one finger in the air, "is the era
of proof."

I was fucked. I could neither sing nor play a kazoo, let alone a
guitar. I didn't even know where Central Park was located in
Manhattan. At the time, I shared a broken-down house off campus with two goalies from the hockey team. The more sensitive of
the netminders played guitar, so I casually strolled by his room
and asked him how long he thought it would take me to learn, say,
a simple blues tune on the guitar well enough to sing it.

"You?" he asked, eyeing me in a bemused way. He was a clean-cut boarding-school kid and his room was covered in plaid banners and posters, forever reminding me of that pedigree, a degree of whiteness higher than my feeble beginnings. "Play and sing at the same time?" he asked, slicking back his neat hair with the palm of his hand.

I shrugged. "That's kinda the idea."

He nodded toward my hairstyle, what some called "business in the front, party in the back." "About as long as it would take me to grow my hair like that."

I needed to find someone talented enough to play the guitar and another person stupid enough to film me getting the crap kicked out of me. Luckily, our mediocre soccer season had ended, so the guys who'd stayed clean all fall had gone out and bought enough drugs to last until Christmas break. At Diversity University, there was a place on campus where you could buy drugs 24/7. In the front window of this small, low-rise apartment hung a two-sided cardboard sign. If the face on the sign offered a smile, you could go in and choose from the drawersful of pot, mushrooms, acid, or sometimes more exotic fare like mescaline and Ecstasy. The sad face meant you had to go back to your Grateful Dead albums and smoke the seeds. The refreshing thing about the house (and its sign) for those of us who got into the school based mostly on athletics was its distinct lack of academic snobbery. Like restaurants in El Paso with color photos printed on the menu, illiteracy wasn't a barrier to nourishment.

I went to see two soccer buddies who were known around campus for their good looks, cavalier sense of adventure, and ability to smoke copious amounts of weed. They were handsome Aryan versions of Beavis and Butt-Head. Luke, the guitar player, was strikingly tall and thin, with a deep stoner's laugh. Wes, my future cameraman, had a cherubic face that let him get away with the kind of crimes money can't buy

When I called on them at their apartment, the duo had just pulled an all-nighter. This was fairly common for them after the season. It was not unusual to fetch them for class only to find them giggling like two drunk monkeys at typewriters, producing unintelligible essays. On this day, they had been trying to construct a two-tiered loft without plans or instruments of the measuring kind. I don't even know if they had tools. When I arrived, each man-child was in a hysterical mass in opposite corners of the room. The loft looked like it had been nailed together by the construction team of Ray Charles and Stevie Wonder. The top level was too narrow, so the stained futon curled like a moldy burrito; the bottom boards had been sawed too short, so the futon flapped over the end like a diseased tongue. Even with its monumental flaws, they ended up keeping the splinter dispenser. Wes figured that since they didn't really fall asleep per se, just kind of collapsed each night, the wooden mess would do just fine. And, since they'd run out of nails, they were ready for a road trip.

All that week I'd been searching for the most simplistic blues song in the listening library and settled on "Love in Vain" by those damn culture criminals, the Rolling Stones. I felt I could connect with the lyrics even given my severe racial and cultural handicaps. It was possible that I'd be waiting for a train in a station sometime during my life with a suitcase in my hand. And hell, most of my love for girls on campus was in vain, so I had that to inspire me.

After a take-out order at the Casa de Smiley Face, we all piled into my Chevy Chevette and drove the forty-five minutes south to my father's house, marveling at the fall foliage, swirling like col-

ored oils along the Merritt Parkway. I think *wow* was the opera-
tive word on that ride, covering everything from the crimson oak
leaves to Luke finding that his pants actually had a zipper. When
we reached Hillandale Lane, I instructed the pair to dash into my
house like criminals, pick up the video camera and whatever supplies we could scavenge, and then get the hell out. My dad was in
the yard, stacking wood left over from a recent splitting. Once a
year, he rented a log splitter and cleaved more wood than Lorena
Bobbitt. The three of us fell out of the compact car like stoned
Shriners. "Hi, Dad," I yelled, waving as I ran onto the porch. We
ducked into the house, trying to gather everything as fast as we
could. I grabbed the dusty camera and a tape that read "Eddie's
First Steps." I figured we all knew my brother's goofy walk by
now; why would anyone care if I erased the meager beginnings?

I walked into the kitchen and froze. My dad had his arms
crossed over his sweaty white T-shirt. Wood chips in his graying
hair, he was staring at Luke and Wes, whose faces were smeared
with Baker's chocolate. Each stoner held a candy bar in one hand
and a slice of leftover pizza in the other.

"Rob?" My dad raised one eyebrow, extending my name into
three or four elongated syllables. He cocked his head. "Is this
some sort of fraternity stunt?"

"It's for a class, Dad," I said, throwing him the excuse I still
employ today to get me out of tight jams or embarrassing situations. This academic alibi gets me a 20 percent teacher's discount
at Borders even if I'm buying chapter books for London's birthday or the latest Green Day CD for Poppy. In the English office at
Prep, it comes in handy if the image of a scantily clad Heidi Klum
on my computer screen seems a bit randy for the department
head peering over my shoulder. But back at my house in Westport,

the excuse stalled my father long enough for us to pile back into
the car while he scowled on the porch, arms crossed over his barrel chest, waiting for a wheel to fly off the car.

Even though we looked like three messed-up musketeers, no one
seemed to notice on the busy streets of Manhattan. Wes filmed us
stumbling down Central Park West, but the video camera jammed
up, and he stopped to fix it in front of the Dakota. I was about to
say something to Luke about John Lennon when Carly Simon
walked out of the building. I shouted to Wes to start filming and
for Luke to pull out his guitar. Carly had a rather large head with
fanned Farrah Fawcett hair and teeth the size of sugar cubes. I
couldn't believe my luck. Here was a fellow cracker who had actually managed to shed some of her whiteness by singing soul music. I vaguely recalled that my dad had done some business at the
bank with her family, so I had a valid reason to engage her and
describe my quest. I walked up and explained who I was and who
my father was, and described my project for Professor Cool. Her
famous mouth shifted from a wide smile into an O of deep horror. I now realize what she saw: a stoned slob in stained thrift-
store clothes with a Lurch look-alike waving a piece of glossy
wood around behind him. I crept closer to the singer-songwriter,
babbling nonsense while Wes swore loudly at the malfunctioning
machine and Luke struck some dissonant chords. Our bum rush
must have seemed like a musical act based on the life and times of
Mark David Chapman because I couldn't believe how fast a
woman Carly's size could run away in heels.

Even though I had freaked out the singer who had supposedly
balled Cat Stevens, Warren Beatty, and Mick Jagger, I was not to
be deterred. Professor Cool and all the other hipsters would see

that I was not destined to wear web belts with whales, mono-grammed shirts, and Top-Siders the rest of my life. I would never speak in Larchmont lockjaw, use *summer* as a verb, or name my children Chip or anything that rhymes with *fluffy*.

We walked across the street to the park, which looked more like the Killing Fields than Strawberry Fields. This was 1985, five years after Lennon was shot and four years before *wilding* would become a term for something other than Elizabeth Taylor's second husband, years before Rudy Giuliani swept all the homeless under the concrete rug. I nudged over a sleeping hobo so Luke could sit next to me on a slatted bench. This area of the park was swarming with an obscenely eclectic group of people. The kooky congregation was like my music class, only larger, more menacing, and with many visible wounds. As Luke tuned up, I watched as tourists snapped photos, panhandlers hassled the tourists, and junkies and drunks mixed it up like trained bears in a Russian circus during an earthquake. I realized that soon mine would be the loudest voice in this clusterfuck and that all these people would be staring at me. My heart rate started to speed up, and my ass seemed wet. What the fuck was I doing? I couldn't sing. Why did I need to prove anything to a group of people who saw me as an oppressor? And what had I been thinking when I got this haircut?

"Okay, dude." Luke patted his guitar. He was ready.

"Hurry up, battery's dying," Wes called from behind the camera.

Luke strummed the guitar, and I began to sing, "Well, I fol-lowed her to the station, with a suitcase in my hand." At the sound of music, people turned to face our bench. Wes was standing across from us, so the gawkers didn't really notice him, even though the camera was the size of a child's coffin.

"Yeah, I followed her to the station, with a suitcase in my haaannd . . ."

"Shut the fuck up, asshole," a homeless guy in a wool cap yelled, shaking a fingerless-gloved fist in my general direction.

"It's hard to tell, hard to tell, when all your love's in vain." It felt like I was singing in the middle of a tornado, only instead of houses and cars flying past me, it was all these different kinds of freaks. They say that music hath charms to soothe the savage breast, but in Central Park it incited the opposite. The guy next to me snored away, but others hurled urban profanity at me and anyone within shouting distance. Japanese tourists snapped my picture with the same sense of odd enthusiasm they had when photographing a building or purse snatcher. I sang the whole song, three verses and chorus, without stopping even though I almost got punched and one angry guy launched a spit gob just past my eye.

"What'd you think?" I asked Wes as I stood up from the bench.

He shrugged. "Battery died a while ago. I think I got you singing the first line, though."

"Dude, you were sitting in that guy's chunder." Luke pointed to my spot on the bench. Sure enough, the sleeping guy's vomit was smeared all over the slats and on my ass.

On the tape I showed during our final presentations, you could see me singing with my pale chin sticking out and my small hands slapping my thighs, trying to eke out something resembling soul. The class laughed at a close-up of the homeless guy sleeping next to me, but Professor Cool kept quiet, rubbing his beard as he watched my free fall concert in the park. When the tape ended, you could hear Wes cry, "Oh fuck!" as the battery died, then my father's voice came on without pause, urging my brother Eddie the toddler to take a few more steps before he fell, like me, flat on his face.

"Give me that tape," Professor Cool yelled to the AV geek running the video player. Even though he never addressed me directly, you could see that he was pleased with the effort. "This is what I'm talking about," he shouted, slapping the cassette. "Those deans say I don't teach a rigorous class. What the hell is this?" He slapped the tape again. "I taught a white boy to sing the goddamn blues in Central Park! Stupid mothers. Wait till they see this."

As Professor Cool left the class muttering to himself, I couldn't help believing that somehow, like my brother on the video, I was taking my first steps toward something bigger—a new way of walking, talking, and thinking about the wider world. This white boy from Connecticut actually had had a hand in sticking it to the Man. And even though I still wasn't invited to the café that final afternoon with all the young radicals in Etch A Sketch facial hair, I had a place that would welcome me with a smiling face in the window, no matter the color of my skin.

Part III:

Family Ties

Old Yeller

The spring of my first year teaching at Prep, my father came to visit. Poppy was almost a year old, and Lala was a few years into her business transforming empty matchboxes into sacred objects. Lala and I both have rather animated fathers, and dealing with them in public can be a tricky (and sometimes embarrassing) issue. Lala's dad never saw any problem with charging into the hotel where Lala and I once worked, wearing checkered pants, white shoes, and a hat that should have been buried with Eisenhower, yelling "Where's that son-in-law of mine?" even if such behavior made Lala cower behind the steam table. My father, not to be outdone, is always eager to conduct an impromptu English class with the Mexican vendors at our local farmers' market as I'm trying to purchase my weekly produce. I know better than to try to out short what he considers community service, so I wait patiently (read: hide) in the car.

So it wasn't an easy thing bringing my father to school with me for a day, but I had little choice. He would have driven Lala nuts puttering around the house, picking up glitter tubes and peppering her with questions about the viscosity of Elmer's glue in the temperate summertime months. My teaching was going pretty well—the kids seemed to respond to my mix of rigor and humor—and I was worried that my dad might blow it for me. Any new teacher will testify that during those first years, you worry about everything, especially keeping your sense of authority in the classroom. You dread the smarty-pants kids asking questions that expose gaps in your knowledge of grammar or the way books were bound during William Shakespeare's time (if there even was a Shakespeare). In my off hours, I skirt situations where people might believe a teacher's supposed knowledge could come in handy. You'll never see me joining a book club, and I'd rather gulp motor oil than come within twenty feet of a goddamn crossword puzzle.

Because of my concern about my dad's predilection for being somewhat of a big mouth, I summoned the courage to speak to him on our drive up to Prep. Our family does not talk openly about much other than our children, travel plans, the weather, and the best way to microwave an omelet in a Ziploc bag, and most of that is done via the detached safety of e-mail. So approaching my father on such a delicate topic was a direct challenge to my emotional avoidance disorder.

"Dad," I said, downshifting, "we need to talk."

"Shoot."

I tried to be diplomatic, explaining how I was still new at my job and I really needed him to downplay his usual enthusiasm when speaking to anyone with a pulse. It's not uncommon for him to stop joggers to ask what type of fabric their jerseys are woven from.

He stared straight ahead at the newspaper vendor in front of us. "A gag order," he said.

"No." The myriad possibilities for disaster flashed through my mind like a best-of episode of *Cops*. "Well, you could put it that way. If you don't mind."

He nodded in a way that told me I'd stung him. I'm sure it's not easy for a father to get a talking-to from his son about behavior, but my dad didn't complain or argue or pull out a wooden spoon to start spanking my ass. He did what many men do: find a totally unrelated way to deal with emotion. Some men drink a lot when they're upset, some drink while watching television, some just drink. I drink while cooking an elaborate meal based on recipes torn from the slick pages of a gourmet magazine. Since I don't keep booze in my truck as a rule, my dad needed a way to address his pent-up emotion. For some reason, don't ask me why, my dad chose jazz drumming.

I had switched on the radio to fill the awkward silence after my talk and a particularly catchy REM song was playing. My dad began his two-mile-long career by tapping a rolled-up newspaper on his leg. It was his way of distracting himself from what had just happened between us, but I didn't acknowledge it in the manner of a therapist or policeman. I let him think that I believed he had taken the criticism well. Much family drama, I've learned, can be avoided through the art of illusion. But soon his left hand joined the band too, providing a counterbeat to the right's frantic whacking. After he got both hands moving, the newspaper explored other timpanic possibilities in the truck—the lip of the dashboard, the window, even the ceiling, which I thought was a bit too heavy metal for what he was trying to achieve. To someone driving alongside us, it must have seemed as if my passenger was allergic to bees and was desperately trying to swat one before the little sucker killed him.

The first part of our day at school together went pretty smoothly. I introduced my dad to my colleagues, and he performed like a real trouper, shaking hands and keeping the conversation light by talking mostly about the intricacies of moving from Connecticut to Florida. The few times I spotted potential for him to jump in and offer his conservative (read: fascist) views on American education, I shuffled him along into the janitor's closet.

Toward the end of the day, I was scheduled to teach my seventh-grade English class, which was rehearsing a mock trial based on a book we were reading, *Bless Me, Ultima* by Rudolfo Anaya. The book centers around a boy whose elderly friend is suspected of being a *bruja*, or witch. The classroom was arranged inquisition style that day—long tables in a U shape, facing the place where I told my father he could sit. My fifteen or so seventh-graders were already wound up, having just been assigned their parts for the upcoming hearing. The characters in the novel were wild and unruly, and the class, especially the boys, had adopted their attributes with great relish.

"*Chingada!*" Frank yelled. He stood in front of his chair by a trio of computers, a shiny Halloween patch covering one eye. I had worried whether to give the part to Frank. With his uncontrollable energy, he was the instigator who poked, prodded, probed, and insulted the others into general crankiness. But he was still a genius. Frank had written a 120-page screenplay, and I was amazed at its merit. I believed I could teach him to channel that manic energy into something more productive, like writing fiction or changing tires in a pit crew.

I called the class to attention, asked them to sit down, and reminded them that today was one of their few prep periods before the actual trial next week. "And this is my father," I said, pointing to my old man, who nodded hello. I had announced the arrival of this special visitor the day before.

"He's come to see Poppy," one of the girls announced loudly enough to qualify for extra credit.

"Yes, Katie, he did," I acknowledged. "And if all goes well during class, I'll give you five minutes at the end to ask him questions."

Frank shouted out: "Does it have to be appropriate? It can't be one like—"

"Appropriate only," I said, cutting him off. I quickly got the class started by separating the two sides: witnesses for the defense, witnesses for the prosecution. Three boys raced to the computers in the corner, almost crashing into the same number of girls running to claim the three beanbag chairs. The lost souls waited by the windows that looked onto the grassy quad. These were the tender kids, the ones whose hair never stayed horizontal; their shoelaces and shoes were often misplaced, and their books and papers continually exploded from lockers and backpacks. With a hand placed gently on each back, I escorted them to their sides, whispering to each of the lead student attorneys to check on these sheep periodically.

When I turned to glance at my dad, I saw him sitting between Frank and a kid I secretly called David Tape Recorder because he frequently threatened to record my sarcastic jokes and irreverent asides and turn them in—à la Watergate—to the headmaster. My father's voice boomed, low and dramatic like he was back onstage in college, "Now why are you on trial here, Tenorio?" I thought he might actually cup his ear to adjust his pitch.

The kids all turned around to see who the hell was channeling the voice of Gary Owens. Frank was a smart kid and immediately spotted my twinge of embarrassment. Adjusting his eye patch, he spoke in a forced Chicano accent. "Is not meee, is that *pinche bruja* Ultima. *Chingada!*" I winced at both the profanity and the racist overtones. If I didn't help him, David Duke would be slipping a hood over his head in no time. He pointed across the room to a girl named Kyra standing near the pencil sharpener.

"*Chingada!*" Frank cried, shaking his fist at her.

"Frank," I warned, "you can save the accent and swearing for the trial."

"Does your dad know what the words mean? I mean, like, should I tell him?"

"I don't think that's necessary." I imagined Frank translating curse words from Spanish to English, and my father trying to recall the root words in Latin.

"I can handle it, Bob," my father offered, holding up his palm. "I'm helping the boys get ready for the trial." He slid down his glasses and winked conspiratorially. "I'm grilling them." Frank and David Tape Recorder waited for me to respond to my dad's teasing me by a bastardization of my first name that I never tolerate in others.

"That's fine," I answered quickly (read: like a coward), then walked to the blackboard to check on the defense. Behind me the two boys giggled and whispered, "Bob." I thought I heard my father stifle his own laughter, but I wasn't sure. Either way, I didn't want to escalate the potential beast of disruption by feeding it. Just like with family, if you ignore students long enough, they might not call back.

I had been pointing out a flaw in the defense team's line of questioning when a commotion broke out in the corner. Casters squeaked, table ends jammed together. Frank was standing on top of his chair, his eye patch in the middle of his forehead like a third eye. He jammed his finger downward at my father. David Tape Recorder looked on anxiously as if he was anticipating a fistfight. The whole scene reminded me of *Dead Poets Society* on crack.

"Your dad said I was wasted!" Frank yelled.

"That is not true, Frank," my father said stoically, sitting up in his chair, not looking in my direction. Folded in his lap, the hands that not long before had worked a funky beat now languished like two dead fish.

The class buzzed, waiting to see how their usually composed teacher would handle this one. I wondered too as I looked upon my father. Should I kick my dad out of my own class? Send him to the headmaster's office?

"If I had my tape recorder . . . ," David said.

"I didn't say he was wasted," my father clarified to the class. "If you want to know what I said, I'll tell you. I said he was a waste, a smart kid who is practicing to be a smart aleck. I hope you all know the difference." My dad now had a podium and an audience, all he needed to get rolling. I expected him to stand up and plot Frank's path to juvie on the chalkboard. "You know, Rob had friends like that. Kids who started out funny but ended up nothings in life. In fact, back—"

"That's enough, Dad. Thanks," I said, and turned my back on him, a move that would have caught hell for me as a boy.

David Tape Recorder whispered, "Busted," the *s* slithering from his mouth. It was too early to dismiss class, yet the students would never regain their focus now. My dad sat quietly, looking slightly pissed about being shut down, while the kids fidgeted in their places. I wondered what I'd been thinking when I decided to bring him without the aid of a flare gun or decent escape plan. The defending attorney, Glenda, chosen because of her tendency to come to the aid of unjustly accused fellow classmates, thrust her hand into the chalky air.

"Yes, counselor?" I said, secretly hoping she could save my fired ass by projectile-vomiting on her desk.

"Mr. Wilder, is this the time where we can ask your dad questions?"

"I don't know if we'll get to that today."

She uttered the two words that any teacher or parent dreads most: "You said."

"I know I did, but . . ." I didn't know how to finish this sentence. I was in a lose-lose position. My dad could continue his lecture and embarrass Frank, me, and most of my friends in high school in one fell swoop. On the other hand, when you break your promise to a bunch of swashbuckling middle-schoolers, you can bet on a mutiny straight out of a Johnny Depp movie.

"That's not fair," Glenda continued. "Some of us have questions all planned out and we'll never get a chance to use them since this is the only day your dad will be here."

I looked out the window onto the quad, hoping something or someone was on fire or bleeding so we could all rush out in a memory-erasing frenzy. No such luck. It was another goddamn lovely day in Santa Fe. "Fine," I mumbled. "Get back into your assigned seats. Remember: appropriate questions only."

The twelve- and thirteen-year-olds raced back to their seats, musical chairs fashion. I went to my father, who was now seated between Kyra and David Tape Recorder. Leaning over so my butt hit the chalk tray, I quietly asked if the Q&A session was all right with him.

"Sure. Love to," my dad said, as if the "waste" thing had never happened, as if it was his job to judge and insult my students when I was trying so hard to be a good teacher. I reluctantly whispered, "Thanks," and backed away, wiping the white dust off my buttocks.

An awkward pause ensued. Neither my father nor I called on anyone. I caught myself automatically deferring to my father's authority as though we were back in Connecticut and he was showing me the correct way to handle a lawn broom. In his chair, the old man sat smugly, hands in the pockets of his windbreaker, as if he could read my mind.

"Miss Douglas," I finally said, too quickly, to the girl who held one of the three major female roles in the trial.

"Yes. Are you a teacher?" she asked, seemingly satisfied that her query was a good one. The faces of the boys showed they vehemently disagreed.

"No, I'm a retired banker." Then he realized that he had the uncontested floor again, and he just couldn't let opportunity go. Never give a Wilder a microphone or a podium. Like an infomercial, we'll be on all night. "You could say I was a teacher in a sense," my dad said. "All parents teach their children, don't they?"

Uh-oh, I thought, *we're in trouble now.* I love my dad, but he seems to know something about everything. If you mention something rare, like performing brain surgery on chimps in outer space, my dad knows someone who tried it, or at the very least he's on a first-name basis with a monkey who lives in his building.

"My father taught me how to make green chile stew," Miss Douglas offered eagerly. "With meat." She nodded like a midget Stan Laurel in drag.

"That's right. See, there ya go. So I guess I was a teacher. What did I teach you, Rob?"

"Lots. Next question," I said, trying to speed things along. This Q&A could only end in tragedy, probably my own. Frank rocked in his seat, waving his arm frantically as if he had to urinate. I swung my gaze to the other side of the room and called on Vern, a seriously studious boy. Short black hair, glasses, and requisite pencil case.

"Did Mr. Wilder—your son, of course"—Vern chuckled to himself awkwardly—"Did he ever do anything bad, you know, get into any trouble?"

Here we go, I thought. Like Gary Busey, I've seen some bedlam in my time. Car wrecks. Obstruction of justice. Girls in my bedroom. Aggravated chest acne.

"I don't really remember him in any trouble," my father said. "I'm not saying he was a goody-goody, but he was a pretty good kid."

"Okay, then." I moved swiftly to call on the next member of the jury, but my father interrupted me.

"He was his own person. I will tell you this: we had a rule at our dinner table, no hats. But one time Rob came in wearing his favorite baseball cap from Little League—just like mine here," he said while pointing to the crest of his hat, "except mine is from a professional team, but no matter. I told him to remove it. Well, he looked down and scrunched up his face and said, 'No.' " My father did an impression of how he'd seen his young son—scowling and pulling the brim of the cap over his glasses. "He said he didn't want to. So I told him if he didn't take it off he'd have to eat alone in his room. And you know what he did?" He snapped the brim off his widened eyes and gawked around the room like a drunken camp counselor trying to tell a scary story without falling into the campfire.

This was a total lie, I realized. Unless I was concealing fresh wounds from my car crashes, I never wore hats of any sort. My noggin was too large and head coverings drew attention to my Frankenstein's-monster-sized cranium. Why the hell was my dad making up stories, and dull ones at that? Why didn't he have me do something more exciting that involved albino lesbians and mutated farm animals?

"I'll tell you what he did. He carried his plate up to his room and ate alone sitting on his bed. And that baseball cap was still on his head." All the kids turned to eyeball me, but I couldn't tell if they felt enlightened at discovering some hidden aspect of my character or confused at the relevance of this tale of the stubborn headpiece. My face got hot. I was blushing even though the story was a complete and utter fabrication. The only rule we'd had after my mom died was to be home for dinner at six o'clock. Once seated, all of us Wilders ate like savages—silverware and pants strictly optional. Girls were actually afraid to eat at our table. I think they slept with us in the backs of cars just to avoid coming over for meat loaf.

My dad rolled on. "The reason I tell you this is because I always knew Rob was his own person, and that's why he's such a good teacher. You must know. Isn't he a good teacher?" The girls all nodded, while the boys' faces took on looks of *What the hell are we listening to?* As I lifted my hand to call on the next one, I noticed my palms were slick with sweat. I slipped them into my jeans pockets and called on Mary.

"What grades did Mr. Wilder get in school?" she asked quietly.

"I bet he got Fs," Frank called out, his uncovered eye jerking back and forth like a goldfish on speed. "And Ds."

"Which level? High school? Junior high?" my dad asked. Before Mary could redirect, Frank stood up and slapped the table with both hands. Excited, he trembled as he spoke. "Who thinks Mr. Wilder got Fs and Ds? Raise your hand. Raise your hand!" He chanted this rallying cry as if he was Mel Gibson in *Braveheart* sans the soccer hooligan makeup. David Tape Recorder raised his paw high, almost lifting himself out of his chair. I slid along the board and drew closer to Frank to place a hand on his back, trying to calm him down and ease him into his chair, but the sound of my dad's bark halted him. "If you would shut your goddamn mouth for one minute, Frank."

"Dad, that's enough. You're out of line," I said.

"You know I'm right, Rob. Frank needs to be told that he cannot—"

"I'll decide what to tell Frank."

"See, this is exactly what's wrong with our classrooms today. A perfect example. Lack of discipline. Look at him," he said, pointing to the frothing pirate. "He knows it."

I sidled up and, cupping my hand to shield my words, spoke close to my father's ear: "You don't know what the hell you're talking about. Just close your mouth."

"*Chingada!*" Frank yelled. "Hold him in contempt. He said I was wasted!"

"Frank, shut it," I yelled. "Shut it *now*. No talking from *anyone* until I say." Even though I've never actually seen it covered in any manuals on pedagogy, it's simply not okay to put your father in time-out. So unfortunately I had to punish the many for the sins of the few, a practice more useful in the military during wartime than in a muggy seventh-grade classroom. I'd vowed never to lose my cool as a teacher, but here I was, yelling at my class (with my dad strangely in it) the way my father once yelled at the four Wilder boys for stealing bottles of his Rolling Rock beer. The apple fell closer to the tree than I ever would have imagined.

I knew that later, on our drive home, I would be sullen, and my dad would act as if the day had been a resounding success. The roles of father and son echo those of teacher and student. Expectations are rarely in sync; outcomes and levels of satisfaction rarely converge.

"Now I *really* wish I had a tape recorder," David sighed.

Interzone

In the town where I live, navigating the educational landscape for your child can be quite complicated and potentially treacherous. Our elementary schools struggle, like their cowering counterparts across the country, with overcrowding, underfunding, teacher recruitment, and many other complex issues that plague public schools today. One of the ways that our board of education tries to remedy the obvious inequity and public dissatisfaction is by allowing parents to apply for their child to attend a school outside of their home zone. Instead of a lottery, spaces are allotted based on a first-come, first-served basis, like a going-out-of-business sale at a discount tire store. The year before Poppy was to start kindergarten, interzone transfer applications were being accepted at 7:30 A.M. on February 1. That meant whoever got to Wood Gormley Elementary (our chosen school) first would have the best shot. In January, I tried cozying up to the principal, explaining that I was a fellow educator and surely there would be some professional courtesy even though my school was of a more, ahem, private nature. Besides, on that fateful morning, I was scheduled to teach at 8:00 A.M.; I did not have an in-service training day like the public schools had. Weren't all children equally deserving of an education, regard-less of their financial background? I pleaded. It wasn't my stu-dents' fault they had summer homes in Maine, housekeepers and cooks, and a fleet of SUVs. The principal nodded kindly, having dealt with parents like me before, then handed me the transfer form in canary yellow and said she hoped I didn't have to get in line too early. Then she shut her office door in my face.

Lala and I agreed that she'd stay home with Poppy that day. And since I was a teacher man and anything to do with education was my responsibility, the same way anything to do with clothing the children was hers, I'd go down to the school. I set my alarm for 4:00 A.M. but woke up with a start around 3:30. I'd been hav-ing a nightmare about oversleeping and missing the deadline, forcing Poppy to spend the rest of her days in an educational sweatshop, chained to outdated textbooks and a rusty abacus while an old battle-axe standing by whacked a rubber-tipped pointer against her chalky palm.

I filled my thermos with coffee, grabbed a clipboard and a few pens, and drove the lonely two miles from my house to Wood Gormley. The streets were empty except for a few sleepy cops looking for homeless people stealing newspapers. Even though I was doing something noble for my child, I felt oddly like a crimi-nal. When I was a teenager, the local elementary school was a place to go at night to drink stolen beer or learn about the com-plicated clasping mechanism of a training bra. Sometimes kids got carried away and broke in to the school to try to access their permanent records or smashed windows out of sheer suburban boredom. In my experience, people on school grounds at this hour were usually up to no good.

The jungle gym was dark and eerily deserted, the swings absolutely still, like the world was in lockdown. Two cars were parked in front of the main entrance to the school. I'd been sure I'd be the first by arriving at around 4:00; the previous year's first-place winner had clocked in at 4:45 A.M. First place would have guaranteed Poppy placement; I couldn't be sure after that. No one knew exactly how many spaces were available, so it was better to err on the conservative side. I stepped out into the frigid morning and walked up to the car in front of me. In the driver's seat was Jeff, the father of Poppy's best friend, Devin. Jeff is an easygoing native Santa Fean who lives in the house he grew up in. We had agreed over some Tecates a few nights before to try to treat this ridiculous exercise in as civilized a manner as possible. We'd heard stories about people setting up tents and sleeping bags on the brick patio in front of the school like it was the ticket line for a Foghat reunion concert. We wanted none of that shit.

"Looks like the twins beat us," Jeff said, sipping from his stained travel mug. "That means you are number three, but technically Poppy is number four." He handed me the lined paper, numbered from one to fifty in blue ink. As I was slipping the sheet onto my clipboard and printing my name, we saw a man in a wool hat with earflaps and an overcoat dragging a suitcase the size of a steamer trunk down the sidewalk. With the dim light, he appeared out of the shadows like some vaudeville performer. I half expected a midget in a tuxedo to pop out holding a squirting bouquet of flowers. The man calmly unlatched the trunk and pulled out a folding chair, card table, and heavy horsehair blanket.

"We should stop him," I said.

"Hold on. Let's see what else he's got in there. I may want to eat some of his four-course breakfast." Jeff took another long sip of his coffee, then moseyed over and approached the man, pointing to the clipboard. Buster Keaton nodded, signed the list, and then, as methodically as he'd unpacked, stowed his gear and walked back whence he came.

"Where's he off to?" I asked Jeff when he returned.

"Guy lives down the street. He'll be back at seven. Next one's yours."

We were like census workers for some strange refugee camp, signing up folks in cars as they arrived. Most of the people seemed relieved not to get out of their warm, radio-filled automobiles, but a few Limbaugh listeners weren't so sure they wanted to trust guys in jeans with shaggy hair carrying a clipboard.

A woman pulled up in a Chevy Cavalier, dressed as if she worked in a real office of some sort. She had on a blue polyester suit, white ruffled shirt, and scuffed black pumps. When I approached, her head was in a downward position as if she was studying an abnormality woven into the seat cloth. I knocked lightly on the window. She didn't stir. I thought maybe the radio was turned up too loud, but I heard nothing besides the slight rattling of the engine. I tapped again, using my wedding ring for timpanic effect, and this time the woman turned and scowled as if I was one of those guys who wants to clean your windows for a mandatory donation. I motioned for her to roll down the window, a silly movement indeed, especially that early in the morning.

"May I help you?" she asked me coldly.

"I'd like a cheeseburger, fries, and a large martini, please," I joked. She looked away. I sighed, then explained how I was here trying to make our early elementary existence easier.

"I don't think so, no," she said, and started to roll up her window.

"Wait. What? You don't think so?"

"I don't want to sign."

"This is not the registration. It's just so you don't have to wait in the cold. It's close to freezing out here." I didn't see any sign of winter wear in her car, just a half dozen binders and a very full ashtray.

"How do I know you won't just put all your friends ahead of me?"

"What friends?" I held my palms up in confusion and glanced around the barren streets.

"Guys like you always have *friends*." She said the last word as if it was a synonym for *STDs*.

I showed her my clipboard. "You can look at the sheet. We've already numbered it. You'll be right here after Mr. Sandstrom." I pointed to the empty space next to her number. We were still under ten signees. She maybe had a decent shot of getting her kid in.

"You'll probably switch sheets."

"Jeez, lady," I said, growing frustrated, "I'm a teacher."

"Like that means anything," she said, and scraped her name across the paper.

An hour passed with Jeff and me popping out of our cars about every three minutes or so. Most of the parents were there to claim a desk in the kindergarten class, the gateway to an education that would keep their kids off the probation list, at least until middle school. It was far more difficult to interzone into the higher grades since, like tenure in college, once you got into the school, you never left. Desperate for a decent education, parents had begun buying houses in this area just to send their kids to Wood Gormley. Those with money simply bought second homes and rented them out, retaining the address rights for registration. They figured that private school cost well over $12,000 a year, equal to a partial down payment for a two-bedroom/one-bath. I know some middle-class parents who got the zoning map from the Board of Ed and bought the least expensive homes on the shaggy fringes of the zone, giving up square footage, a bedroom, half bath, or backyard. People were desperate. One of Poppy's friends, Zelda, pretended to live at her mother's coworker's home, located a half block from the school. Her real residence was over twelve miles away, and with the hectic morning commute, Zelda was late almost every day her first semester. When her mom let it slip about traffic being bad along a road they weren't supposed to live on, the jig was up. Even though the principal let them stay, they were known around the monkey bars as "that family of liars."

"Getting hairy out there," Jeff said, handing me the growing list. The cars had crowded the entrance to the school, turning the street and adjacent faculty parking lot into a used-car dealership. The sight of those cars with eye-like running lights and plumes of exhaust, the muted voices of Rush, Don, and NPR pulsating from the cabins, made me feel like this was some horror movie, *Night of the Helicopter Parents.* I could hear the voice-over now: *In a world where getting into a decent school is like finding Saddam's gold . . .*

A Crown Vic pulled in to the lot, so I dutifully trudged over. Even though we still had a good hour to go, people kept a close eye on the entrance to the school as if, like Willy Wonka, the principal would throw open the doors and invite the crowd into a world full of pure education. The heads behind dashboards noted me also, making sure no money exchanged hands or a new list appeared from inside my coat. The guy in the cop car was in a dark suit, red tie, and tinted eyeglasses. His hands hung thick on his wrists like a pair of pork roasts. Opening his window without looking at me directly, he said, "Hey, pal, how's it going?"

"Okay," I guessed, and spewed my by now well-rehearsed spiel. I handed him the clipboard.

"I appreciate you doing this, pal. If things get ugly, just give me a holler."

"Ugly?" We were waiting in line so that our recently potty-trained kids could finger-paint in a room without vermin.

"You know. If you need support. If anyone disrespects you. Stuff like that. I hear this deal can turn sour."

"Should we have a secret wave or something?"

"That's probably not necessary. I'll be able to tell by the look on your face." He eyed my jeans and wrinkled oxford shirt. Then he noticed my sneakers. "What do you do?"

"I'm a teacher, though not at this school."

"There ya go," he said, as if teachers were always the ones best suited to stand out in the cold.

The sunrises in New Mexico can be quite breathtaking—light blues and dark reds layered in an open sky like an Impressionist painting. But on this morning it struck me more as what God's vomit might look like after a heavy night of vodka and Red Bulls. As the sun started to illuminate the dozens of idling cars, the machine in which we were all cogs started to churn. People emerged from their steel cocoons even though an employee from the school had yet to arrive and it was still freaking cold outside. No one spoke. Forty or so adults leaned against their cars as if they were their own chauffeurs. I desperately wanted to be the level-headed guy who didn't succumb to the hysteria of not-yet-higher

education, but I couldn't help myself. Even though I alone held
the almighty clipboard, I reached inside my car and shut off my
engine, trying not to appear anxious or uncool. All around me
men and women jerked their heads from one to the next, saying
nothing. We were like a bunch of goddamn birds waiting for
someone to throw us a mackerel to fight over.

A woman came stomping down the sidewalk, yellow highlights shining in her spiked hair, big plastic hoop earrings trying
to keep up with her frenzied pace. "Goddamn. Goddamn.
Goddamn," she said. "What time did y'all come here?"

"Three forty-five," the father of the twins happily offered,
since he held the golden position. Next year it would be midnight, I figured, once the word got out.

"Shitshitshit. That principal told me not to wait out here all
night. It wasn't necessary, she said."

Someone behind me stifled an ironic laugh.

Jeff lazily stepped up onto the curb. "We've been taking numbers here," he said calmly, showing her the list.

"I'm sorry, but I'm not getting behind all you people." She
clawed her fingers through her hair. Her eyes seemed to be sizing
us up, wondering how she'd get around waiting behind a group
larger than the most oversubscribed classroom. "No way." She
crossed her arms across her tidy chest.

Her comments and attitude seemed to set the crowd on edge.
People broke their silence and started murmuring to themselves
and the nearest ear. The opening chords of a riot in G minor.

"Listen, my girl needs this more than any of yours. She
really does." The woman wasn't pleading; her tone suggested that
she was willing to do anything to get her daughter behind a tiny
desk.

The faces of my fellow worriers grew tense, their hands fidgety. I caught the eye of the Regulator next to his Crown Vic. He pointed to his chest in a do-you-need-my-services gesture. I waved him off.

A guy in a green fleece vest and hiking boots strolled up with a look of surprised confusion slathered across his face. You could tell that he'd had no idea fifty other people wanted to do the same thing he did that morning. Spiky Suzy grabbed him by the arm, yanking him next to her. "Don't sign anything. We'll go in together. We don't have to do what they do. They can't make us."

The guy just shrugged, startled by the aggressive antics of his new partner in tardiness.

"What should we do?" Jeff handed me the clipboard.

"I'll just write 'crazy lady' and 'sheepish friend.' "

"Sounds good to me, brother." He looked at them again. "I'd love to meet that guy's wife."

By now, all the cars had been shut off and locked and everyone seemed poised for something dramatic to happen. The tardy pair hooked arms and paced up and down, Spiky Suzy talking rapidly into the ear of the guy outfitted by REI. Even though we were next to a sandlot filled with colorful playground equipment, there seemed to be a distinct lack of children in this odd equation. I hadn't thought of Poppy once in the last hour, or why Lala and I wanted this school so badly anyway.

Then the doors opened. As if by magic, the smiling secretary unlocked the double doors about a hundred yards from the front of the group. Even though we had all signed the list and agreed to act like a civilized contingent, when Spiky Suzy and REI Guy set off running, we all followed close behind—heavyset men in suits and ties, fit young mothers in velour sweatsuits, hipster parents in designer eyewear, tattoos leaking out from under shirt collars.

I could tell by our motley gaits that this was the first hundred-yard dash most of us had done in decades.

When I slipped into the lobby of the school, I saw Spiky Suzy yanking on the office door, swearing rather loudly. The mob milled around like a bunch of soccer hooligans, eyeing each other but keeping mum. REI Guy was smart enough to figure out what was about to happen and slithered to the back, near the entrance to the cafeteria. I knew if someone didn't do something, there would be an altercation. Someone would get hurt. All in the good name of children's education.

The Regulator gritted his teeth like a pissed-off Jack Nicholson and headed toward the frantic mother trying to jimmy the office door lock with a hairpin. Did the principal know about this? Was she pulling a Knute Rockne on us, hoping that we'd all sort ourselves out so she wouldn't have to deal with the "twins on first, Jeff got second" routine? Just before he reached her, I patted my bodyguard nicely on the back, asking him to hold up. I addressed the congregation, employing my most pedagogically sensitive voice: "Would it help everyone if I reminded you where you are in line?"

Spiky Suzy turned with clenched fists and was about to dissent when she saw all those faces glaring at her, each parent as angry with burning love as she was. Her face, and hopes, fell like a truant student's grades.

"Mr. Apodaca, I believe you are number ten." Like he was my own student, I guided him to his place in line. "Mr. Whitehurst, you are lucky number one." The father of the twins smiled at us and waved as if he was running for mayor. "Jeff, you are number two." I sounded oddly like the boyish host of *The Amazing Race*.

"Thank you, bro." He shook my hand so all the rest could see that even though he had held the list, I was now the one in charge.

For me, it was just like the opening day of school. The bodies before me might have been older and lumpier, but they too were frozen with apprehension, insecurity, and awkwardness. Just like their younger counterparts, these individuals welcomed my touch as I guided them, one by one, onto the long conveyor belt of American education.

Breachers

Every year my family flies to Florida to remember what moisture feels like and to visit with my father and brother Crazy Eddie and his family. This past year I decided to go down a few days ahead to spend some time with my brother alone. For close to a decade, Crazy Eddie was a character actor for Walt Disney World. He wasn't a mouse or a duck; Eddie was more of a circuit performer, playing roles ranging from a disc jockey and talent agent to a hippie paleontologist who could explain the five major theories of dinosaur extinction while acting like Keanu Reeves after ten bong hits of skunkweed. In any level of show business, roles come and go, and my brother was eventually laid off and forced to find another, supposedly steadier line of work. When Eddie was exploring his employment opportunities, he reflected upon his characteristics and skill set—peppy, not easily depressed; an extensive knowledge of pirate jokes, one-liners, pratfalls, slapstick comedy—and everyone immediately pointed him toward the teaching profession. Following their advice, Eddie busted his ass for a few years getting certified during the day while acting certifiable at conventions and comedy clubs by night. He ended up becoming king of his own cafetorium by starting a drama department at a large middle school in Orlando. Now that we were brothers in teaching, or "breaching," as I referred to it, Eddie would call me and in his rapid-fire dude-speak try to find some educational touchstones we could share. It was true we were both teachers, but only in the same way death by natural causes is similar to death by strangulation.

"Bro, when you got certified did they assess you using that dude Bloom's taxonomy?" he asked over the phone, racing through those thirteen words in the time it takes me to say hi.

"I'm not certified. I teach at a private school where you don't need to be. Our tech guy never even finished college. I've been here ten years, and we just got fingerprinted."

"No way."

"Way."

"Dude." He sighed. "I get fingerprinted every time I use the freakin' bathroom."

Once he'd phoned me to complain that when his students performed scenes from *Fiddler on the Roof*, he was required to have them meet a grocery list of educational objectives and categories ranging from aesthetic and critical analysis to historical and personal connections.

"Aren't they in seventh grade?" I asked, remembering my own experience in that production as Nachum the beggar. It had been my first real break in the drama game, so I went way over the top, dressing in dirty rags and gluing an excessive amount of orangutan fur to my face. I even adopted a clubfoot, something I thought would add character to my very minor role. During the production, I ended up dragging my leg and shouting so loudly even my parents thought I was playing the part of a deaf and homeless werewolf.

"Yeah, seventh- and eighth-graders mostly." Eddie sounded a bit daunted by the idea that everything in his life, every future spit take, arm fart, and Cockney accent, would have to include a rubric to measure its holistic educational value.

"How are you going to apply *Fiddler* to all that crap?" I asked him, being about as helpful a brother as a Sheen is to an Estevez.

"Dude, I dunno. They all want to be rich men, even the girls, so I can work with that."

Without kids, flying from Albuquerque to Orlando was like being at a tranquil spa in the sky. I got to read more than two pages of a novel without being interrupted, and the businessman next to me never once asked me to play Buzz Lightyear, read him a story, or clean his ass with flushable wipes. Without my son tagging along, the airplane bathroom seemed quite spacious, and when I returned to my seat, a barely attractive woman nicely asked to serve me a cold beverage. I don't know why people bitch so much about flying. Try spending fourteen hours lugging around a few kids, some car seats, a stroller, and a wife who's scared of crashing and you'll realize that even with security checks, flying commercial by yourself ain't so bad. Without children to worry about, even the pat-downs are kind of like a chair massage.

My brother Eddie is more optimistic and energetic than Ned Flanders on a field of magic mushrooms. My dad used to joke that if you punched Eddie in the face, instead of storming away, he'd offer you his groin to kick. Even though he missed being onstage and the bureaucracy of the public school system confounded him, he was sure that he could make this teaching gig work. I arrived late in Orlando, so after he gave me a brief "Dude!" and a suffocating bear hug and then flashed me the peace sign, I hit the hay. By the time I got up the next day to get ready to go see his school, Eddie'd been awake for an hour trying to decide which coffee I would enjoy most. Maybe my brother gets some of his sweetness from his diet, because his house is filled with soda, ice cream, frosted cereals, and coffee that tastes more like Pixy Stix from the Candy Baron than beans from Juan Valdez.

"Do you want Peppermint Sugarbush or Hazelnut Amaretto?" he asked, holding up two bags in packaging the color of crayons.

"What a choice!" I exclaimed, grabbing the phone book to locate a twenty-four-hour dentist in the area.

"Tell me about it," he said. "I don't know what I'd do without good coffee."

We drove in separate cars just in case I got thrown out of his school for not having been fingerprinted often enough. On the way, Eddie kept up his teacher bonding energy, pointing to a prefab school being thrown up only a block away from his house. He shot me the thumbs-up sign out the window as we passed the construction as if we were the sole owners of McDonald's and here was another Golden Arches to add to our fleet.

The traffic in Orlando was abysmal, stop-and-go, white cars like teeth on a black mouth of road. It took almost an hour to go thirteen miles. At home in New Mexico, when I get on the road to go to work at 5:00 A.M., I'm practically alone. I can even manipulate the traffic lights by flashing my high beams on what my students call "zombie boxes," machines that control the traffic flow in the wee morning hours. I get pissed off if I have to slow down for a darting rabbit, so waiting in rush-hour traffic made me rather anxious. I think Eddie sensed this because he did routines in his car, break-dancing to music I couldn't hear, waving his arms out the window like the wings of a large metal bird, and performing mime shit stolen from Shields and Yarnell. The other commuters didn't find it as funny as I did, and more than one pointed to my brother, held a pretend roach to their lips, and inhaled deeply.

We pulled in to the parking lot as most of the other teachers were arriving. They all stepped out of their cars in a line, shut the doors, then slipped lanyards over their heads. It reminded me of the cop shows I'd watched as a kid where the police would tuck the billy clubs they never used into their belts after exiting their vehicles. I could see that some teachers tried to personalize their educational choke collars by adorning them with buttons and badges related to their hobbies of hot-air ballooning or cat worship, while others replaced the school-standard "Reach for Success" lanyards with the scary "What Would Jesus Do?" ones. So much for separation of church and state.

Eddie wore a fanny pack pushed to the front, so I guess it could be more accurately called a scrotum sack. He also carried a shiny briefcase that made him look a bit like a fruity bond salesman. I asked him what was in there, so he flipped it open. The case was empty except for a few manila files that were, I realized after further investigation, also empty.

"Why do you carry that thing if you don't use it?"

"I don't know, dude," he said, running his fingers through his hair, where some crimson still remained from when he was a redheaded boy. "I got it playing the talent scout at the park and thought a teacher would carry something like this." I sensed he was about to open up to me about being torn between the acting world and the teaching world, but then he caught sight of an

African American faculty member entering the building. "Hey, Ronald, rock on! Peace, my brother!" Eddie shouted, and held up the black power sign. My brother is one of the rare white guys who gets away with using racial greetings and signifiers with anyone he meets, regardless of their point of origin. During the course of our day together, I would heard him say, "*Domo arigato, Mr. Roboto*" to an Asian American and "*Hasta la vista,* baby" to a Mexican national. I think people immediately sense by my brother's boundless kindness and positive outlook that he truly sees and treats everyone the same. I try to practice tolerance and understanding too, but the last time I called a Hispanic guy I didn't know "bro" at a local nightclub, they pegged me for a narc and I almost got stomped.

Eddie's school was built mostly of whitewashed cinder blocks and steel painted Dodger blue. It looked as if the Board of Ed had taken over the public swimming pool and never gave it back. We walked to what I would call a library but what Eddie and the rest of the staff referred to as the "media center." The large room held books just as a library might. As far as I could tell, the name was a misnomer; no members of the media were present to cover the event.

Before we sat down, Eddie grabbed my arm and swung around on one leg like Charlie Chaplin, pulling me back outside. "Hold on a sec. I need to sign in."

"Sign in?"

"Yeah, don't you sign in every day?"

I shook my head and felt slightly outraged by the idea, though I couldn't say why exactly.

"How do they know if you're there or not?"

I thought of all the ways I'd witnessed unsupervised kids drawing attention to the fact that their teacher hadn't shown—

loud profane music, face licking, erotic chalk diagrams on the board, one kid inserting his head into a whole watermelon and attempting to smash it off.

"They just know," I said.

Eddie's school had just completed nineteen days of the Florida Comprehensive Assessment Test, the grueling grand-daddy of standardized exams in America. As a morale booster, the principal had ordered breakfast for the staff—crates of hash browns, towers of Egg McMuffins, columns of yogurt parfaits, and buckets of orange juice. Having two kids, I know my way around a McDonald's drive-through menu, but seeing boxes of greasy food under fluorescent lights near books and pasty-faced librarians—I mean media center staff—made me lose whatever appetite the sugary coffee had created in my poor gut. Eddie elbowed me. "Take some hash browns, dude." Then he uttered the words that all teachers invoke in times like these, words that I've used often, yet which make me question our place in the hierarchy of American society: "They're free." Eddie had obviously joined our cult, and looking at the average weight of the faculty, the rest were pros at exploring this particular idea of freedom.

The principal opened the meeting by thanking the FCAT team, a weary group of administrators and teachers who, you could tell by their gritted smiles, would never pony up for that crap duty again. The rest of the crowd seemed in pretty good spirits, happily munching on McThis and McThat, wiping their hands on copies of *Highlights* magazine.

"Okay, we have our raffle now!" the principal exclaimed, clapping her hands together like the captain of the adult pep squad.

"Raffle?" I was confused.

Eddie leaned toward me and said in a stage whisper: "Okay,

dude, here's the deal: because of budget cuts, we only are allotted a few new computers every year, so now we get to see who gets them next August."

"Joseph Jackson!" the principal cheered, and a young guy with a shaved head raised his hands in the air as if he'd just won a Gates Millennium Scholarship. Reaching her hand into a fishbowl, the principal pulled out another square of yellow paper. "Sally Rutin!" she squealed. As she drew the names, the mood in the room darkened considerably. People put down their hash browns, wiped their greasy fingers on the Xeroxed agenda, and wrapped their heads in their hands. Some fingered their lanyards as if they were considering using them as nooses.

"Oh man, oh Manischewitz," my brother laughed ominously. "They're all new teachers. That dude over there has only been here since January."

"So? It's a raffle."

"Dude, you don't get it. That teacher over there has been here since we opened fourteen years ago and her computer is older than the one in my room. And mine still has Pong installed on it. People are gonna be pissed, bruddah."

As if on cue, the principal explained that now that the raffle was over, she had news that was not as light. If playing Russian roulette with vital teaching materials for underpaid workers was cheery, I steadied myself to hear about some invasion of locusts in the crotches of the band uniforms or an outbreak of dysentery spread by the drinking fountains.

"Because of the hurricanes this year and their possible impact on the FCAT, we will have to include another reading period in addition to Wally Walrus time." There was an audible groan. According to Crazy Eddie, Wally Walrus time was an extra study period for the tests; it had displaced music, art, and any activity

that didn't use a calculator. The administration named the period
after their mascot because as union members, teachers were not
allowed to teach outside their discipline, but every teacher had to
teach to the test, regardless of his or her calling.

"Even the PE teachers?"

"Dude, you should see those coaches wrestle with the over-
heads in the gym."

The principal continued to discuss the extra class, which
would, in turn, create a total of six lunch periods for the thirteen
hundred students. This meant that some kids would eat lunch as
early as ten-thirty and starve for the rest of the day, while others
had to pop appetite suppressants and wait until after one-thirty
to drink their sloppy Joes.

The news just kept getting better. The principal droned on
about the possibility of a ten-year hurricane cycle and the ardu-
ous task of trying to schedule for hurricanes in the school year's
calendar, like snow days. Unfortunately for my brother, his last
day of teaching would be on June 1 and the next school year would
begin on August 1. Instead of experiencing a full three-month
summer break, he would now have to settle for the Cliff's Notes
version of the original.

Just like their students would later in the day, the faculty
started looking at their watches and toward the exit sign over the
double doors. The principal never slowed down, though, contin-
uing with her information barrage even as people marched out
past her: "Don't forget to remove all items from the walls and un-
plug all appliances!" she yelled, waving the agenda like a distress
flag. "The district will deduct energy points for anything left on
or plugged in. Thank you for all that you do!" she shouted to our
backs as we shuffled into the courtyard and the energy of school
life, away from the doom of what we had just witnessed. Unlike

faculty who dread any form of modification, the smallest event or change always fires up students. As Eddie and I walked to his class, kids swarmed around us, pointing and whispering. The bold ones excitedly lobbed questions at my brother, hopeful to be the first to receive the exciting news that I was indeed visiting.

"Mr. Wilder, who is that?" a boy asked, shoving a finger under my nostril. When Eddie answered, all hell broke loose, as if aliens had just landed and demanded to rapture the lunch ladies from under the sneeze guard.

"Look at Mr. Wilder," a pigtailed girl screamed. "He has a brother!"

"Mr. Wilder," another panted, "is that really your brother? Omigod! Omigod! Why haven't you ever told us?"

"Hey, is that your twin?" a kid in thick glasses asked, but didn't wait to receive an answer. Instead, the gifted one came to his own conclusion. "Mr. Wilder's twin is here!"

I don't know how Corey Feldman or the guy who played Urkel feels or acts when they are treated like minor celebrities, but I performed like an awkward dork. Eddie has no problem with any situation, really, because he's always onstage and treats everyone—student, teacher, cabbie, dockworker, Sally Struthers—like his audience, or "guests," as they called them back in the theme park. He nods, waves, and smiles his head-shot grin at any and all passersby. But not me. As the brooding and moodier brother, I scrunch up my face as if I don't speak English, trying not to reveal a grin that makes me look as if I have rat's teeth, small and pointy. That day I stooped so low as to give a pack of kids the thumbs-up sign, something I had vowed never to do again after viewing a horrifying picture taken of me at a drunken fraternity party in college.

At the end of the courtyard, I almost wept at the sight of

America's educational future: rows and rows of gray metal portable classrooms, all exactly the same, equipped with handicapped ramps and black metal handrails. All over the country, schools are trying to keep up with expanding student numbers and lean budgets by using these white-trash housing units. The trailers in front of me had long ago taken over the basketball courts and now were creeping across the grassy playing fields as well. I felt like Charlton Heston at the end of *Planet of the Apes* when he sees Lady Liberty buried in a skirt of sand.

"You bastards," I mumbled, and Eddie heard me. "I mean, oh my God, look at all the trailers."

"Welcome to Portable City," Eddie said, and waved his empty briefcase in what I suppose was a welcoming gesture but wound up almost hitting a passing kid in the temple.

The inside of Eddie's Roomable or Portaclass was as bleak as the outside. No matter how Eddie had tried to cheer up the décor with psychedelic peace signs, district-issued motivational cards, or oversized props stolen from central casting, the lack of natural light and building materials that could be found in nature sucked all the life out of me.

The class trickled in. The boys were dressed mostly in black T-shirts advertising some image of bleakness—Scarface, WWF, or post—Marilyn Manson glum glam bands. The girls wore barely enough to cover the dress code. After they all had shuffled and signed in, Eddie started to roll. His teaching initially reminded me of a fishing trip the Wilder men had taken a few years back. It was still dark when the five of us were trapped in the same vehicle once again, only this time Eddie was no longer the short, defenseless redhead with a few teeth coming in. He was now a professional comedic actor and wanted revenge for all the times he'd been the whipping boy of our family. Eddie subjected us to material for close to two hours, doing riffs off every road sign ("Mount Tom? I hardly know him"), bait hut, and flat-footed pedestrian walking by. My older brother Rich would have hit him, but he was driving, so instead he swerved at trees to clip Eddie's side of the car. I could tell that a roomful of sullen pubescents wouldn't slow my brother down one bit either.

"Good morning, ladies and gentlemen, please open your binders to the word of the day. Does anyone know what that word means? Anyone?" He pointed to the board where the word *alliteration* had been written in handwriting far better than mine, which on good days looks like it came from the hand of a blind doctor writing his own morphine scripts in an earthquake.

Before they could wake up, Eddie raced through the definition, explaining about repetition of sound, consonants, and clusters. I could barely keep up with his Buddy Ebsen–meets–*Blackboard Jungle* banter because as he lectured and introduced new ideas, he threw in jokes about inane terms like *ordered pairs* ("Who ordered pears? I ordered apples!") and *metaphor* ("What's a meta for anyway?"). He even connected alliteration to acting by showing the kids a vocal warm-up exercise about a woman with an obsessive-compulsive disorder named Betty Botter who bought some bitter batter. By the time he did the tongue twister twice, the whole front row was drenched in spit. They would have been drier at a Gallagher concert.

I noticed two girls seated in the back row who shared a look of utter panic. They hadn't understood a thing Crazy Eddie said. Their notebooks were open, but the pages were blank and their pens were frozen in their grip. When the class started a few minutes of quiet seatwork around the word of the day, I called Eddie over and pointed to the pair.

"I think you killed them," I said.

"Dude, thanks. I was trying to make it more fun. It's hard to spice up this stuff."

"No, I'm serious. Look at those two." We both watched as the death-mask girls clung to each other for dear life.

"Oh, them. No worries, mate. Li is from Korea and she speaks *nada inglés, por favor.* For some reason, the kids have taken to calling her Michelle. She doesn't seem to mind. The other girl just got here. Just in time for the FCAT, bro. Can't wait to see that score. We're talking single digits."

"Where's she from?"

"Not sure, somewhere in South America. Haven't gotten her file yet."

By the end of the word of the day, I desperately needed a nap. Since there was no couch, I thought at the termination of class I could at least breathe some air that wasn't scented with kid sweat and pressed wood with a hefty component of petroleum derivatives.

"Eddie, let's walk to the bathroom," I said to him after he waved goodbye to his class and explained I wasn't his twin to at least ten kids.

"No can do, Señor Wences."

"Why not?"

"Trip to the bathroom and back, even for a quick squirt, takes, oh, at least six minutes."

"So?"

"To make room for extra study periods, they shaved off passing time to four minutes. My class is either supervised or locked. My next break is at noon."

"That's two and a half hours from when you started teaching."

"You are correct, sir."

"And you've been chugging coffee like an addict."

"Tell me about it, little sister. At first I thought my bladder would explode, but I got used to it. If I don't eat, it makes it easier. Mind over fecal matter, brother, mind over fecal matter."

The next class shuffled in and signed Eddie's log. "Dude, this is the class I was telling you about!" he shouted in my ear, and waved his hands around like a Holy Roller.

"Are they really talented?" They looked the same as the group before except for one boy who sported a full beard and mustache.

"Not so much, but I've got Raquel Welch, Mike Wallace, and Macho Camacho in this one."

In some twisted bit of fate, his next class had two celebrity name-alikes and one son of a famous boxer who loved his boy enough to bequeath him his own manly nickname. In terms of a teacher's mundane life, this was news. I knew the feeling first-hand. During the course of a particularly stale month of teaching, I got positively giddy knowing that in one class I had the grand-daughter of a legendary American writer and the winner of the county spelling bee. I could hardly contain myself from hugging them both on a daily basis.

Even though Eddie's class would be like a mini *Entertainment Tonight* set in a trailer court, I got the hell out of there. But when I was outside sweating in the moist Florida air, I still was not entirely free. During the time it took for my brother to allow Betty Botter to buy some better, less bitter batter, the word had gotten out about the arrival of his twin. I'd left Eddie's portable and was wandering around lost in a sea of single-wides, trying to locate the bathroom, when I came upon a trio of idle kids who seemed to know I was coming. They started off in a coy manner, trying not to startle me, as I made my way toward the main building. "Hey, Mr. Wilder. Wait a second, you're not Mr. Wilder, are you?" a kid asked in his best Eddie Haskell voice.

"No, I'm not."

"He looks a lot like Mr. Wilder," another chimed in, pulling the wintergreen toothpick from his mouth and using it as a pointer. "Well, then, he must be his twin. Hey, everybody, Mr. Wilder's twin, right here in the hallway!"

I don't know if there has been a shortage of matching siblings in the state of Florida recently, but the kids were so fired up that I had to run away. Since I wasn't wearing a lanyard or any other official neck jewelry, I was forced to duck into the student bathroom, which reminded me a lot of the rest rooms at major sporting events or rock concerts held in stadiums. Inches of mystery liquid bubbled on the floor, and toilet paper was stuffed in every commode. As I held my breath and shot sugar syrup into the overflowing urinal, so many questions flooded my mind:

Why did I come here?

What did I hope to learn?

Should Eddie follow his dream and go back to the theme park and possibly get laid off again or stay in the stable world of trailer teaching?

Do I really look that much like my little brother?

My visit with Crazy Eddie ended in the empty teachers' lounge over Styrofoam trays holding cold pizza, Tater Tots, and a cup of the holy trinity of vegetables (carrots, corn, and peas, with the carrots nicely cut into booger-sized cubes). The lounge was like a group holding pen in a county jail, cinder blocks and steel with no hope of escape or natural light anywhere. Against the far wall stood two broken refrigerators like antiquated sentinels, left over from the last failed regime. In an attempt to make the cell cozier, some kind soul had hung a small framed winterscape on the white wall over a pair of abandoned salad bars. This gesture, while noble, had the creepy effect of bright red lipstick on a naked department store mannequin. I shudder to think about it even now.

Eddie was trying to keep my spirits up by creating erotic farm animals from the fast-food condiment packets strewn on the table, but I could see that he was tired. It was the end of March in a hellacious year, and he still had two more grueling months to go. He told me that there was a chance he would land a job at his old theme park that summer if he got lucky. I could tell the opportunity to perform again without educational standards and practices excited him, but for now he was still a teacher eating a rotten lunch in a stale room with his older brother, who also happened to be a teacher. Growing up, neither one of us had planned to share a profession. He'd always wanted to be an actor, and I'd always wanted to be either the thin Elvis or the fifth Beatle.

"Dude," he sighed, shaking his head, and I understood as only a brother can that this was no ordinary *dude*, it was a *dude* deep from the depths of his soul.

In the shadows between the two dead fridges, I spotted a laminated sheet of paper with a floral border taped to the cinder blocks. It was a motivational piece written by an educator in Omaha and was called "That Noble Title: Teacher." The lofty essay listed our profession's nuances and essences, claiming that a teacher is a poet, physicist, maestro, architect, gymnast, diplomat, and philosopher. I read it aloud to Eddie in our high school drama teacher Al Pia's melodramatic voice, full of breathiness and long, drawn-out syllables. At least for a little while I could take on the burden of being the performer and he could be the one sitting back, trying desperately to laugh.

Teacher Turtle

It's always been clear to our family that my brother Eddie was put on this earth to make people laugh. He was the only Wilder boy born with a clownish wig of red hair, always seemed to lose his baby teeth in cute hillbilly places, and on his first birthday took his first pie in the face using his own hands and our mother's homemade chocolate cake. As the four of us grew older, Eddie's eagerness to bring others joy led him into other, more adult situations. He eagerly volunteered to play goalie for the highly competitive soccer games held in our backyard and never quit even though shots were repeatedly fired at his nuts from close range by an all-state midfielder. Eddie was the butt of the jokes spat by Tom and his tobacco-chewing buddies, and Rich used him as a guinea pig when he concocted complicated cocktails with alcohol stolen from my father's liquor cabinet. Sadly, I treated Eddie like an unpaid Sherpa, forcing him to haul my gear to soccer practice or play rehearsal, depending on the season and my mood. Most therapists would label what we did to him as child abuse, but today Eddie just shrugs it off as "younger brother syndrome." Whether he's being called "fruity" in front of a million listeners by a talk show host when he plays a character called Eddie the Shaman on Friday afternoon drive-time radio or "way over the top" by his teaching colleagues, Eddie takes it all in stride. He's cultivated his YBS into quite a little industry for himself.

Since I'd spent a grueling day shadowing him at his middle school in Orlando and followed his relentless teaching responsibilities over the phone, I often wondered how this overt desire to please could sustain itself with more than 150 students a day, many of them carrying the types of issues they imprison you for in countries that end in -stan. So I wasn't surprised when I got a phone call from him and instead of his usual exultant "DUUUUDE!" a diminutive "Dude" deflated over the cell.

"I got some news," he said rather soberly. "I'm leaving teaching."

"Why?" I asked, even though I had a feeling I knew. The clown needed to scrape off the makeup and vent, so I let him.

"Where should I start? I haven't slept in years, I'm crying in my car on my way to work right now, and I'm supposed to teach acting to this Asperger's girl without looking her in the eye or allowing others to come within thirty feet of her in a twelve-by-twelve trailer. How's that for starters?"

"Pretty good," I said, remembering some of my own early teaching days where I thought wearing a barbed-wire jockstrap sounded better than attempting to inspire other people's kids.

Many overworked teachers are forced to create boundaries for themselves when the gum-chewing cannibals with backpacks (and their helicopter parents) start eating them alive. They dress more formally, don't answer their phones at home, and sprint to their Subarus after the final bell. Others I know drink to excess, pop antidepressants, or develop strange emotional outlets like running in extreme marathons held in the Andes or dressing and addressing their dogs like autistic children. Eddie, on the other hand, was not born with an emotional filter, so he took every one of his students and their nests of problems home with him each day. It didn't matter if Robbie Ritalin grunted at my brother from the back row or filed a formal complaint with the principal because Eddie had the gall to make him stand up during rehearsal; my brother wanted all his students to be happy little learners, and no matter how many pirate jokes he told or vaudeville impressions he mugged, he couldn't save them all. And because public schools are killing education in order to retain their funding (by worrying more about test scores than actual learning), his administration never had his back. The culmination of my brother's burnout happened right after Eddie staged a production of *Guys and Dolls* with a cast larger than the rosters of two NFL teams. I saw the DVD of the show, and my brother did his best wrangling those squirmy adolescents into fedoras and checkered coats, but that many kids on such a small stage made each musical number seem like a head count during a prison break. In one song, it took ten minutes for eighty kids to file through a single door, so by the time the opening notes of "Sit Down, You're Rocking the Boat" squawked from the CD player, everyone, including the leads, had forgotten why they were gathered there in the cafetorium.

With that many kids and their tagalong parentals, even the cast party, which Eddie had booked at a restaurant with a seemingly unappetizing alligator theme, couldn't proceed without incident. One mother complained that her son got the wrong sandwich, so Eddie, as supervisor of the event, had to stay late after everyone else had left to watch the little ingrate masticate a ham and cheese cut in the shape of a crocodile's jawbone. My father often says that he envies Eddie, living in a world where everyone is his brother and sister, coupled with the ability to look on the bright side of anything even if you're inside a black hole covered in bull excrement. I don't argue with my father (because it exhausts me), but inside I know that such a happy-go-lucky life takes its toll on Eddie or others who try to achieve my brother's state of bliss through ingesting multiple tabs of Ecstasy with Red Bull chasers.

Sure enough, the night of the cast party, Eddie started to feel very ill. His temperature spiked, he experienced vertigo, and his body hurt more than the time he was working a gig with an untreated hemorrhoid and got kicked in the ass by a mean ex-con inside a Grinch costume. He quickly drove himself to his doctor's office, where he was told his white blood count was as high as a leukemia patient's.

"So I can go to work?" Eddie asked, trying to summon his trademark smile and peace sign, which get him through most scrapes with both Johnny Law and the PTA tribunal.

The doctor, peering over his half-glasses, offered the same question many have asked Eddie in his lifetime: "What's wrong with you, son?" Then he added, "Didn't you hear what I said? You've got the worst case of influenza I've seen this year."

"I gotta go to work, dude. I'm a teacher and . . ." That's how I knew Eddie was deathly ill. He couldn't even deliver the punch line that says there are no sick days for the watchers of other people's children, especially around test time.

The doctor crossed his arms. "Here's your choice: go home and stay in bed for a week or I check you in to the ER right now."

It may be due to some Puritan inbreeding in our past, but for a Wilder, calling in sick is as good as admitting we once wrote fan letters to Yakov Smirnoff. My dad took maybe one sick day a year, and even that was a malingering moral defeat for him. I haven't missed a day of school due to illness in five years. I'm not bragging, because I expect an unwelcome transfer student from heart-attackville will be visiting my classes real soon. All the shit Eddie had been taking at school—extra classes, parent meetings, bogus committees, and the toxic cafeteria food—had filled him up like the liver of an overfed goose, and he collapsed.

On the phone, I asked Eddie if he'd managed to unwind his crazy inner mechanism and actually rest for a full week. This was like asking a hungry shark surrounded by gravy-covered sea turtles not to swim.

"I had to," he said, recalling his fall from grace. "Dude, I couldn't get out of bed. Then the next morning, the phone rang and it was the front office asking me to come in to train for the standardized tests, which started the next week. I could barely talk, so I whispered: 'Dudes, I'm really ill.' "

"What'd they say?" I imagined some gray-haired woman with Lisa Loeb glasses bugging him for lesson plans, attendance lists, or sub suggestions.

"They said I needed to come in for at least an hour. They needed to train me to give the tests."

I was outraged. "Those fuckers."

"Tell me about it, little sister. I told them I was close to dying."

"What'd they say?"

"Could I come in for forty-five minutes, then?"

Even as Eddie relayed the litany of miseries he faced teaching, I still worried about him leaving a set gig. He had a growing daughter who loved to eat, wear clean clothing, dance, and play sports that cost money; his wife, Sandy, was currently pregnant after two rounds of very expensive in vitro, and being the father in a modern family, he still had a living room set, two TVs, and the digital babysitter TiVo to pay for.

"So what are you gonna do?"

"Here's the thing." He took a deep breath. "I'm gonna be a turtle, dude."

"A what?" I thought he'd said *girdle*. Maybe he would sell women's underwear. He'd actually be good at that.

"A full-time turtle, dude. Back at Disney."

I had to see this. From teacher to turtle. Could it be possible? "I'll fly right out," I told him the soonest weekend I could come.

"That's great, bro. You can see me do Turtle Talk on Saturday, but there's one more thing."

"Okay." I readied myself for him to ask me for a loan. How much lettuce could they pay turtles, after all?

"I have to perform a wedding the night before."

Stay with me here. Besides teaching full time, monitoring dodgeball at the YMCA after school to earn extra pay, playing Eddie the Shaman on the radio on Fridays, fathering his family, and coaching his daughter's tee-ball and basketball teams, my brother marries people. For reals, as Poppy's friends say, or so it seems. For his thirtieth birthday six years ago, his wife, Sandy, had him ordained in the Universal Life Church. After deciding that opening his own church was too restrictive, Crazy Eddie started banging those wedding drums for other folks. He began slowly, marrying baked and bankrupt friends, and then happened to mention on the radio show that he'd fused a couple; after that, for reasons that are lost on me, listeners started calling in. I'm still trying to figure out why. So far he's done dozens of ceremonies, from something called a Celtic handfasting to a Native American cleansing ceremony at the Disney pavilion.

My brother was presiding over a wedding at Orlando's oldest municipal golf course, Dubsdread, which, when Eddie had mentioned it to me, sounded more like a recording studio for Rastafarians than the old moss-covered stomping ground for Slammin' Sam Snead and Ben Hogan. For the ceremony, I sat in the last row in a banquet chair that had been draped in sheets and ribbon like a transgendered ghost trying hard not to be mistaken as male. I felt as though we were kids again, playing some elaborate prank on the Charletons next door, pulling a fast one on all these Floridians even though Eddie had met with them, conducted the rehearsal with sober family members present, and made sure the couple had a license to legally wed. Eddie told me people had come from all over—including the son of the groom, who flew home from the war in Iraq. This shit was real, I could touch it, but something felt as if at least one of us was pretending. Then I was overcome with guilt for doubting my brother and the joy he had brought countless others, whether Native American, Celtic, redneck, or perpetually stoned. Maybe these people were not unlike Eddie's students in wanting some of my brother's loveducation. Turns out I wasn't the only doubting Thomas in the crowd. Two older couples were seated next to me, and from their catch-up chatter I surmised that they hadn't seen each other since the last wedding or, judging from their age, funeral they attended together. After the canned Yanni music punctured the balmy air, my brother strode up the floral runway, his back erect and his grin as wide and white as the bride's train.

"That there's one strange minister," the man next to me

grunted to his fellow elders. "You should have seen all his ear-rings at the rehearsal. Looked like a goddern pirate."

"Bangles? On a minister?" The woman next to him slapped her Miracle-Ear.

"Yeah, I don't know where they located him, but it sure weren't in no church I never heard of."

The voice Eddie used in his sermon was different from the one he employed as a teacher. His "preacher brogue," as he later referred to it, sounded like Alistair Cooke playing a Puritan cleric in a James Bond film. *Far* was pronounced "fah" and the pause before the last two words, "as one," was longer than it took to get his entire *Guys and Dolls* cast and crew onstage. Even though he knew these people by now and really wanted their marriage to survive, he was doing shtick. All through the ceremony, I recognized the many voices my brother had cultivated over the years, and suffered the accompanying flashbacks. During the middle of the ceremony he channeled Marcellus Washburn from *The Music Man*, the role made famous by Buddy Hackett. I recalled driving home from college to watch Eddie do the stiff-legged "Shipoopi" dance on our high school stage. So as he recited something about love and trust in that the same nasal whine the seagull employs in *The Little Mermaid*, all I could see were my brother's two legs kicking up and down like an overfed Rockette.

If I had to sum up the text of Eddie's wedding ceremony, I'd say it was a chunk of raw wisdom from Jerry Garcia put through the Hallmark meat grinder. The funny thing is, just like with his teaching, I knew my brother meant every cosmically convoluted word. I didn't really want to change Eddie or the many roles he plays not on TV but in his day-to-day life; I just wanted to understand him a little better, especially now that he was leaving teaching for pursuits I was still trying to get straight in my head. I sat back in my gift-wrapped chair, closed my eyes, and tried desperately to ground myself because I knew that the next day we were heading to Disney, which would catapult me in the opposite direction.

I've never liked thrill rides very much, the kind that shake you around and spin you like a tennis shoe in an industrial washing machine. So when I was racing with Eddie and his daughter, Marcy, across Disney's Epcot Center, I wondered what exactly I was in for. I'd only wanted to go to (read: tolerate) the park to see my brother in his new post-teaching gig as a turtle. Because I'd visited often during the ten years my brother worked for Disney before he started teaching, I have no trouble remembering the magic, and frankly, it's lost on me. Before Eddie's call time at Turtle Talk, we were heading to a new ride called Mission: Space, and because of my brother's shortcuts, we were first in line, which, according to him, is a real honor.

Mission: Space is a ride that simulates the actual takeoff, weightlessness, and landing of a rocket going to Mars. In the briefing room, we stood patiently like good students and watched a video where Gary Sinise plays a Pollyanna-ish astronaut telling us about our mission. During his talk, we were warned three separate times that if we were too old, too young, too short, too tall, or too pregnant, or if we suffer from back pain, neck pain, motion sickness, seasickness, fear of heights, or claustrophobia, we should abort the mission immediately. I realized that I suffered from all those things, so I asked Eddie, "Why do they need to warn us three times?"

"At Disney," he said proudly, "cast members need to tell everyone everything three times to make sure they understand. If someone is hurt, you have to ask 'Do you need help?' three times before you can leave the scene."

"Sounds right."

He smiled devilishly. "And also because this ride is really fucking sick."

As we moved into the area outside our capsule, people started bailing, including this huge tattooed dude and his canine-looking kid in the pod next to us. These guys looked like they could shit railroad ties, and even they were chickening out. That didn't make me feel any braver. Neither did the fact that by the time we entered the ride, I had been warned over thirteen times that I would definitely be ill.

I was seated with a stranger on one side, my brother on the other, and his five-year-old daughter, Marcy, to his right. The compartment was very small and dark, and once they closed the door, the front console moved close enough to my face that I could lick it. As I looked around the detailed interior, I saw stacks of white barf sacks on either side of my joystick. "Eddie, they have airsickness bags on a ride in a goddamn amusement park."

"I know, dude. They had to," he explained. "People were hurling all over the place." He readjusted the rings adorning his fingers. "We don't call it hurling, though. We call it a 'protein spill,' " he said, holding up two wiggling peace signs acting as quotation marks.

I knew I could spill more than just protein, so I grabbed the joystick and stared straight ahead. According to the warning briefs, I absolutely could not move my head, close my eyes, or look anywhere but the screen ahead of me. "Are you sure Marcy's going to be okay?" I asked Eddie without moving my lips.

"She's the navigator, aren't you, Binks?" he said, using her pet name. "She's been on this ride more times than I have. She'll be fine."

I heard nothing from the navigator's seat, so I figured she either was calm or had smartly passed out already. Either way, she is my brother's spawn, weaned on Disney magic, so she'd no doubt fare better than I would.

After static crackled over the speakers, mission control began the countdown. Our seats tilted back and the screen made it seem as if we were inside a rocket looking up into a clear blue sky. Maybe this won't be so bad, I thought, when all of a sudden we went from a stationary position to 1.5 Gs in one second. My cheeks were melting off my face, my small intestine was rolling around inside my mouth, and I thought I was going to vomit and pass out, but I wasn't sure in which order. The guy next to me started groaning, then gagging, and I prayed he wouldn't reach for the bag between us, which would undoubtedly trigger a chain reaction. On another planet, Eddie was laughing and hooting like we were five drinks into some strip club. I don't know what my mother was smoking when Eddie was in utero, but he is not from this earth. When we hit the weightlessness stage, where you feel as if you are spinning around in space like a pinwheel, my brother acted like a seasoned steward on a Delta flight to Newark.

"Push your button, dude," he told me. In my effort not to chunder all over the screen, I'd ignored Gary Sinise telling me to push some flashing yellow light the size and shape of a tab of acid.

Eddie was unaffected by anything this ride had to throw at him. He whipped his head back and forth to look at Marcy and me, closed his eyes, and during one bout of bravado scrambled his skull like that dude does in the movie *Scanners*. If Eddie could, he would have removed his over-the-shoulder harness restraint and given us all neck rubs. The man next to me had no idea what to think. Who was this superhuman seated next to a guy who wanted to die quietly just like he did?

Of course the ride couldn't end calmly with a smooth, peaceful descent. We had to crash-land on Mars and then hang precariously over the edge of a red cliff, igniting a fear of heights I didn't even know I had. "Why do we do this to ourselves?" I yelled to no one in particular. "Why didn't you just take me to Turtle Tits or whatever it's called?"

"Because it rocks!" Eddie said, holding an alien fist in the air.

" 'Cause it rocks!" Marcy echoed, fully enrolled in the school of dizzying Disneyness.

"It's like I got food poisoning during a lethal car crash," I said, feeling as though a zit the size of a grapefruit had just popped in my mouth.

"Amen to that!" the guy next to me said. "Get me out of this thing." He fell out of the cabin door like a handful of tools as soon as the hatch opened.

I couldn't get my sea legs for the rest of the day. Every time I turned my head, that queasy feeling revisited me. Marcy wanted to run around the undersea playground while we waited for Turtle Talk, but this sissy missy preferred to wait staring straight ahead with his rubbery arms at his sides. Even though I didn't dare to glance over my shoulder, I could sense the line growing very long behind us, and it was still early in the morning. I asked my sister-in-law, Sandy, who met us after that damned Mission: Space ride, why so many people were gathering to just sit and watch a turtle. Shouldn't they all be punishing themselves on thrill rides like I just had?

"It's the most popular child attraction in any of the four parks," she said. "Just wait until you see your brother. He's amazing." I remembered those were the exact same words Eddie's colleagues had used to describe his teaching. Could the life of a teacher and the life of a turtle be at all connected?

The Turtle Talk room was set up so that kids sat on the floor in front of a small movie screen and the parents sat on benches in the back. After what Sandy had said, I couldn't help but see a classroom shape in all this—kids sitting in loose rows facing something a little larger than a chalkboard. On the screen was an animated underwater scene with a school of red fish darting back and forth and long blades of green grass waving serenely in the water. After a brief introduction by a mumbling Disney cast member with a microphone, we all screamed for Crush, and sure enough, the most famous turtle alive rolled in riding a wave that none of us human dudes could actually see.

"Whoaaaaa—righteous righteous righteous—whoaaaa, dude!" my brother yelled in his Crush surfer timbre. It was surreal. I was watching my brother speak through a computer-generated turtle in a voice not unlike Jeff Spicoli's in *Fast Times at Ridgemont High*. Still dizzy from my Mission: Space disaster, it was hard for me to unpack the dialectical contradictions in front of me. I tried to imagine all six feet of my brother somewhere manipulating this image on the screen, who was actually putting on one helluva show. Crush told jokes, did tricks, made funny faces, and interacted with the little "hatchlings" in the same kinds of ways I'd seen my brother do for reals in his porta-trailer at the middle school. My brother chose one British kid from the dozens of raised hands and answered all his questions about what turtles eat, how fast they swim, and where they go to the loo. As he left, I saw the biggest grin on the little shaver's face, showing teeth that had yet to be spoiled by the bad diet and poor dentistry favored by what my brother would call "our brothers and sisters across the rockin' pond." So maybe the show wasn't as educational as a day in school, but he did slip in some facts about turtles and sea conservation, and the kids were free to go outside after the show. They weren't denied fresh air and exercise in order to pass some fascist standardized test that taught them nothing but the right (read: stressful) way to fill in bubbles with number-two pencils. Even though what I had just witnessed was all an illusion, Eddie was still my brother, and his act had triggered the kind of joy in those kids that would register on any lie detector test.

Since I was leaving early the next morning, I asked Sandy and Marcy if we could watch the show one more time. I knew the routine would be basically the same, but I wanted to remember all the briny details to tell Poppy and London when I got home. I knew those two would be as proud as punch to have their uncle pursue a career as a surfing turtle. Most of their friends had studied *Finding Nemo* a lot more closely than they did other, less important subjects like long division or the Bill of Rights. As the audience was filing out, I spotted a leash kid lying facedown on the floor having a whale-sized tantrum. I don't know if he was upset that my brother hadn't chosen him or he wanted to see Crush with that hilarious bikini top around his neck again, but the urchin was really pissed, and his parents were on the ground trying desperately to reason with him. I recalled a story my brother had told about that Asperger's girl who freaked out in his class one day. She thought someone was pulling her long hair, and it was all my brother could do to calm her down without touching her, looking her in the eye, or invoking her Christian name. I knew Eddie, in his secret booth somewhere, could see the leash kid struggling, and I wondered what it felt like to watch it safely from a computer screen instead of being directly on the killing floor.

A Disney cast member came over and asked the parents three times if they needed help dealing with their harnessed hooligan. Even though the seas were calm on the screen in front of me, no turtle in sight, I swear I heard a whispered but celebratory "dude" echo over the loudspeaker from a person who had no responsibility for another couple's child. I told Sandy and Marcy that we could go now. The transformation was complete.

Jesus Box

In terms of religious upbringing, Lala and I share the same oil-and-water beginnings followed by two very different paths down the Holy Rolling aisle. I was baptized in the Catholic Church, donned the wax-stained robes of an altar boy, and spent four terms at Sacred Heart Catholic School followed by a few more years of religious instruction whose lessons were as forgettable as almost all of the minor saints' miracles. I learned more about the complexities of being my brother's keeper watching my brother Rich lose fistfights in the rectory parking lot than I ever did from any catechism missal. I stopped going to church mostly because of the oppressive dogma, numerous unanswered questions about sex and dying, and the fact I was forbidden to choose Elvis as my confirmation name. What can I say? To me, the man was a saint.

Lala was christened in the Catholic Church too, though thousands of miles west in Colorado. Since she spent summers on her grandfather's farm in Utah, she was also baptized in the Mormon Church, which I suppose makes her a switch-hitter in the church-going department. Even though Lala has spent most of her life hiding from the doorbell-ringing Latter-Day Saints, she hasn't forgotten what she learned in Merry Miss A.'s Sunday school class. Lala rarely drinks, but if you do happen to convince her to imbibe, she'll sing her Mormon songs louder than Donny or Marie.

Lala and I successfully avoided discussing all that abstract God business with our kids until we signed London up for a Lutheran preschool. We enrolled him in Gentle Shepherd because the three half days suited our schedule, the church-subsidized fees fit our limited budget, and on his visit day, London had taken a test drive in a plastic pedal car and it passed his forty-point inspection. We understood there'd be some minor religious instruction included in the package deal—blessings before snack, happy songs about a father who was not biological, and pictures of a hip Jesus riding a motorcycle slipped discreetly into their coloring books. As long as he didn't come home dressed in a hair shirt and speaking in tongues, we were fine with those lovable Lutherans running the show for our little congregant.

London had been at Gentle Shepherd for two weeks when I went to pick him up early because after preschool we were all driving eight hours north to Golden, Colorado, to see the blessed savior of the railways, Thomas the Tank Engine. When I arrived, his teacher asked if we wouldn't mind staying for chapel, which happened for just ten minutes each Friday. I figured that if we were going to spend eight hours in the minivan for two hours of traintopia, what was another ten minutes? Might actually keep us safer from all those heathens on the highway expressing what London calls "rude rage."

I got on one knee and asked him quietly, "Do you want to go to chapel, buddy?"

"Apple?" He furrowed his brow and leaned forward to whisper in my ear. "I already ate my apple, Dad. For snack. Jeesh."

"No, do you want to go in there with your class?" I pointed toward a large room with what looked like felt banners the color of Easter eggs hanging from the ceiling. "I'll come along if you like."

"Sure," he said, but then again he'd given the same answer to other invitations just as unclear in his mind. Immunizations, for instance, and hair cutteries that accept discount coupons from grocery stores.

London's fifteen or so classmates were already seated on the thickly carpeted floor in front of the altar. A bald man with a handlebar mustache was perched on a chair above the kiddy congregation. Even though he was dressed more like a real estate agent than the priests I remember, I could tell by his cheery voice that he was the pastor of the church. I had spoken to him the day before London started school to alert him of the possibility that we might not have London's immunization records since his former pediatrician had told the corrupt insurance companies to screw off and converted her office into a tanning salon. When I finally tracked down his chart, I called the pastor back and kidded him that he must have prayed for the lost to become found again. He answered, "Well, Bob, I surely did." I let the Bob thing go because, after all, he was a man of the cloth.

For a Lutheran preschool, the flock of kids was pretty diverse. A pair of adopted twins from China were seated next to a few Hispanic kids, who huddled with London's towheaded friend

Lark, who, with her white hair, looked the closest to a real Saxon. The oddest one in the lineup was a slobbering boy who had to be cradled by the teacher's assistant, even though he weighed well over forty pounds and was old enough to get his own paper route and start tithing.

"Good morning, children," the pastor said.

"Good morning, teacher," the rug rats answered mechanically.

The head holy dude chuckled and adjusted his wire-rimmed glasses. "Well, I guess I'm a teacher, but really you should call me Pastor."

"Good morning, Pastor," the kids dutifully replied.

"That's great, children! And do we know where we are now?"

"Earth?" a long-haired boy with a hemp necklace answered.

"A room?" another said.

London threw in his two cents. "School?"

"Yes, we are at your school, but this room we call chapel."

"Good morning, Pastor Chapel," the kids shouted.

After Pastor Chapel explained that they'd be meeting here every Friday, he pulled a shoebox from under his chair. I recognized the British flag logo from Reebok's line of footwear and wondered where exactly he'd be going with that 1980s prop. London recalled the image too, not from the footwear manufacturer but from the different apparel Lala has purchased connected to the city that shares London's name. This Halloween, she plans to drape him in Union Jacks and have him hold a telephone in an attempt to be "London Calling," the famous Clash song. Lala doesn't love the actual city of London per se; she just enjoys the idea of her son having his own logo.

"Look, Dad." London pointed to the box.

"Yeah," I said tentatively, having no idea what the hell would happen next, especially with a crowd that was a few nuggets short of a Happy Meal.

"Does anyone know what this is?" Pastor Chapel ran his finger along the center of the red and blue box vertically, then horizontally. London raised his hand halfway and whispered his own name under his breath like a prayer.

"A box," Hemp Kid yelled.

"Right, but what do we call this here?" He traced the longitude and latitude again.

"Your finger? It's kinda hairy," a girl said.

"Red?"

A kid in the corner by a flag quoting scripture jumped up like he'd just gotten the Spirit. "Oh, I know! I know!" he shouted.

The pastor seemed relieved. "Yes, Diego?"

"My dad says an alligator can swim in dirt, y'know that?"

The pastor looked in the opposite direction. "Anyone else?"

"Bashama darn shino shin shi," one of the Asian twins mumbled.

"Miss Kathy," the pastor asked, "can you please translate?"

The exhausted Christian caregiver shrugged. "I have no idea."

"Oh well," the pastor sighed. "This, children, is a cross."

"It is?" London asked me. His pinched face told me that his brain was under severe duress. "London is a cross?" He rolled his eyes, then blinked in what seemed to be Morse code. "Dad, I'm a cross?" I thought he might cry.

"Not exactly. We'll talk about it on the way to see Thomas," I answered, which really meant *Please let him forget all about this crazyass talk*.

"I have a cross in my house."

"I have a cross in my room," a kid said, scrunching forward to get closer to the pastor and his box of celestial conundrums.

"That's great, Larry," the pastor replied. "I have one in my bedroom."

"We have two crosses in our house," another boy shouted, trying to show off in front of the Lord.

"My grandma has, like, twenty hundred crosses," Larry replied, and yanked up his pants.

"I can cross the street if a grown-up holds my both ways."

"Okay, children, settle down now." I could tell things were not going exactly as planned since our spiritual leader was starting to sweat. "Do you know who we associate with the cross?"

The accompanying silence, even for a church, was quite overwhelming.

"Jesus." The pastor nodded solemnly. "And who knows the name of our school?"

"Preschool?"

"Chapel?"

"Pastor?"

"Gentle Shepherd," London said. He knew the name only because we had tried to gear him up for school weeks before he started. Lala and I had sounded like cheerleading idiots, jabbering, "Excited for Gentle Shepherd? Ready for Gentle Shepherd? Psyched for Gentle Shepherd?" until London finally said, "Enough already about that stupid Gentle Shepherd. I get it. Jeesh."

The pastor pointed in our direction. "Right you are, London, and I want everyone to welcome London's dad, Bob, here with us today."

"It's Rob, actually," London said, and shot his pals a look that said they'd be taking a vote of confidence early next week.

"Jesus is the gentle shepherd," the pastor explained. "Look behind you."

We all turned around to face the back of the church. The area was fairly dark, and it was hard to tell if he wanted us to see Jesus himself come out of the bathroom or the pastor was tired of looking down at noses encrusted with snot.

"Miss Debbie, will you please turn on the light so the children can see the stained glass?"

The teacher's assistant pried Baby Huey from her lap, wiped off the boy sweat from her groinal area, and started down the aisle. About half the kids stood up and blindly followed her like she was the Pied Piper of candy or cartoons. She fumbled with a few switches before illuminating a picture of a long-haired man surrounded by furry farm animals. The perspective in the stained glass was a bit off, so the Son of God was the same size as ewe and me.

"What do you see?" the pastor asked those of us remaining who did not, like Lazarus, decide to walk the walk.

"Teacher?"

"Pastor?"

"Chapel?"

"Cross?"

The pastor clapped in what I guessed to be a gesture of restrained frustration. "Jesus is the gentle shepherd for what animal, children?"

"An alligator!" Diego yelled.

"I love animals," Lark sighed.

"I have a dog, two cats, and a fish."

London nodded eagerly. Animals were a subject he could weigh in on. "We have a fish, his name is Turkboys. Right, big fella?" He elbowed me in the ribs and winked. I decided not to reveal that the name of the fish was actually a color, Turquoise, not a gang from Ankara.

"Look closer, children."

"Lambs?" Lutheran Larry proposed.

"Well, Jesus is the lamb, but we won't get into that today."

"Thank God," I said, looking at the hands of my Roman watch.

"Sheep, children. Jesus is the shepherd of sheep."

"Tell them how he's the shepherd for us," Kathy whispered.

"Right," the pastor said, nodding, but you could tell his heart wasn't in it. He closed his eyes and sighed. I wondered if he had better luck on Sundays when his audience was more interested in the Book of Concord than Winnie the Pooh. "Jesus is always with us."

The kids searched around the room as if the Savior was hiding behind the heavy curtains or under the pews in some cruel version of holy hide-and-go-seek-and-ye-shall-be-found.

"You can't see him, but he's always with us. He is our shepherd."

The kids looked more confused than Paris Hilton in a discreet math class at MIT.

"Now let's get back to this box." The pastor held the cardboard container in his hands. "We call this our Jesus box."

It's funny to think about now, but I had my own Jesus box when I was eight. After two years of Catholic school, I covered a shoebox in one of my father's handkerchiefs, stole a crucifix from my grandmother's rosary, jammed it in the cardboard, added some birthday candles, and created my own mini altar. Unlike in London's case, my inspiration came from fear, not confusion. The ruler-yielding nuns literally frightened the hell out of me, as did the idea of confession every Friday in a dark box the size (and odor) of a phone booth. I used my Jesus box to invent sins and practice confession so I wouldn't freeze up in front of Father Scare-You-Shitless. I wasn't a particularly bright kid, so my trespasses usually included hurting my older brother

Richard, which was a laugh given that he was already the patron saint of kicking my meek ass. Just for the record, I have yet to inherit the earth.

Pastor Chapel lifted the lid of the 3-D British flag, and Lutheran Larry yelled, "Stickers!" He had obviously viewed the miracle of the Jesus box the year before. This Christ-centered clusterfuck had been longer than ten minutes, and I was itching for Pastor Chapel to hand out religious stickers so we could get out of there and on the road—if not to salvation, at least somewhere less confusing. A place where trains ran on uniform tracks and overtired parents ran on fumes and highly caffeinated beverages.

"That's right, Larry." The pastor pulled out half a sheet of brown stickers, fewer than the number of kids present. The stickers themselves opened up a whole new hosanna can of worms since they featured only a silhouette of the water-walker with a halo over his head.

"Who's that?"

"This is Jesus, the gentle shepherd."

"Where's the cross?"

"It's not on here."

"Where are the sheep?"

"This is a different picture of Jesus."

The kids looked to the three remaining adults, but I, for one, wasn't getting near any of this. I closed my eyes, folded my hands, and pretended to pray for our salvation.

"I want a sticker!" Larry demanded.

"I need a sticker, mine falled off." Hemp Boy pointed to an orange stain on his T-shirt.

"Stiff gite shan cho choe," one of the twins said, and I swear I thought I was starting to understand her more clearly than the idea of a three-part, omniscient God.

"I'll tell you what I told the three-year-olds yesterday," the pastor whispered, trying to calm down the frenzied addicts. Three-year-olds? I would have loved to see how an even more re-medial audience responded to such abstract connections. I imagined something out of *Boys Town* meets *Lord of the Flies* with Pastor Chapel harpooned on the end of a shepherd's staff. "I don't have enough stickers in the Jesus box today, but if you'll come to chapel next week—"

"Good morning, Chapel." The kids were tired, but their Pavlovian responses still worked.

"I'll have enough then," the pastor said, dabbing his brow with the paper. I wanted to make a joke about loaves and fishes, but London was tugging on my shirt.

"Dad, let's go. I don't get this Pasture Apple guy and his X box," he said, leading me toward the door. "Thomas is way better than this."

"Amen!" I said, and we raced to the car before the Holy Spirit could catch up to us.

When I was growing up, my parents pawned off any religious in-quiry to the priests, nuns, and laypeople at Sacred Heart or our local church. Our family dinner table never addressed the foren-sic possibility of a Holy Trinity over my dad's beef hearts in red wine sauce. Even when I did gather up the courage to ask Sister St. Ignatius why she wore a wedding ring when she never even met her husband or let him carry her over the threshold, I couldn't get a straight answer from the flat side of her ruler. The discovery of scrotum hair was mystery enough for me; I didn't need more unanswerable questions when I went to a place that supposedly offered solace to the sick and the weary.

With Poppy, Lala and I got away with my teacherly "some people believe" speech after she wanted to know about crucifixion, a term she learned not from school or catechism but from a *Simpsons* episode on the rapture. Now that London was enrolled in a preschool that equated British running shoes with crosses, farm animals, and resurrection, I knew we were basically fucked in the most holy of ways.

"Dad, where are we going?" London asked from the padded manger we call a car seat. He was happy now, sucking on the same two fingers Jesus offered as a sort of gang sign for the peacefully inclined.

"To Colorado to see Thomas and Sir Topham Hat."

"Who's coming with us?"

"Mama, Poppy, you, and me."

"Will Jesus be there?"

I imagined the hordes of parents and children from all over the West, gathered in worship of a pagan god capable of producing scalding steam and highly annoying theme songs. In a vision I saw full-grown adults dressed in striped overalls and engineer caps, while children wrapped in polyurethane costumes overheated, vomiting cotton-candy goo onto HO-scale villages and towns. At the Colorado Railroad Museum, Nietzche's controversial quote about God not being a useful engine might actually come true.

"Will he, Dad? Will Jesus be there?" London repeated.

"Not unless he has a ticket, son. I think the bloody thing is sold out."

Low Blow Showdown

School life rarely ends after the final bell. Teachers are expected to support the whole child, which translates into suffering through atonal band concerts, clumsy dance recitals, and student films that look as though a razor-wielding drunkard has edited them. The hardest events for me to sleep through are the musicals. Last year, I saw my twentieth reincarnation of *The Music Man*. Even when Prep kindly recruited Poppy to play Amaryllis in the high school production, it wasn't easy for me. Wasn't it enough, I wondered, that I'd been in the play before and seen performances in various schools, community theaters, and nursing homes across the country? As Poppy's stage dad, I had to endure hundreds of hours of rehearsals, multiple viewings of the film at home, and the soundtrack playing incessantly in our minivan. Even after I tried to clear my head by scrolling to the Sex

Pistols or Clash in my iPod, I couldn't get the fucking Wells Fargo ear-worm wagon out of my skull. I'd walk into first-period class like a drunken Broadway has-been, groaning "Oh, the Wells Fargo wagon is a-comin', grrr, grrr, it's a-comin', dammit."

I don't mind attending sporting events I can understand, like soccer and basketball, even if we get trounced by teams that grew up dribbling the round ball instead of caffè latte out of a paper cup. I've played and coached soccer for many years, so I think nothing of throwing Poppy and London in the van like athletic equipment and driving across town to watch Prep play the local Catholic school, our archrival archangels. Such school-related jaunts give Lala some time alone, and watching priests scowl at the referee is as close as Poppy's ever going to get to my early childhood experience.

London had just received some Transformer action figures as a reward for not swearing in front of the Lutherans at his preschool, and he decided to haul them to the soccer game in a Scooby-Doo lunch box. I usually discourage lugging toys to such events in order to avoid the heartache of some cybertron losing his head or wheel, depending on how you configure the asexual contortionists. When we arrived at the stadium, Poppy recognized some kids from her own soccer team and asked if she could play with them. I told her she could, even though they were little brothers and sisters from the rival school and would probably try to sway Poppy to join a side that believes immaculate conception is a fine way to explain away the issue of teen pregnancy. London, on the other hand, was in a social quandary. He could sit in the stands with the Prep parents and me and safely transform a robot into a plane, or he could try his hand running with Poppy and the big dogmas. When London is deep in thought, he freezes and rolls his eyes around their sockets.

"What do you want to do, Londy?" I asked, trying to save him from triggering his first seizure with his creepy Marty Feldman peepers.

"Can I go with Poppy?"

"Sure."

"Can I bring a Transformer?"

"No."

"Do I have to wear my hat?"

"Yes."

Happy with the parameters we'd set, he said, "Okay. I'll be right back." It was the girls' soccer team's first game of the season, and even though this was my tenth year at the school, the summertime hangover made me forget that any school function, no matter how supposedly fun it's intended to be, is still work. As soon as I sat down, the parents starting asking for a few minutes of my time to fill me in on how the recent grads were faring in college or to inquire how we could possibly get my current students into one. That day I needed three heads (or three drinks) in order to listen to the parents, watch the game, and periodically check to make sure London hadn't fallen between the bleachers like a dropped chili dog. I'm usually pretty good at multitasking—making dinner, proofreading Poppy's homework, and acknowledging Lala's list of my failures as a handyman—but I was out of practice and out of my kitchen.

". . . and they placed Peggy in the International House with a bunch of foreigners since they thought she was from Mexico, not *New* Mexico," one parent rattled on behind me. London disappeared down a ravine, so I stood up and asked a member of the Booster Club to guard my Transformers, something I'd never dreamed I'd ask another adult in my lifetime. I walked over to an elevated cement slab, built probably for a pep band or ancient alums who needed to be wheeled in for homecoming. I side-stepped some kids gathered in a clump and peered down at London, who was sliding down the dirt ramp on his butt.

"Hey, Dad," he said, waving a filthy hand. He seemed happy to be included with the older kids even though he still employed some juvenile ambulatory ass moves.

"You okay?" I asked before a rock stung me in the back of my leg. I turned around and barked, "Hey!"

Like the Bible had taught them, the kids behind me all had small stones in their hands. Behind the little Pharisees sat a row of adults who were far too busy showing school spirit to notice their kids tossing rocks into the crowd and onto the field.

"Let's not throw rocks," I said in my best PC teacher voice. "It's not Christian," I added, just to be a pagan smartass.

Poppy and London and the rest of the brood were below me playing a game of tag. Prep had just scored a goal to tie it up, 2–2. "Now we have ourselves a ballgame," I said to myself, then deeply regretted sounding like an extra in the Appalachian version of *Field of Dreams*.

From below, London let out a yelp. "Someone hit him in the neck with a rock," a blond girl said. I clenched my fists and was ready to have a serious "come to Jesus" meeting with the little miscreants, but London stopped me.

"I'm okay, Dad. I'm okay. *Je*-sus," he sighed, and I knew two things: he wanted to be treated like a big boy, and with a mouth like that we'd be getting a call from his Lutheran preschool teacher in the next few days.

I have the distinct male trait of zoning out if the entertainment in front of my face is even remotely interesting. Poppy has recited whole plays during *Monday Night Football* and I don't remember a single line. Lala has alerted me to automobile maintenance issues during *The Simple Life* and I claim innocence when the car seizes up due to lack of oil. At the game, I was so engrossed in our team trying to spank God's side that when London started wailing, I realized I'd been mentally gone for at least ten minutes. He was crying with two eight-year-old girls at his side. The temptresses had evil grins smeared across their faces. Behind the devilish duo was a red-faced boy twice London's size, doubled over in pain.

"He hit him in the privates!" the first floozy yelled.

"We told him to and he did it!" the second one screamed while jumping up and down like she was trying out for the cheerleading squad.

Like Orpheus, I descended into Hades and retrieved my son, still in shock from having committed such a violent and neutering act. I led him away from the scene of the crime and past the bleachers, where I would have received an earful of parenting advice from the spectators on how to handle the incident.

The account I got from London was that the girls had set up their own kangaroo court and sentenced the rock thrower to a *Jackass*-like punishment of a punch in the nads. As I rubbed London's back, I tried to think of the right way to respond to being ushered into confrontation, however unwillingly. How should I tell London how to react to these types of situations? As I was stalling for time, I saw the cluster of rock throwers with their crooked grins, and they reminded me of my own run-in with a bunch of hooligans years before.

One May early in my career at Prep, before London was born, I was leaving the upper-school quad to go to my car, parked at the bottom of the hill. May in Santa Fe is the gateway to summer—

warm days, cool nights, and a sky as blue as a supermodel's contact lens. My last class didn't meet that day, so I was exiting early to spend time with my wife and young daughter. I was at the top of the hill, bag in hand, saying goodbye to some students and faculty, when a Jeep full of bare-chested teens smoking cigars raced onto campus playing loud hip-hop music. The Jeep screeched to a halt right in front of the school and, rather unfortunately, me. I couldn't believe it. I was only five minutes from leaving campus and heading to the open arms of my family and the open door of my beer cooler. Now I had to play Officer Krupke to these jerk-off Jets. It's a drag being the only adult in these situations. I rolled my eyes to myself since the group of faculty I had just been speaking to had magically disappeared behind classroom doors and inside garbage cans. Unhappily, I sauntered over.

"Could you please turn the radio off?" I asked.

"Sure thing," the driver said. He was slighter than the other goons, and his tiny head was shaved, which made him appear even younger and far less intelligent.

"You guys gotta go."

"How are you?" the driver asked, holding out his hand for me to shake. I passed. "We're just visiting your lovely school."

"I'm sure you are, but you need to leave." It felt as though someone else was saying these words, my father maybe, or all the disciplinarians I mooned from the back of yellow school buses.

"What's your name?" the driver asked, still trying to be charming.

"Pete."

"Pete what?"

"Pete Moss." I glanced over my shoulder, naively expecting someone to show up and help me out—a maintenance man, secretary, receptionist, our FedEx guy—but no one was around.

When they give out free doughnuts or breakfast burritos, teachers come out of goddamn retirement to stuff their gobs, but when there's trouble, good luck finding even a lowly aide. I had a hard time believing that no one happened to notice a group of half-naked teens smoking cigars in a Jeep. Later, when the incident would be brought up at an after-school meeting, everyone would feign surprise as if the entire faculty had been bused off on a field trip to dumbassville that day.

"Can't we visit?" Driver Boy pleaded.

"Nope. Not like you are now." I crossed my arms.

"Oh, pretty please?" He chuckled to his pals, who blew smoke rings over my head.

I walked behind the Jeep, took a pen out of my pocket, and wrote the license plate number and make and model and color of the vehicle in my moleskin notebook. What's amazing about troubled teenagers is how a feeling of invincibility often goes hand in hand with some modicum of stupidity. These mooks forgot that cars have license plates that are registered at the DMV to their parents. They also didn't realize that my own students couldn't wait to tell me who these guys were after they left. Five minutes after they were gone I would have their names, ages, where they went to school, who they slept with on our campus, and whether they called the next day to say "Thanks, I had a great time."

"What are you doing, Pete?" the driver said as I scrawled away.

"You're a bright kid. Figure it out."

"Why would you want to do that?"

"Because I'd love to sit down and have coffee with you guys sometime. Maybe light some aromatherapy candles. That sort of thing."

The other guys started to look nervous, as if their plan wasn't working out the way they had imagined. They had come to cause trouble, maybe start a *Fame* dance scene on the quad or the great American smoke-in. I was their buzzkill, and being teenage boys, they had to do something or lose face in front of the thirty or so kids now gathered to watch the showdown. The driver rammed the cigar in his mouth, slammed the Jeep into gear, and burned rubber down the asphalt, stopping where the circle met the driveway to the road. Then, one by one, each kid started gesticulating and lobbing at me the real language of boys who've had their fun taken away, and there was nothing I could do but stand there and take it: *asshole, motherfucker, cocksucker, pussy, faggot*.

Unlike London, I didn't go hit them in the groin, which might have made me live under Megan's Law the rest of my life. Instead, I felt old and embarrassed, even though I hadn't lost my cool or overreacted by padlocking the gate, trapping them in, and dialing Homeland Security. Even with all that was right on my side, I was still a nerdy, pathetic teacher confiscating the dirty note and reading it aloud in class.

I turned my info in at the front desk and they called the police, who paid a visit to each boy's home. One of my advisees, Mary, was a friend of theirs and let me know that their parents busted each and every one of them. "They really hate you, you know," she told me, smirking, one day on the quad. "And why did you say your name was Pete?"

In the manner of goldfish or actresses like Farrah Fawcett, schools have very short memories. This week's naked boys in a Jeep are replaced by next week's rigged student council elections. Beloved teachers fired one year are never spoken of the next. Expelled students just disappear like Yahoo Serious. It's simply the nature of the beast. I forgot all about my run-in with the cigar sissies as I was buried in piles of end-of-year paperwork. Graduation came and went like elective surgery, and I was invited to a host of parties of various tones and motifs. I attended the Dutch-themed clogfest because of the fresh herring, but decided to skip the Mexican fiesta due to the distinct lack of mariachis. Like a hemophiliac's menstrual cycle, these parties stretch for over two weeks, starting well before graduation and extending into late June. One of the last ones I attended was at Mary's house. Her mother was notorious for giving her two girls a fair amount of freedom, which translated into their house becoming a speakeasy for the baseball-cap-and-baggy-pants set. When I arrived, the adults were hobnobbing in the kitchen while the kids huddled outside by the basketball court. I could tell that this was a party that would go all night. There was some discussion by the toxic parents in the kitchen about taking kids' car keys, but I knew from experience that the "leave your keys" plan doesn't work. Kids never hand them in, or they steal them back while the confiscator's getting loaded herself, and unless you live in Fort Knox, you cannot control the comings and goings of such sneaky creatures.

I excused myself and walked outside to spend some time with Mary and her classmates before I left. As a teacher, you develop relationships over the years with these kids and then they leave. Most you will never see again. With some kids, you wish you had one more year to work with them on their remarkable essay writing or close reading of *Hamlet*; others you wish would leave as soon as they plant their nasty asses down in a schoolroom chair.

The basketball court was a crumbling patch of concrete about the size of the one I'd been standing on when London delivered his low blow. Kids were sitting around the edge, talking, drinking, and watching a group of sweaty boys playing a hot-dog version of two-on-two. I approached Mary and some of her classmates and said hello. Some faculty members had just left, she said, trying to make me feel less like a total loser. I asked about their collective summer plans. Mary was running the day care at a local gym, while others were lifeguarding or traveling to Europe on a quest to find the perfect handbag.

Out of the dark field next door came three guys, each carrying a small cooler. They placed them down on the edge of the court across from where I was standing. Mary went over to them, hugging each one in succession. Two boys opened their coolers to grab a beer, while the third one, slightly smaller than the other two, used his as a stool and sat down to view the game. As he followed the bodies sprinting down the court, he caught me watching him. At first he smiled and nodded hello, but then he squinted as if he was trying to locate my face in his drug-addled memory. He scanned the perimeter, most likely to see if there were any other adults bold enough to hang out in the ring of teenagers. He stared again with a look many people call the "stinkeye." Then he pointed at me, nodding in a ghetto dawg way.

"Look, it's Pete!" he shouted to his two buddies. Mary slipped inside the house, where I should have followed her. For some stupid reason—pride, righteousness, a misplaced Clint Eastwood complex—I didn't want to appear cowardly to these punks. But here I was alone, without a host, holding a margarita with under-age kids who were also drinking.

"Hey, Pete!" the thug wannabe called.

I nodded.

"You won't say hello to your old friends?"

I nodded again.

"You had a lot more to say the other day, didn't you?"

"Yup." I gritted my teeth and tried to channel Clint Eastwood, but without a serape, I felt more like Vivienne Westwood.

"Well, you got us in trouble with our parents. They were definitely upset." With the mention of the P-word, the murmuring crowd quieted their conversations and watched us. I wanted to say, *Well, that's what you get*, but even my nine-year-old daughter wouldn't sound that nah-nah infantile when the boys pull her hair on the playground.

"What do you say me and you go take a walk?" He jerked his thumb over his shoulder toward the scrubby field.

"No, thanks, I'm married," I said, a very lame comeback even for me. He was the smallest of the three, and I probably could have taken him in a fair fight, but with my luck, I would have tripped over the basketball and broken my nose before either one of us took a swing.

Driver Boy just flashed me a *Deliverance* grin because nothing could pop his fantasy bubble of getting revenge on an adult who had ratted him out. I thought of my own such fantasies as a teenager, wanting to crush my cigar-chomping boss with a roller when I laid asphalt one August, dreaming of slugging abusive soccer coaches or short-fused assistant principals with Napoleon complexes. I had my own issues with authority, still do, and here I was on the other side of that line. Just like London and his rock throwers, there are no easy answers for these types of showdowns. I never imagined going out the way I was about to go, but I have to be honest. Teachers are supposed to be honest, aren't they?

"I gotta take a piss," I said, loud enough for everyone to hear and deep enough not to feel like the star of *She's the Man*. Driver Boy rose to his feet and started walking over. I ducked inside the house and could hear the kid behind me, feeding all the hammered parents his best Eddie Haskell horseshit. My friend Nell tells this story about a crazy Zen master who, when asked about enlightenment at a cocktail party, raises a finger and says, "What a fine question, but first I need to use the bathroom." When he finds the rest room, he locks the door behind him, climbs out the window, and runs home before anyone has a chance to notice. I am no Zen master, but boy, was I glad that the bathroom window that night was large enough for my sorry rear to fit through.

When London finally calmed down, I wiped away his tears and held his two little hands in mine. I didn't want to teach my boy to be a coward, but then again I didn't want his playmates to cover their crotches anytime Low Blow Londy stepped into the sandbox. There had to be another way. I led him back to our seats in the bleachers and offered him an apple from our snack bag. His Transformers were still there, frozen in fighting poses reminiscent of the Rock 'Em Sock 'Em Robots I played with as a kid. This gave me an idea of how I could avoid the thug life for my son while not turning him into a total nancy-boy.

I grabbed a red Transformer. "Londy, watch me." I held the action figure by the waist and rocked it side to side. "When someone throws a rock or bothers you, I don't want you to fight or hit like this." I crashed the toy into the overblown image of Scooby-Doo on the lunch box.

London chewed his apple openmouthed and wiped the hair from his face.

"Instead, I want you to transform into a truck." I struggled to manipulate the plastic pieces forward and backward, desperately trying to automobilize its plastic ass. I could feel the Prep parents' watchful gaze on my little role-playing exercise, but I didn't care. This was good parenting, dammit.

When the reincarnation was complete, I was worried too much time had lapsed between objective and demonstration, but I wasn't going to quit. "See? Once you turn into a truck, you can zoom away from the bad boys." I recalled the little harlots who'd given him the twisted idea. "Or bad girls, and find me, your mom, or another adult." I breathed deeply. Success.

"Let me get this straight," London said, swallowing a chunk of apple and wiping his mouth with the back of his hand. I could see that he was really mulling this innovative approach over in that little head of his. I felt proud. Now my son was equipped to deal with any such confrontations on the kindergarten playground or in the future as an adult, far smarter than his old man. I couldn't wait to go home and tell Lala of my amazing parental instruction. "If somebody bugs me," he said, squinting, "you want me to turn into a truck and ride to you?"

Victory was mine! I nodded rapidly. "Yes! That's right, London. Or to Mama or another adult." The boy truly understood.

"What the heck?" He rolled his eyes and spat a bit of apple onto the seat in front of us. "*Je*-sus, Dad," he said, shaking his head in disbelief. "That's so dumb I can hardly take it."

Snowblind

When the head of my school asked my father whether the Wilders were a skiing family, having grown up in the snowy Northeast, I wasn't that surprised at the lie Big Ben told.

"Nah. We took the boys up to Vermont a few times, but they didn't really take to it," he said, making his sourpuss Walter Matthau face and shaking his head as if that sport was some high-falutin haute cuisine that didn't agree with the collective Wilder meat-and-potatoes stomach.

I've learned by now that the unreliable narration my father offers grocery store clerks, art gallery owners, and the stationary targets who man tollbooths is just his way of feeling connected to a dodgeball game of a world where he doesn't want to be picked last. If he doesn't share the experience with the person he's speaking with, he lies and says he's tried it or at least knows someone who has. Even so, the skiing stretcher was quite re-markable even for a frequent fibber like Ben. By spinning these yarns, my dad has almost passed as a weaver, former thespian, and silversmith, but I'd pay good money to see him on two long pieces of lumber careening down a run called Bubble Cuffer or Ripsaw with a lanky Suzy Chapstick by his side. I'm not much bet-ter. The only skiing I've ever done was one day at a Christian camp in New Hampshire where I was left on the top of a double diamond by two stoners who misquoted the Bible just to get laid more often than the villagers of Sodom. Either way, my fall from grace (and Christianity) came in the form of a series of face-plants followed by a walk down a hill as long and lonely as Mount Sinai.

When it snows, New Mexico has some of the best skiing in the West, and I've been lying to people for fifteen years about why I don't take advantage of a mountain only thirty minutes from my bed. I've blamed two broken ankles, floating kneecaps, altitude sickness, and detached retinas from a faulty Coney Island roller coaster. Truth is, I just don't get it. You get dressed in enough padding to stop a bullet, strap on a helmet, put on boots that be-long on some astronaut, and pay a shitload of money just to slide down the side of a hill. The few times I've been near a ski resort, I head right to the bar, then grab a place by the fire, and enjoy my extreme sport of sitting down. Call me lazy, chicken, or unath-letic, but I do enough racing around during the week not to want to "amp it up, dude" on Saturday.

Like any good (read: guilty) parent, I don't want my kids to be as big a pussy as their old man, so I encourage them to try all the things I couldn't give a flying shit about, like riding horses, skat-ing, and being a helpful neighbor. I'm worried, though, that they've inherited my anti-ski gene. When Poppy was four and

Lala was pregnant with London, they flew out to Lala's sister Emily's house in Sun Valley to see if Poppy could be like her cousins and make music videos of her dodging trees with faux gold medals swinging around her neck. Emily was so keen on getting her niece to join the ranks of the snowy set that she outfitted Poppy in a pink Gore-Tex ski suit and hired her a private instructor and life coach, who taught Poppy not only how to stop and turn but also the proper way to snub the tacky Schwarzenegger family in the lift line. While they were away, I had hopes that Poppy would be eventually spending her winter break with her cousins skiing from Sun Valley to Aspen and back again, but instead Poppy showed her true colors by politely thanking Emily and her instructor and then spending the rest of the week soaking in the hot tub like a Hilton.

London fancies himself as an athlete even though he has yet to join a team or don a jersey—unless, like me, you count superhero costumes as a uniform for kids who eventually grow up into teenagers with greasy hair reading graphic novels on the subway. If a sales clerk asks him what sport he prefers, London'll rattle off a list longer than the events featured on the full roster of ESPN channels. In all fairness to my little Bruce Jenner, he can throw a ball fairly well and only trips over his nimble feet after a full day of trick or treating. This past winter, a former babysitter of ours was hired to run the Chipmunk Corner at the Santa Fe Ski Basin, which is a combination rich kids' day care and ski school for the spa set. Julie called us because she needed kids with no ski experience to train the goth teenagers who had applied for the free lift tickets and weren't exactly sure if kids under thirteen could actually speak since they'd never spoken to one. Poppy was already booked to see four different productions of *The Nutcracker* that Saturday, but London was free and naked (that's another story).

When I asked him if he wanted to spend eight hours away from his mother, trains, Transformers, Power Rangers, and private food supply to learn to ski, he shrugged and said "Sure" like he was going to demo a different pair of shoes. I don't think he understood the difference in length between a day on the slopes and a *Cyberchase* episode or the fact that he would be wearing clothing more constricting than the neckwear at Abu Ghraib.

The few days before our journey up the mountain were the coldest of the year. The early mornings trembled in the single digits, and it only warmed to about forty even with the constant New Mexico sun. Lala and I were both hopeful that London would be our sole winter sport enthusiast so that when people asked if we skied or skated, we could push London forth as proof that our family left the couch once in a while. Lala stayed up all night planning his pre-, during-, and après-ski outfits, while I took notes on when to change sweaters, socks, and athletic supporters. I was a little distracted during our My-Size-Ken-doll fashion show since I had 350 pages of *Hamlet* essays to read over the weekend. According to my fantasy, I'd drop London off to be jumped into the alpine gang, and I'd grade essays in the cozy lodge, a snifter of port by my side to help make the sentences appear more attractive.

The time it takes to get to the ski basin from our house is about the same time I'm required to drag my students through Shakespeare's iambic pentameter each day. London was especially chatty that morning, telling me about his week at his Lutheran preschool. Even though the teachers had promised Lala that the religious instruction would be minimal, the holiday season created more and more natural intersections between mindless play and play in the fields of the Lord. Lala and I noticed that God and Jesus were showing up in our house as often as London's previous imaginary Hispanic animal friends Benny and Tico, and whenever we passed a Nativity scene on the street at night, London would exclaim, "Look, there's a Jesus play set! Can I have a Jesus play set?" What the pasture (London's version of *pastor*) and the two female teachers didn't understand is that with kids like London, their instruction gets revised, so Joseph ends up as Mary's wife and the three wise men are keepers of a nondenominational talking zoo.

"You know, Dad, Pasture said that Jesus made us," London exclaimed while chewing on some nonkosher pretzels.

"How did he do that?"

Pursing his lips, London searched for an answer that obviously hadn't been provided by the big man back at school. "Dinosaur bones?" He shrugged. I thought it was a pretty creative answer and some nice common ground for the fans of both evolution and creationism.

We passed a fleet of long white trucks jammed into a campground parking lot. I knew from a friend that *Seraphim Falls*, a movie starring Liam Neeson and Pierce Brosnan, was being filmed in the woods. I also knew that it was a thriller set during the Civil War, which was just a recipe for box office disaster even with the stunning locale and the sexy foreigners wearing bad facial hairpieces.

A voice rose from the back. "Jesus is everywhere AND invisible, Dad."

These superpowers raised a myriad of questions for me. "How does he get around?" I asked.

"In a car. A yellow one."

"If he's invisible, doesn't he get pulled over by the police?"

"Nah." He shook his head at my ignorance. "The police know him." I could tell he wasn't done with all this Jesus talk and was building toward something, maybe a miracle in his own head, and soon enough, he put his fists in the air like an elfin Cagney in *White Heat* and shouted, "Jesus is the King of the World!"

After that frightening display, I had no further questions, your honor.

Since it was the opening day for the season, the ski basin was lousy with snowboarders, skiers, and what looked like kids orphaned after following the band Phish around for a few years. Loaded with bags, I led London like a shaver Sherpa to Chipmunk Corner. Due to a rash of stomach flu and birthday parties, he was the only four-year-old guinea pig there. Julie met us with her crew of half a dozen teens who looked like they should have been passed out at a Green Day concert instead of working with children brand-new to this hibernal cult. Since he was their only specimen under seven years old, London was run through a gamut of policies and procedures more extensive than what potential astronauts endure. He was weighed, tagged, measured, and fitted for skis, boots, and bindings, all which had to be labeled with London's entry number, blood type, and stool sample.

"Is it always this complicated?" I asked Julie as I filled out the mandatory multitiered next-of-kin section on a stack of forms thicker than an Alaskan snowdrift.

Julie nodded with that weary look of experience. "When you have a hundred and fifty Londons check in by nine A.M. and parents anxious to hit the slopes before they tell us their kid's name, it can be, well, complex."

I felt okay about leaving London in the Corner, since a sea of counselors (who would later prove to be as obedient as any action figure he'd ever bossed around) surrounded him. I lugged my bag up to what I'd previously imagined being a cozy wooden lodge but was more like a cold and septic school cafeteria, only higher in elevation. Where was the roaring fire? The ski bunnies? The overpriced liqueurs? The overweight bearded drunk guy bragging about being an alternate behind Tommy Moe? I chose a table in the corner near an antiquated first-aid poster and spread myself out. Part of me longed to go back to Chipmunk Corner and check on my boy, but the other wanted to carry on my dad's school of bravery and independence and let the little guy tough it out. I had a conflicted moment that often plagues a parent who actually considers his rearing ways. One minute I saw London as a quivering emo boy, crying and pleading for someone's sweater to sniff, destined to live a life of interior design or international relations; the next I imagined him using a small handsaw to cut down trees to fashion his own skis before learning to chew tobacco and spear a bobcat with a ski pole to grill for lunch.

Either way, I had fifty essays awaiting me like a pile of rusty penile clamps. For the last paper of the semester, I give my students a wide range of options, some barely relating to *Hamlet*. Some kids choose a critical analysis of women's roles in the male-dominated Elizabethan era; others film a movie where dogs dressed in tights lick light poles, then urinate on them. I started my chipping away with the more academic projects. Most competent teachers I know get at least partly invested when reading student essays. My department head nods as she reads, agreeing with the good parts and shaking her head at the ones that suck. Once in a while she'll actually wag a finger. I take it a step further, though most of my nutty behavior is unconscious. Ever since I was a boy, I've hummed. Not musical ditties or during meals like Matt Dillon in *The Flamingo Kid*; it's far closer to an annoying buzz, more akin to the grating sound of an old fluorescent tube. Sometimes an officemate will walk in on me humming like an angry beehive and will walk right out again. I don't even hear it myself until someone asks if the computer is broken or the physics teacher left his Geiger counter on under my desk. I had a friend in graduate school who was studying such aberrant behaviors and diagnosed it as low-level Tourette's and advised me to keep away from heavy drugs and chant "I have Tourette's, but Tourette's doesn't have me" whenever I feel stressed out.

In the sad café, I delved into the pile as people started strolling in to meet up before they hit the slopes. Like any ski area near an affluent town, the downhill freaks were dressed in the latest gear. I saw futuristic helmets straight out of *Tron*, with stealth compartments for an iPod, headset, or those annoying Bluetooth earphones that make *Star Trek* gear worn by adult virgins look cool. I gawked at goggles in more colors than a psychedelic rainbow; some were as small as a pair of marrow spoons and others larger than Bono's wettest of eye dreams. To this nonskier, it looked like an invasion of really fashionable insects from a planet that had no poor people. The stomping creatures all stared at me as they applied sunscreen to their few patches of uncovered skin. Unlike the swarm, I had no boots or goggles or even gloves, just a Pilot pen and enough paper to create a faux snowstorm of my own.

I delved deeper into the essay before me. Hooray! One of my students actually defended Ophelia's suicide as an act of power, which (a) impressed me due to the logic of her argument and (b) scared the shit out of me because teens and suicide are a really bad mix. The next paper, loosely inspired by the plot of *Hamlet*, was about a group of worms who joined a frat house and committed revenge against a worm who cruelly hazed another worm. I could forgive the idea of reading about worms for seven pages, but when the frat house entered the scene, I could no longer suspend my disbelief. The beautiful vermiform dream of fiction was interrupted. I could feel my mouth start to work up some serious crazy noise. Somewhere in this pile of what some could call prose, I was hoping for a surprise of any sort, a gem in the midst of all this twelve-point excrement. In a zone fueled by bad coffee and worse writing, my mouth started to hurt, which is always a bad sign. Then I looked up and saw one of my seniors with a ski pass stuck like a spit wad to the zipper of his jacket.

"Dude," he said quietly, peering around, "everyone's looking at you."

It was like a scene out of *The Birds* meets *Rain Man*. While I was spitting and sputtering and talking to myself, all the Gore-Tex-enrobed aliens had closed in for a better view of the paper-pushing creature.

"You ski?" the student asked nervously, not wanting to be seen for long with the drooling special ed guy in the corner.

"No, not really." I wiped my mouth on one of the essays.

"Why would you come *here* to grade papers?" He looked pained.

I explained about London and Chipmunk Corner, but I was coming out of my marking trance and knew it sounded like bullshit. Then I noticed that somehow I had kicked off my shoes. Probably had ink smudged on my face. I was too frightened even to look at my fly.

"Okay, whatever," the kid said, giving me a halfhearted wave. "See you Monday." He went back to a huddle of kids and shook his head sadly.

Since my spell had been broken, I put on my shoes and searched out the window in the direction of where they said London would be learning to fly. I spotted him almost immediately since he was the shortest person around, smaller than some of the high-tech boots. He looked fine, clapping his hands in front of him as he skied on one ski with an instructor. At least someone was happy.

I grabbed the video camera and my jacket, leaving the essays in a heap on the table. I ignored the stares as I walked through the cafetorium to get outside. On the bank of a small hill, the ski school had set up an L in Astroturf so when the kids cruised down, the verdant swatch stopped them and they could step on the putting green and easily stomp back up the hill. I switched on the camera and hid behind a dormant ski lift. I could hear London's cheers echoing off the trees behind me. I grabbed my cell to call Lala with the good news, but there was no signal. She needed to hear the sound of one Wilder skiing. We could now call Emily and tell her London would need a permanent room in Sun Valley because pretty soon he'd be joining his cousins on the front page of the *Idaho Mountain Express*.

Wanting to get a better shot on video, I stepped from behind my hideout and crept closer, trying not to interrupt this most historic day for my boy. The first thing I noticed was that London was hatless and the goggles we'd inherited from Emily's kids were wrapped around his neck like a dog collar. Even though he was clapping to stay upright, his cheers were actually hysterical sobs.

"I can't take it anymore!" he screamed, loud enough for the actual skiers on the slope behind him to hear. They must have thought from London's wails that Chipmunk Corner was actually a toddler torture training area. Then he saw me with my mouth open and the camera dangling at my side taking a fascinating video of my inappropriate footwear.

"I want my dada!" London screamed. The instructor tried to rally him but then gave in and led London over to me. My boy fell to the ground with his skis sticking straight up in the air.

"Snow angels, London," the guy said in an Irish accent. I guess they waste no time in ski boot camp.

London dutifully slid his arms and legs up and down, still crying like a fat baby bird that had fallen out of its nest.

The instructor leaned on his poles as he sized me up. His face was red from the cold, though his eyes were piercing blue. I felt oddly naked without skis strapped to my feet. "Can I ask you a question?" he said.

"Sure."

"What do you do?"

I thought of the papers curling inside. "I guess I'm a teacher."

"Your wife?"

"Artist?" I thought we had somehow failed the interview to be with these outdoorsy folks and they'd pull London's transcript at the Corner, strap us to the back of a snowmobile, and haul our warm-weather asses out of there.

The instructor pushed his hat back on his head and scratched his hairline. "I've never heard a four-year-old boy say 'I can't take it anymore' and 'Get me outta here!' They usually complain of being hungry or tired or hot or cold or sore, but your boy definitely has a way of saying things."

"Amen to that," I said, and thought of my fallen angel calling me a "dirtfag" only days before.

I checked London out of Chipmunk's Corner, bought him a muffin and hot chocolate, and gathered up my limp essays. On the way back down, I thought he would sleep, but instead he just stared out the window at the landscape as it changed from wintry to woody to a horizon of parked cars that signaled our reentry into snowless suburbia. We didn't spot Liam or Pierce on the way down, nor was there any talk of that water-walking King of the World. I even stopped myself from telling London to tell Pasture that Pope John Paul II was a lifelong skier. I thought this day would be the end of the Wilders' brief flirtation with the sport of embezzlers and coke addicts.

But then, like an excellent essay in a pile of mediocrity, a miracle occurred. I don't know if invisible Jesus cruised by us in a yellow car with a trunkload of dinosaur bones, but in the driveway, London ripped himself from the car seat and ran like a felon to the house. He pounded on the door with his cold little hands until Lala finally opened it.

"Mama, Mama! Guess what?" he said excitedly, his face exploding with news.

"What is it, London?" Lala asked, wiping her hands on a glitter-covered apron. She cocked her head and gave me a sideways glance. I shrugged.

"I learned to skate!"

Kind of a Drag

When I ask parents what they were like in high school, they never tell me any juicy stories about sex, drugs, or why Burt Reynolds was considered such a heartthrob back in the day. Most of them stick to school-related themes and say that they never took advantage of the opportunities that they had in terms of good teachers, interesting classes, and valuable resources that a decent education provides. They hope their children will do better by adding a photo class and utilizing the darkroom at Prep or signing up for an art history course even though it's a museum-load of work to get through in one semester. And you can be damn sure that all parents want their kid to fully utilize (read: exploit) the real pimps of high school: the college counselors.

I understand that I'm a representative of the school whenever

I talk to the parentals, so I tell Mom and Dad purely positive stories about their children capitalizing on their educational opportunities—preparing questions for a best-selling author during his visit or volunteering to join the student council. What I don't tell them is that there are two sides to this carpe diem coin. When we encourage kids at an early age to take advantage of any given situation, we don't realize that such a go-get-'em attitude can land them places we never dreamed of. And it starts when they are the age of my own children.

Some moons ago, Poppy's elementary school saw that the students (and their parents) had turned Halloween into an excuse to run amok on school time. The faculty and staff had grown weary of the frenzied atmosphere of wee ones running around in costumes and makeup, shoving sweets down their gobs until they vomited on the hamster cage. As a teacher who has survived many of those candy-bloated D-Days, I sympathize. You can't really teach Tyler about long division if fake blood spews all over his worksheet, and if you join the little freaks and dress up yourself, then you just add to the hysteria and mayhem as they yank incessantly on your Urkel suspenders. Veteran educators know that there's just no winning on Halloween. So the administration decided to cancel school and move its fall parent-teacher conferences to Halloween and the day prior to that most haunting of holidays. That way, the parents, not the school, would have to deal with the freakish festivities. But then a whole new batch of teachers were hired at Poppy's elementary, a youthful crew more open to the whiny appeals of their students and still at an age where they themselves partook in their own nocturnal parties of the ghoulish sort. The younger faculty petitioned the principal, who, after some reasonable resistance, reinstated Halloween festivities the day before parent-teacher conferences. For parents like me, this proclamation meant that Halloween would be extended into a four-day-long torture session, starting on Thursday and ending on Monday. For the students, it meant crazy day was back on the academic calendar.

Personally, I've never been a huge supporter of dressing up as someone else and waddling around in greasepaint with warts cemented to my lips. Even as a kid, I loved the candy part of the deal, but the whole disguise thing was lost on me. If people were already willing to give us candy for free, why go to all that effort? Everyone knows that disguises should be saved for armed robbery or a decent B&E.

Lala, on the other creepy hand, adores Halloween to the point of obsession. While our neighbors spend weeks creating a realistic graveyard in the front of their homes, Lala holes up in her studio for months, concocting the perfect outfits for our little monsters, making and remaking our kids' costumes after having spent the previous twelve months discussing possible ideas that were beyond the pathetic and uninspired fare of witches, ghosts, and goblins. Just like a kid, Lala takes advantage of the holiday to suit her own needs. Her mother, Beverly, did the same. Each year after I complain about her obvious lack of sleep or how the house has turned into a garment and vestment shop, Lala tells me stories about her mother using permanent dye to tint her sister Becky's hair green just to be the best damn pumpkin Cheyenne, Wyoming, had ever seen. As a child, Lala suffered outrageous outfits of her own that she didn't fully understand, just to amuse Beverly's sense of chicanery and control. One October, Lala impersonated oval-headed Stan Laurel in a miniature suit and tie; the next it was Yosemite Sam with a mustache and beard so thick it covered her face and dragged on the ground as she stumbled toward the I'm Not OK Corral. Basically, Halloween allows Lala to openly brag that her parents tortured her far more creatively than mine ever did.

This year Lala and Poppy huddled together and agreed that Marilyn Monroe was a good choice for our daughter the drama queen. Lala wanted Marilyn to be freshly ripped from the grave, skin rotting off her face and an empty prescription bottle dangling from loam-covered pearls. But after Poppy followed her mother's strict training regimen by watching *Some Like It Hot* and *Gentlemen Prefer Blondes*, she wished to inhabit Marilyn in her blond bombshell years. Sadly for Lala, no one wants to be the fat and dead Elvis, no matter how hard it makes her laugh.

London wasn't as easy to boss around. Like so many other boys his age, he wanted to be a Power Ranger, a character from a show we have yet to let him watch, but that's no matter. He's still managed to cobble together an ass-kicking backstory from his friends' inarticulate misinformation in preschool, colorful television commercials for kids with ADHD, and images ripped from the napkins and tablecloths of thematic birthday parties. Lala wouldn't hear of a store-bought costume, so she promised London he could be a Power Ranger next Halloween if she could choose for him this year. She was betting on our son's future amnesia but forgot about his issues with time, so this Christmas I expect a boy in a red nylon suit and plastic mask will be a bigger force than the fat guy with a similar, though less flashy, outfit.

Lala ended up creating a visual pun for London, constructing a costume based on the Clash's "London Calling." London wore a Mohawk-wig headpiece, a Union Jack shirt, and baby Doc Martens; his jeans and cape were wallpapered with the British flag and color copies of the 1979 album cover. Around his neck twisted a telephone that, when prompted, the little hooligan would lift and say "Hello? London calling" to the joy of all the ex junkie parents in the mall.

I picked up Poppy on Halloween. After the final bell tolled, she clip-clopped out in high heels like she had been partying all day with the Kennedys, all while trying not to bump into the vague princess, pumpkin, and hobo set. Accustomed to being a roadie for my kids even on less auspicious occasions, I grabbed her book bag and lunch box and escorted her to my car. All the other adults were doing the same, dragging these shrunken, wobbly freaks home so they could reapply makeup for the second set, which started in only a few hours. The parents of the pumpkins and more swollen costumes had it the worst, struggling to wrap seat belts around their little Augustus Gloops and Veruca Salts. Once we got rolling, I shifted into our usual gear and asked Poppy about her day. When I checked my rearview mirror, I almost swerved into a minivan next to me, forgetting that I had what appeared to be a happy gnomish hooker strapped in my backseat. Still giddy with too many Kit Kats on a day that rivaled Mardi Gras for the up-and-coming middle schoolers, she relayed tales of the confection lovers' cabal.

"Yeah, Dad, you know, and Ms. Geier? She, like, dressed up as Pippi Longstocking with wire in her hair and like—"

"Easy, whiskey. Slow down. Breathe. Can you please talk like a human being?"

"Okay. Sorry." Her lipstick-mottled mouth opened and allowed some air to squeeze through. I didn't want to imagine what her teeth looked like, covered in chocolate, caramel, nougat, and strings of mystery meat from the cafeteria. "All the students and teachers had a parade in the gym. It was so fun, Daddy."

"Hold on." I slowed the car. "The entire school? Every grade?"

"Yup." She nodded proudly, full of Panther pride.

"How long did that take?"

She shrugged. "About an hour, maybe longer."

I shuddered to think of those poor teachers, especially those I knew who had over twenty-five years' experience, trying to keep their own students calm without using sedatives or weapons while two hundred other crazy kids did the hoochie coochie in front of them.

"Dad," Poppy said in a tone void of Valley Girl lilt, the one she uses to let me know she's actually formulating a thought, "a lot of boys dressed up as girls this year."

"Yes?" I wondered where this line of questioning was going.

Her face twisted in thought, causing her makeup to peel off in white flakes. "And they seemed to really like it. It was kinda weird."

"Did any girls dress like boys?" I asked, knowing the answer before she gave it.

"Not really."

I've sat through numerous sexuality courses in grad school and in-services as a teacher, and I know the theory that says there are over twenty types of gender variations from hetero to homo to andro, but I can't say I fully understand this soupy human mess, and I was damn sure I couldn't explain it to a nine-year-old still jacked up on Snickers and SweeTarts. So instead I told her about watching powder-puff football games when I was a kid, where girls played tackle football and boys dressed as cheerleaders. "The girls were really aggressive and competitive and took it seriously," I said, "while the boys acted ridiculous and silly the whole time." I left out the part about the cheerleaders fondling their own makeshift breasts. Bros before hos, after all.

She nodded. Something about that aberrant behavior struck

Poppy as familiar and confusing at the same time. "Why do the boys do that?" she asked.

I had no answer other than that the Halloween gods give them permission to. I remembered that I'd read about a small school district in Texas that had outlawed something called TWIRP Day, an acronym for "The Woman Is Requested to Pay." According to the article, on this unfortunately named holiday, boys dressed as girls and girls dressed as boys to reverse social roles, so the girls could now ask boys out on dates. A parent, new to this tranny tradition, thought TWIRP Day promoted cross-dressing and, in turn, homosexuality. So they decided the only remedy was Camo Day, where kids dressed like they were going to war. Puts a whole new deadly spin on "don't ask, don't tell," if you don't ask me.

The truth is I don't know why some boys like to dress as girls. At my school there are certain male faculty members who jump at the chance to raise money for whales displaced by hurricanes or jump-start school spirit by donning fishnets and a bra made from split coconut shells. Year after year, while the kids scream at their male teacher's sense of abandon, I scratch my head wondering why this married guy with kids waxed his whole body for such a brief stint as Baby Jane.

In the car with Poppy, I did as any confused parent would do— I sweetened the age-old change-of-subject move with a decent bribe. "Got any candy?" I asked my backseat Marilyn.

She raised her painted eyebrows conspiratorially, like she wanted me to drive her to the Hollywood Walk of Fame.

"You can have another piece," I told her. "What the hell? It is Halloween."

———

Prep has slowly surrendered to both Halloween and cross-dressing over the past few years. Our entire academic calendar is based around October 31, the only school day the kids feel they can treat as their bitch. When I first started working here, students wore costumes and handed out candy during the biweekly assembly, which lasts about as long as it takes to boil a lobster. Our student body grew larger, however, and those twenty minutes turned into thirty and then forty. So the admin surrendered and manipulated our annual schedule so that Halloween always falls on a full, fifty-minute period previously reserved for nationally recognized speakers and ex-students who have kicked one addiction or another and want to come home and tell us all (yawn) about it. This past year, after losing every battle, we raised the white flag and forfeited half the school day to these Hedwigs and their angry inches.

This October 31, I arrived early as usual and prepared the silent in-class essay I give every Halloween so I don't have to listen to the banal conversation about how great it is that Jordan stuffed the crotch of his leotard with a sock stolen from the volleyball team. Before my first class began, I sat in front of the plate-glass window and watched the students arrive one by one as if I were a tower guard on Ellis Island and these were the most flamboyant foreigners that Lady Liberty had ever seen. Many faculty refer to this holiday as Inappropriate Day, the one chance the students get to break every rule in the handbook without getting suspended, expelled, or arrested. Some kids try to break all the rules at once, so it's not uncommon to see a sophomore dressed as a gangbanger with headphones on his ears and cell phones and pagers clipped to every band or hem possible, carrying an arsenal of toy knives and guns, and smoking a cigarette while riding a skateboard propelled by a dog on a leash that advertises whiskey.

It's also a day where the usual rules of political correctness and decorum are thrown out the window, and so the kids capitalize on the opportunity to poke fun at the fat, homeless, religious, addicted, and immigrant in nature without fear of retribution by the administration. The banter is like what you'd hear UN delegates say with their mikes turned off after a few strong cocktails. The antics are just as deplorable. I've seen a mooning Pope make out with a slurring Speedy Gonzales, supermodels with eating disorders dressed in skeleton costumes, and the bloody reenactment of Siegfried and Roy's tangle with that most *ungezogen* tiger. Warms my heart each year to think how far we've all come as people. We are the world. We are the future.

After lunch, Lala drove the kids up to campus to be a part of the faculty children's segment of the all-school Halloween assembly. This year's bacchanalia was in the gym, and the bleachers were packed with what looked like soccer hooligans who doubled as interior decorators. After Poppy's remark about crossdressing, I started searching past the scantily clad girls posing as feline prostitutes toward any boys dressed as girls. I spotted a pregnant nun, a female sumo wrestler in a bikini fashioned from dental floss, and a six-foot boy dressed as the hairiest Tinkerbell you've ever seen. Poppy and London soon earned their candy stripes next to the other faculty kids by being cute and speaking clearly into the microphone.

After they cleared the staff and their children from the viewing area, each grade level would fall down the bleachers and reassemble onstage, and when asked by the MCs what they were dressed as, every mumbler would quickly remind us how much our school desperately needs a public-speaking program. My mind wandered after seeing yet another unimaginative kid dressed as the Grim Reaper, and my peripheral vision caught one boy who was done up as La Femme Nikita. He held a compact in front of his face and was delicately (and expertly) touching up his makeup. Like me, he seemed lost in this halcyon haze of drag, but his look was a more enchanting one, as if the mirror was telling him he could have been a star if only he'd been born with indoor plumbing instead of the nasty outdoor type. But when it was his turn to stand in line onstage with his less rakish peers, he got the crowd screaming by slapping a butt sheathed in skintight rayon and dropping a few choice and androgynous delegates of the profanity party. Since we surrendered the day to the opportunistic (read: possessed) students, there wasn't much we could do about this one. It was his one chance to shine.

"He looks better in heels than I do," Lala said, rubbing her legs, sore from the work in her self-imposed sweatshop.

During this chaotic chorus line, Poppy's expression varied from wide grin to slack-jawed confusion as the costumes changed from a giant farting outhouse to the more complex messages sent by that sexy spy from some French town that encourages loud swearing, sleek weapons, and widespread gender-bending. All the older kids were laughing at the femme boy, but I could tell Poppy was wondering why exactly he/she was such a funny sight.

After about ninety minutes, I'd had enough. My head was throbbing, London was calling, and the place had started to smell like a shaken cocktail of stale sweat, sweet candy, and the kind of cheap perfume strippers favor. But the suggestive show wasn't over yet. The kids were going to take full advantage of their one day of free expression. The inmates would not surrender control of the asylum just yet. Over the loudspeaker leaked the alien-spacecraft sound of a 1970s synthesizer followed by a low-down guitar. Out of one of the locker rooms strutted a lean kid dressed as Dr. Frank-N-Furter with large-mesh fishnets, black eyeliner, thick pearls, and a wig like the head of a giant black Q-tip. At first, I couldn't tell who it was because of the thick makeup and nondescript body type, but then I saw that this unknown student had stuffed her panties with what looked like a lumpy dinner roll.

Poppy had never seen *The Rocky Horror Picture Show*, but Lala had viewed the film numerous times with her sisters at the Lincoln Theater in Cheyenne, so she was happy to take this trip down memory lane even if it was in a gymnasium with basketball nets and a blue griffin painted on the hardwood. My older brother had taken me to a midnight showing of the cult classic in Norwalk, and my recollection of that experience was more like a soggy food fight in a theater that didn't bother to wipe up any of the mystery fluids on the seat backs or the sticky floor. Even though it was Halloween, it didn't help explain to Poppy why a girl in high school would dress as a boy who dressed as a girl who called itself a "sweet transvestite from Transsexual, Transylvania." And as this creature swaggered in ten-inch heels on a floor more accustomed to sexless sneakers, I wondered who in the stands would be titillated by its bragging of being "one hell of a lover." The boys? The girls? Boys who secretly wanted to be girls? Girls who wanted to be boys who liked boys wanting to be girls? I needed a combined degree in anthropology and statistics to figure all this shit out.

Turns out I didn't have to. Maybe it was because Poppy knew the girl with the knurled package from starring together in *The Music Man* or the fact that this faux Frank-N-Furter invited everyone in the bleachers to come stomp on the gym floor or that

Poppy was still only nine, but she grabbed her brother by his telephone-cord leash and dragged his punk ass onto the mock dance floor, where they boogied along with the other monsters, forgetting all about what past, present, and future complications lurked inside the intersexed costumes and masks.

Learning to Scrawl

In what I guess to be an effort to modernize, the maintenance men are ripping down the chalkboards at our school and replacing them with new dry-erase ones. At first I was eager to get rid of those archaic slabs of slate, happy not to have my lecture on Emerson's *Self-Reliance* interrupted again by the snap of my bleached writing stick, relieved that I wouldn't be forced to breathe enough chalk dust to put me in an iron lung. I often joke with my students about how, with technology, the tires on our cars can check their own air pressure, but here I am employing the same instructional tools they used in goddamn *Little House on the Prairie*. There have been days where I had so many pieces of chalk break during what I considered brilliant discussions on syntax that I ended up throwing the whole box against the board and scaring the shit out of my students, who believed most teachers were brain-dead or lacked a significant pulse. Poor little Willa in the front row couldn't believe that a teacher who so loved the music of Shakespeare's language would demonstrate rage equal to that bipolar Macbeth or self-absorbed mama's boy Hamlet.

Otherwise known as dry-erase boards and marker boards, the first whiteboards began appearing in American business meeting rooms and corporations in the early 1980s. By the end of the 1990s, over 20 percent of American schools had already converted from chalkboards to whiteboards. The new markers that accompany these boards offer various colors, no chalky mess, and a new item for the stoner kids to sniff.

After giving the new whiteboards a trial run, now I'm not so sure I want to get so current. The slick, easy-flowing lines remind me of the difference between a term I've always admired, *teacher*, and one that sounds too much like corporate America for my mouth, *educator*. The hard scratching of chalk on chalkboard linked me to famous academics of the past, both in my own life growing up in suburban Long Island and Connecticut and in uplifting movies like *Blackboard Jungle*, *Stand and Deliver*, and *School of Rock*. None of those pedagogues ever wrote with an Expo bold color marker or introduced themselves as an educator to little Jimmy Sadsack on his first day of class. No boy has ever run his nails down a slick sheet of plastic to send shivers down the spine of the girl he secretly pines after.

Just before our school modernized its visual aids, I painted my car with chalkboard spray paint. I can't in good conscience claim a connection between the two, but they happened around the same time. Lala had an extra container of the black stuff lurking around the house and my Daihatsu Charade looked tired, so I decided to spruce it up. I couldn't predict how that one afternoon's spraying would change my life. After I let Poppy and her friend Sierra try out the round mobile chalkboard with new boxes of colored chalk, I darted about town running errands. Inside the vehicle I couldn't see the pink-and-yellow sunsets or the multi-colored surfer girl riding the gnarly wave on the black hood. I'd forget that the car looked like a box of Fruity Pebbles as I deposited my paycheck at the Century Bank drive-up window or picked up my dry cleaning at One Hour Martinizing. I don't think it's that surprising how people reacted to the car. They behaved as you'd imagine at the sight of a hatchback covered in chalk the color of crayons. Homeless men waved eagerly, Bluetooth-using professionals stared, kids pointed. Some artsy folks even gave me a thumbs-up. The more disturbing part was how I dealt with these reactions, forgetting that my daughter and her pal had now tagged me as a freak, a radical artist, or a seemingly heterosexual man looking to switch teams. When people would wave, I'd search my life memory for where I knew that drunk guy or newspaper vendor from. I'd start at my first job waiting tables in Santa Fe and run through all the spheres of my life, trying to locate a connection loose enough for me to forget. If people pointed or laughed, I'd check to see that I didn't have a big coffee stain on my chest or a booger hanging from my nose or that my hair wasn't in some origami-like shape after I removed my sunglasses from their lofty perch. Sometimes I'd get angry at staring soccer moms in their SUVs or glaring rich motherfuckers in their BMWs because I thought they were looking down on my two-door, three-cylinder car that was worth less than five hundred bucks and a case of diet beer. I'd feel almost political in my workingman's auto next to their environmental rapists that cost as much to fill up as it takes to feed an African village whose name I can't pronounce.

The other thing about having a car that doubled as a chalkboard is that Lala and I started feeling as though we should be doing something important with a machine with this type of creative potential. The vehicle now had worth, even if it didn't translate into American dollars or a number printed in the auto-biblical Blue Book.

"We should have a party around the car," I told her one afternoon. We were standing in her studio, surrounded by her little pieces of art, admiring the oversized black turd languishing in our driveway. God's tears had already washed the chalk from Poppy's artfest away. "All our friends could come over and draw something. I'd get a keg and we could hire Joe Ray to DJ."

"Why do you always want to turn everything into a frat party?" She gave me a look that suggested she'd never actually seen me before. "No," she said, turning back to our black metal canvas, "Becky should come out and do something cool on it." Lala thought her sister, a talented artist in her own right hiding out in California, had the type of skill set perfectly matched to this odd project of the motor vehicle type.

"What about the rain?"

She nodded, crossing her arms. Her mind, it was a-churnin'. "We could spray it with glaze."

"That defeats the purpose. Shouldn't art like this be, well, temporary?" Even though my question was clothed in philosophical undergarments, my concern was really that once Becky had her way, I'd be stuck driving her mind's creation to school every day. I'd seen some of her previous projects—hideous dolls with long clay penises, blood-red hearts with arrows sticking out of them—and although they were cool to examine, I didn't want to have to explain to the old-school bio teacher why I was so obsessed with advertising oversized male anatomy or deadly lost love.

"I wouldn't want to fly Becky out here to do this if it's only going to last a day or so."

"Fly Becky out?" I asked, wondering if I had missed something. "When did we say we were going to fly Becky out?"

"If we really want to do this right, we should at least fly her out."

This is the point in our conversations where I usually exit to tenderize meat or clean the toilet since I know from experience that the longer I stay, the more elaborate Lala's schemes become. One time we were discussing changing a light switch in her studio and we ended up buying more flood lamps than surround your average penitentiary.

Before Becky could come out and pull a Christo on my poor car, I wanted some kids to enjoy it. On Thursday afternoon, I drove the Charade to Poppy's school and parked it in the middle of the playground, a safe distance from the line of treacherous tetherball poles. Since I came to teach writing each week in Poppy's class, I told her school that my car was part of a poetry project and that the kids would write original verse on my traveling chalkboard. For some reason, even with the concern about graffiti on public and private property, they bought it. I didn't even have to fill out any district-mandated paperwork. What luck, I thought at the time.

When the kids burst out of the doors in front of the school, you could tell they didn't know what to make of me grinning like a jackass next to my shitty car. Poppy has a hard time keeping a secret, so the whole class knew they were about to do something usually reserved for guys in masks covered in spray paint or inmates doing chunks of time. The gaggle gathered around the vehicle, looking for some sort of catch—maybe the principal hiding in the backseat, ready to spring a surprise standardized test on them. I went over the rules with the crowd: write anywhere but the mirrors and windows, no profanity or mean language, share the chalk, and, in the future, they should never write on anything without permission from the owner. As I said this, I noticed a few girls with crude hearts markered onto the backs of their hands. I wondered if I could be held responsible if my little idea led to any future tattooing.

I handed Poppy's teacher some boxes of chalk, and we started distributing. The kids went at it like maggots on a corpse, which is a pretty fair comparison if you have seen children swarm and the state of my car. Some students drew small pictures of stars or happy faces in yellow and blue. Most of the boys wrote their names, adding benign verbs that told the world, or in this case whoever I happened to drive by, that these young men ruled, rocked, or were totally cool. One of the misguided males added his phone number next to his name, and instead of educating him on the types of calls he should expect from advertising on this particular billboard, I had him erase his digits. There wasn't much poetry going on, but the kids looked happier than I'd ever seen them before. They'd never considered a car as a canvas to express themselves. The kids lucky enough to claim a door or section of the hood sketched elaborate sunsets, and one girl actually wrote a few lines from a poem we had worked on in class. I grabbed a chair so one of the vertically challenged third-graders could start on the roof. I hoped a DEA helicopter or flock of birds would enjoy the view from above.

As a teacher who tries to make literature relevant to teenagers on a daily basis, I am forced to make connections between *Walden* and *Survivor* or between *The Office* and *Bartleby the Scrivener*. As I watched twenty kids go nuts on my car, I couldn't help thinking of the chalking controversy that had plagued Wesleyan University, my alma mater, only a few years earlier. It had been a tradition at

Diversity University that students could express themselves freely on the sidewalks with chalk the college actually provided. When I was there, the ashen messages focused mostly on divesting from apartheid and asking you to choose if you were gay, bisexual, or questioning. It all seemed fairly harmless when I was there, probably because even though I was pretty sure about my sexuality, I was questioning everything else. From what I've heard, the chalking got out of hand. Messages became more personal, attacking teachers and students by name, and more elaborate in a sexual manner, as "gay, bisexual, questioning" (GBQ) evolved into an acronym (LGBTQQ) that wouldn't even fit on my car in chalk or spray paint. Wesleyan's president actually called a chalking moratorium, two words I thought I'd never see scribed in the same sentence. However, those moments where the juvenile meets the adult are always fun to watch, and such was the case at Poppy's school.

"I'm going to ask my mom if we can do this to her car," a boy with Bazooka Joe's ball cap chirped. He was well into a picture of a skateboarder, and he seemed cheerier at that moment than he had all semester. I could tell that this project touched something in him, connected his passion for art with his love for cars in a way no other project could.

"What kind of car does your mom drive?" I imagined a Ford LTD station wagon, the kind my mother rattled us around in.

"A Lexus," the boy said, and I strolled to the other side of the Charade to admire a blotch of yellow on the rear quarter panel. From this new and safer vantage point I could see parents pulling up in their SUVs, shiny minivans, and expensive foreign imports. It was a sunny New Mexico day, and they all stepped out of their vehicles in fine footwear, content to wait outside for the final bell. Our project was hard to miss—a car getting tagged en masse smack dab in the middle of the playground.

The parents stepped toward our project, bemused at the sight of buzzing children, but as they got closer their faces took on visages of confused fear, as if they recognized the familiar details in the image—kids, chalk, car—but weren't sure how those pieces all went together. They started leaning in my direction, and I clamped on a smile that my brother Crazy Eddie refers to as the I'm-not-afraid grin. A parent in a greenish-gray suit walked over and asked me what we were doing. I explained how the project allowed the whole child to unify many disciplines and modes of learning and expression, and connected with our weekly writing workshop, which was part of the nationally recognized service-learning component of my school. I knew as I was talking that he wasn't buying any of my New Age crap. I probably should have shut my mouth, but when I get nervous, I just keep talking like I've got a nose full of the white stuff. When I ran out of breath, I ended with "And look how much fun they're having!" pointing like Bob Barker in front of a Cadillac Escalade dripping with supermodels.

"Huh," the man grunted, and I knew as he walked away he was thinking, *What the hell does fun have to do with education?*

As the available space disappeared on the black-painted metal, the kids drew in tight clumps, leaning over the hood, roof, and each other to add a few final scrawls to this mobile monument. Right before the bell, the principal came out, and after the father's gruff reaction, I expected a dressing-down. As principals are known to do, she walked around the perimeter of the car, withholding any comments until she surveyed the entire scene. Poppy's teacher was busy playing Kissinger between two boys arguing over who had the property rights to the last patch of black on the car's hood. As the principal finished her inspection, the kids started to leave the Charade, realizing that there was nothing left for them to draw on. Even my hubcaps had been duly flavored. As they tore themselves away, I saw that their clothes had been sifted with all the colors of the gay and straight rainbow. All the skirts, shirts, and pants looked as though they had walked a long way in the great Lucky Charms dust bowl. It was an amazing sight to behold: the unwavering principal in the foreground with a mob of kids holding sticks of chalk behind her, standing next to a car that looked like someone's abstract idea of an acid flashback in the shape of an oversized testicle.

"Where's the poetry?" the principal asked, and I thought, *If she can't see it, nothing I can say could ever make her.*

Helicopter Crash

In what I consider to be one of the most logical things a prep school could do, two members of our English department traveled to the West Coast to visit colleges and universities to see if they were still buying what places like ours continue to sell. It's funny that many high schools roll along, doing what they've always done, without checking to see if colleges still make freshmen wear felt beanies or require morning calisthenics before chapel. During their trip, my two colleagues expected to mull over curriculum, rubrics, and reading lists, but what they spent a good chunk of their time doing was lending a sympathetic ear to college professors needing to whine about issues high school teachers consider old hat. These tweedy academics bemoaned a distinct lack of passion in this millennial generation, a far cry from the vocal rabble-rousers of the 1960s, 1970s, and, God forbid, even the decade when Reagan ran roughshod over our country. The profs confessed that they weren't equipped to deal with coeds text-messaging lovers in the same class or posting last night's party photos on Facebook on their wireless laptops during what Mr. Chips considered a stimulating lecture on Brontë. The final item on their undergraduate bitch list was helicopter parents, a subject my colleagues could get an advanced degree in. Colleges, universities, and boarding schools have long been sequestered from this breed of hover-parents, who micromanage every aspect of their child's life from womb to tomb. My friend Tom says it started with those goddamn "Baby on Board" placards stuck to the rear windows of 1980s station wagons, as if having children in your car held the same street status as a Blaupunkt stereo system with Jensen 120-watt triaxial speakers. Some say these alpha moms and dads are just trying to keep their children safe in an otherwise unsafe world; others chalk it up to the rising cost of education, with parents simply wanting to protect their investment, even if that investment just wants to drink copious amounts of beer from a plastic funnel and then get laid on the fifty-yard line.

Because of the battalions of helicopter parents, colleges and universities are now forced to offer symposiums on "having to let go" because Mom and Dad won't, and with the world's longest umbilical cord—the cell phone—they don't have to. Not only do these parentals wish to drop off their kid (as my dad dutifully did), but they also want to help Johnny choose his courses, roommates, dorm room, and meal plan, and even sit in Johnny's classes and take notes for him when he has a bad case of the sniffles. If the message "It's not mean to wean" doesn't sink in during those tutorials, parent-bouncers, hired by the college, escort the folks away from the students toward more intense counseling. But even that immersion-style intervention doesn't always work. Some über-parents continue to keep contact, offering daily wake-up calls, visiting monthly to clean their kids' rooms, cooking their meals, and doing their laundry, all in the name of love. But what impacts these professors most are calls from parents to argue due dates, grades, and the finer points of curriculum. In conferences during a professor's office hours, it's not unheard of for an undergrad to flip open his phone after an impasse and say, "Here, dude. Talk to my mom."

Elementary, middle, and high school teachers have had to deal with the parent issue ever since the invention of the abacus. At a prep school, it starts before the child is even admitted, when an overzealous mom or dad will submit a thirty-point questionnaire and expect an answer in writing or a full hour with the headmaster on everything from a school's mission statement to what kind of music the bullies and queen bees listen to. Most parents I deal with behave pretty well overall and pounce only when they spot me trying to figure out how to thump a ripe melon in the produce section of Albertson's. I've learned over the years that if I spell everything out ahead of time in my syllabus and answer e-mails promptly (and when parents are sleeping), I can escape the 9:00 P.M. calls when I'm drying London off after playing tsunami in the bathtub. That doesn't mean I haven't had my fair share of helicopters threatening to get me fired if I didn't offer a makeup exam after their kid overslept, or begging me to help Sally make the honor roll because she suffered from acute self-esteem depletion disorder.

The week before my colleagues presented the findings from their West Coast jaunt, I was in my office packing up my books and papers. The barn where Poppy rides her borrowed pony was throwing her an equine-themed birthday party complete with all the beasts we would forever deprive her of. I'd had a decent week teaching Toni Morrison to mostly white kids, and the final essay of the year was due the next day. I make it a policy never to read a draft of an essay the day before the due date. The primary reason is to teach my students some time management skills, but the buffer day also gives my eyes a break before they cross over four hundred pages of twelve-point type.

As I was buckling my messenger bag, I heard a sharp knock on the door, which is never a good sign at the end of a school day. There have been heavy marking periods where I've covered that window embedded in the blue steel with old exams, but, sad to say, this wasn't one of them. At the door was Charlotte, one of my juniors, and her super-fit mother, who would fit neatly in the heliport holding all the other helicopter parents. I should say that Charlotte has learning issues that, along with the alpha mom's cattle prodding, turned her into quite the little perfectionist. I served this kid all year to the best of my ability by reading multiple drafts of her essays and cutting her slack in terms of tardiness and the fact it took her a full *Boston Public* episode to complete a ten-minute pop quiz. I had great empathy for her and knew school wasn't easy, especially with a mom who smiled like her jaw had been cemented shut.

While Charlotte studied the pattern of the water stain on the carpet, the mom stood fiercely grinning, only inches from my stale coffee breath. "Charlotte says that you didn't read her draft today," she said.

"That's right."

She crossed her toned arms. "Can you please explain to me why?" Sometimes if you listen close enough, the word *please* can mean so many different things.

The truth was that Charlotte hadn't e-mailed the paper to me until after midnight (which technically was against another policy of mine), and the computers were down all morning, so by the time I could read it, I was in class. I had told Charlotte all this earlier in the day, but I guess that hadn't dissuaded her from calling in her momstrocity for backup.

When I'm in conferences with students and their parents, the best thing is to let the kid speak first, so I said, "Charlotte, I already explained about today. Haven't I read every other draft you've given me all year? Sometimes at five-thirty in the morning so you could have time to revise?"

Her mom didn't give her a chance to speak. "So," she said, tight-lipped, "you should give her the same opportunity now."

"I'm going to my daughter's birthday party." I glanced at my watch. "Actually, I'm already late."

The mother didn't move, blink, or even acknowledge that I had a life outside this cramped (and rather close) office.

I spoke to the daughter but kept my eyes locked onto the mom's icy gaze. "Charlotte, you'll probably get some flavor of an A on this one. What's the real problem here?"

She pressed her lips together and shook her head slightly before looking up. "You did give me that B-plus."

It was true. I once had had the gall to award her a grade lower than an A. She was a very talented writer, but her critical reading skills weren't maturing. According to Charlotte, Steinbeck and Fitzgerald had nothing on some of the better anime plotlines coming out of Japan. So I'd given her a slightly lower grade to motivate her. What the hell was I thinking, trying to teach her something?

I sighed. "What would you like me to do?"

"I think you should give her an extension," the mother said.

"Based on what?"

"The fact you refused to read her draft."

"I didn't refuse. Besides, that would be playing favorites. No one else gets breaks like that. A lot of kids here have issues."

"No, they don't. Charlotte has special needs. She deserves an extension."

You *have special needs, you beeatchh* is what I wanted to say, but I was late to my daughter's tenth-birthday party and this hover-mother was blocking the door. If I fought a woman with teeth and arms and free time like that, I'd be ass deep in meetings through graduation. Not to mention the possibility of a lawsuit, which I'd been through before after supposedly "underserving" a student who did everything short of manslaughter trying to get himself kicked out. I have the summons framed on the wall of my office at home as a reminder that paper cuts and a chalky ass aren't the only occupational hazards for a teacher.

"Fine," I said, in as chilly a voice as I could muster. "Whatever you want. How long would you like?"

"Monday."

"Swell by me." I moved toward the doorknob, but my obstruction wasn't letting me pass.

The momster hoisted a phony smile. "What about her draft?"

"What about it?"

"We'd still like you to read it."

"Just leave it on my desk."

Because of parental bullies like these, I think I've gone too far the other way as a parent at Poppy's school. I'm always saccharine-friendly to the elementary teachers and administration, asking how their days and families and TIAA-CREF investments are fairing. When I taught writing in Poppy's class as part of Prep's community service program, I brought her teacher coffee every week, not as a grade-grubbing tactic, but more in the I've-been-there-sister school of pedagogical pity. Some of this learning through negative examples of helicopter parenting has been a good thing for Lala and me. Recently, Poppy spent two weeks with her wealthy cousins in California and came back home in a hurried-child lather, having had private instruction in golf, tennis, surfing, windsurfing, shopping, and guitar. Here in Santa Fe, she was already involved in horseback riding, rock climbing, and voice. Luckily, we have no water nearby for her to surf on, yet she still wanted to add tennis and guitar to her already busy lifestyle.

"Easy, whiskey," we said, reminding her of our three-activities-only rule, and sent her off to watch a few hours of network television to purge all those silly dreams of overachieving right out of her.

But by trying not to fall into the hover-dad category, I made a terrible mistake when Poppy was in third grade. It happened on a Thursday. I was asleep in a study hall when the receptionist came in to tell me I needed to call home as soon as possible. Even though Lala can at times be a tad hysterical, most of the alerts and bulletins usually wait to be announced until I'm trying to fall asleep at night. So as I dialed, all the terrible things that could happen to my wife and kids flashed in my mind like a music video on the tragedy channel.

"Poppy's in the principal's office," Lala said, obviously upset.

"Thank God." I was so ecstatic no one was in the hospital, I almost yelped.

Lala gasped. "What did you say?"

"Forget it. What's she in for?"

"Not sure, but one of us needs to go, now. Can you do it? London's asleep, and I'd probably start crying before I hit the playground."

I told my yawning study hall that they should sleepwalk to the library and sped to Poppy's school, only a few minutes away. The receptionist nodded toward the principal's office, a place I dread entering even though I'm forty years old and have given the woman at least a dozen forms of baked goods during my tenure as a parent. Poppy was sitting with her head bowed like a death row inmate about to take the long walk. I tried not to hug her, weep, or scream, "What the hell happened?" in my dad's foghorn-like tones. The principal asked Poppy to wait outside.

"Well," she sighed, leaning back in her swivel chair, "Poppy and some friends were quite cruel to a girl on the playground today."

"Really?" Poppy, like any sister worth her salt, could be sadistic to her brother, but outside the usual family terrorism, she'd never been one to pick on others.

"The girl went home crying and now doesn't want to come back to school."

I nodded, forcing myself to listen to the whole story first instead of arguing right away like those parents I'd been on the receiving end of.

"I know," the principal said. "The last one I'd expect to have disciplinary issues with is Poppy. Let's call her in."

Poppy wouldn't look me in the eye, which I had to think was some sort of admission of guilt, even though the whole episode still didn't sit right with me. She nodded along with the brief list of accusations, and every time I wanted to go *Law and Order* on her and ask how or why it all went down, or request some forensics, I thought of those combative parents who denied or justified every felony their little angel had committed, even if he was caught naked smoking pot in the headmaster's office.

Soon Poppy was shuffled out, and the mother of another accused party came in to listen to the punishment. I guessed they'd make the girls stay in for a couple of recesses to write "It's nice to be nice" on the chalkboard a few hundred times.

"Well, I'm in a bind here," the principal explained, "because their teacher is out tomorrow and I'm in meetings all day, so I can't really supervise a detention. Neither can a sub. And tomorrow's Friday and our policy is to deal with issues like these immediately so the child can learn from his or her mistakes, make reparation, and move on."

We both nodded like bobbleheads from our side of the desk.

"So tomorrow, I'll place your girls in in-school suspension." At Poppy's school, when a child gets suspended, he has to sit silently in another class all day reading and studying. I know the topic of suspension, and discipline in general, is a tricky one for schools. Sometimes suspension at home can be a Roman holiday. I remember the trendy mother of a middle school student squeaking, "Super! We can go shopping!" when her fourteen-year-old daughter got suspended for leaving campus. I always thought, though, that making a student sit in the corner while a classful of kids stared at you was as close to a dunce cap as you could get without the pointy headgear.

When the principal said "suspension," I should have screwed in the rotor blades and argued that the punishment did not fit the catty crime. I should have taken Poppy aside to find out the truth, which, as I discovered later, was that she was just taking the rap for one of her friends and the teased girl had previous truancy issues based on a general allergy to school in the first place. Poppy, I learned, is nothing if not fiercely loyal to her friends. After her sentencing, she refused to speak to Lala or me and cried all that night, and I had to drag her out of the car the next day to shame-fully serve her time. I know a dad who says the proudest moment of his life was standing up to a headmaster for his son when he believed the boy was treated unfairly in a disciplinary case. On the other end of the spectrum, I've sat in a meeting with a mom who, after shipping her daughter off to rehab, said, "I guess that's what I get for ignoring my daughter for thirteen years." I believed that being around all these examples of parenting would help me be a better dad, but in Poppy's case, I floundered miserably. I learned during that episode that you can't gain your identity by trying hard not to become the person (or parent) you most de-spise.

The other day I was in the car with the kids en route to sign Poppy up for a tennis camp to see if tennis would replace rock climbing for her fall lineup. London was strapped in his car seat, flying his Buzz Lightyear figure into a fierce draft whooshing from the open window. Poppy was nose deep in the final part of a young-adult novel titled *East*. The book is centered around an ancient myth that in the rural villages of Norway children inherit the qualities of the direction in which they are born. Nymah Rose, the central character, was a North-born baby. In the book, North-born babies are said to be wild, unpredictable, intelligent, and destined to break their parents' hearts because they all leave home to travel to far away. I reminded Poppy of her suspension and asked, now two years later, what she thought of the whole episode.

"Why do you want to talk about that?" she asked, marking her place with a glittery strip of plastic.

"Because I wonder if we should have done things differently."

"I don't think about it. Why are *you* thinking about it, Dad?"

"Oh, no reason."

What I didn't say is that I worry about what I'm doing now as a dad because, like the North-born babies in her book, Poppy will someday break my heart by traveling far away to an exotic (and expensive) land called college, and I do not want to become a helicopter parent who follows her there.

What I didn't say is that while she's still young and still at home, I do want to hover (just a little bit).

Part IV:

School Daze

Teentales:
High School Students' Retelling of Classic Literature

The Great Gatsby

The Great Gatsby is about this guy, Nick Canary or something, who hangs out with all these rich-ass people including a guy named Gatsby who lives in this sweet house and drives some sweet car I've never even heard of. Nick spends a lot of his time talking about other people which I think is totally normal but some of the kids in my class say it's sketch because he never talks about his own relationships with girls. I don't think it's a big deal if you don't really know why you like a girl, you just do, and you don't really want to talk about it even if you probably talk about other people's relationships a lot. There's nothing wrong with that. I also think it would be normal to break up with a girl if she had a mustache of sweat on her upper lip. Nick does that which I think is fine because if I ever saw a girl shoot sweat out of her lip, I'd probably hurl.

The Grapes of Wrath

This really really really long book is about a bunch of hillbillies called the Joads who leave Oklahoma because it has way too much dust. A lot of people die including a dog which is pretty sad especially since no one seems to give a shit. The dialogue is really hard to read because of the funny way those people talked back then. The book spends way too much time talking about dust and starving kids and turtles. It gets pretty depressing and boring. I think John Steinbeck gets bored himself and ends the book without tying up any of the loose ends. We don't know where Tom Joad goes or where his brother Al goes and then they end up in this barn where the daughter with the weird name Rose of Sharon, what kind of name is that anyway? Rose of Sharon ends up, this is pretty gross, breast-feeding this diseased old man. It's pretty sick and all the boys in my class got really freaked out by it. So did some of the girls. That's how gross it was.

Song of Myself

Walt Whitman was so gay. And really boring.

One Flew Over the Cuckoo's Nest

I don't know what the big deal is about this book. All the guys in the nuthouse are crazy or wasted or both. The Nurse is obviously a bitch. McMurphy is cool but he dies which totally sucks but that Chief is fucking insane so I don't know why we bother to try to figure out what the hell he's saying. I think the whores are cool and that stuttering guy Billy gets laid but he dies too which sucks especially since his mother and the Nurse are such bitches. Why do all the books we read have to be depressing? Why couldn't McMurphy and stuttering Billy live and kill the Nurse? That would make so much more sense and the book would probably be shorter which would be a total bonus.

Hamlet

Dude, I hate Shakespeare. All those *thou*s and *thee*s. Half the time I can't figure out what the hell anyone is saying. Why can't we read those plays translated into English? It takes me an hour just to figure out what some stupid guard or messenger is saying. My friend at another school says they get to read comic books based on Shakespeare's plays. He says it's totally easier cause you can see what people are doing and I think they shrink the play or something so there aren't as many words. My teacher said *Hamlet* is Shakespeare's longest play. Is that supposed to get us excited or something? More confusing language? Oh, hooray. Then he said we should watch the movie with the guy who played Professor Lockhart in *Harry Potter and the Chamber of Secrets* but the movie version is over four hours long and that dude who plays Hamlet is way too old anyway. So that gives me at least two reasons not to see the movie.

A Streetcar Named Desire

On the cover of our book was a picture of Marlon Brando without a shirt on. The girls got all excited but it made me sick. What if I brought in a book with a picture of a topless woman on it? I'd probably get expelled or something worse. It's totally unfair so I took a Sharpie and gave the guy a black wifebeater and a mustache while I was at it which was pretty funny if you ask me. Some of the other guys made fancy shirts out of paper and glued them on but that was a little too *Brokeback* for me.

As I Lay Dying

This is a book full of weird names like Jewel (not the lame singer), Anse, and Vardaman. This family is all retarded I think because they let their mother's dead body rot in her coffin then drag it around by a crazy horse. One of the really retarded kids drills holes in the coffin and then says, "My mother is a fish," which has to be one of the stupidest things I have ever read. Some cool stuff happens in this book like barns burning and people being carted away to the nuthouse but you can't really appreciate it because of all the crazy talk. I think if someone were really wasted they might like this book better.

Walden

This book is about a guy who was such a loser that he went into the woods for two years, two months, two days (it was on the quiz). His life was so boring that he actually sat and watched ice crack and melt. For days. Literally. I thought I had a boring life. Not only is it bad enough that he did nothing for two years but we actually have to spend time reading about it. My friend got so bored once that he spent two periods in the library painting both arms with Wite-Out. It was pretty funny but I wouldn't want to read about it and I definitely wouldn't force anyone else to read about it. And Wite-Out is so much more interesting than freaking ice.

Jane Eyre

Two kinds of people like this book: chicks or pussies.

Faculty Feast
(in Three Courses)

I. Slobbatizer

At any small school, part-time employees are hired to fill the gaps the full-timers leave behind. You can be contracted to teach one section of U.S. history, run PE classes, help coach fencing, and be that soggy guy who stands in the rain trying to keep the flow of parent traffic moving. Years ago, our school hired just such a jackoff-of-all-trades, and it was apparent from looking at him why he wasn't qualified to be handing out flyers in the mall. During faculty orientation, I was seated at a table in the library with other teachers wondering how the hottie we call summer had dumped our sorry asses once again. Like my students would in a few days, I longingly looked toward the door and thought, upon seeing the new hire stumble in, that a homeless man had woken up in the arroyo by the school, pissed himself, smelled coffee, and wandered inside. This guy's torn jeans hung loosely below his pale gut, and the red shirt he wore was turned inside out. His gray hair was flat and greasy on the top but billowed on the sides as if the guy had slept in a perpetual headstand. The new hire went immediately to the breakfast buffet and started jamming blueberry muffins in his mouth, dribbling crumbs onto the glass top of the photocopier. Even as the headmaster introduced the new guy, this mess named Stephen just waved and smiled, exposing teeth bubbling with foamy batter and bleeding berries.

Our faculty would not win awards for professional dress. Chalk it up to a temperate climate, academic freedom, or casual Santa Fe style, but on any given day you can see one teacher in flip-flops and cutoffs, a department head who dresses only in purple, and two men who started their own religion by donning robes sewn from leftover denim. My striking sense of mismatched fashion encourages people on a daily basis to ask if I dressed in the dark. Even with our eclectic, tag-sale sense of style, Stephen still pushed it. One day I passed him in the hallway by the guidance counselor's office and had to steady myself against a herpes poster on the health class bulletin board. He was dressed in an outfit that looked as though it had been exhumed from the grave of someone who died in 1982. He had on tight turquoise capri pants, Hush Puppies, and a Members Only jacket with a wet, Chunky soup stain on the shoulder. After I removed the pushpins from my palm, I went to my friend Tom, who supervised the guy.

"What's the deal with that Stephen?" I asked him, peering down the hall, then closing the door behind me.

Tom pushed back from his desk. "What'd he do now?"

"Nothing really," I said, "except dress like he died during the porn version of *Flashdance*."

"Shit." He closed his eyes. "I told him."

"You've spoken to him already? Wow, you're awfully quick for a history teacher."

"I've had to call him in twice. The first time was because his big toe with a huge yellow toenail was sticking out of his ratty Top-Siders. Kids were in here complaining."

"That explains the Hush Puppies." I checked that item off my list. "The second time?"

"You won't believe me."

I grimaced in anticipation. "Try me."

"A week ago, Stephen showed up with what I thought was some sort of decoration on his shirt. On closer inspection, I saw it was half a bean burrito stuck to him."

"Oh my God."

Tom continued: "The dried beans were literally dripping out of the bitten tortilla. I asked him to follow me into the library. He had no idea it was there. The guy was truly surprised. I gave him some Kleenex but he just made it worse, smearing the beans like baby shit all over."

"Did he have a reason for his disgusting new trend of formerly edible fashion?"

"I told him how distracting it is for students to watch a teacher who has food on his shirt or his nasty yellow toenail or all the mooning he does."

"Mooning?" I imagined that big cottage cheese ass smashed against the library window facing the quad.

"You've seen his pants. Imagine what it's like when he picks up dropped chalk."

I clutched my stomach. "I really think I'm sick."

"Get in line. The ninth-graders are way ahead of you." Tom stopped to fiddle with his laptop. "Anyway, he gave me some story about commuting from Gallup, which is three hours away." He waved his hands in a gesture that meant he had given up on this guy already. As a department head, he had other, more immediate, and far less toxic issues to worry about.

Three hours each way for a job that I knew paid very little? Nothing was right with this guy. I starting avoiding Stephen the way I do other parts of the school that disagree with my delicate sense of aesthetics. I skirt certain teachers with overt agendas, like the one who is so obsessed with the Southern writers that she says she has "no time for Shakespeare" in her literature course. Now that I teach in the upper school, you'd never see me in the frenzied, fluid-laden middle school unless I'm collecting a debt. And I haven't been within ten feet of the faculty lounge refrigerator for years now. That death box has more cultures and spores growing in it than a neglected AP biology lab. Opening that door always reminds me of famous gross-out scenes in films like *Jaws* when they slice open that garbage-eating shark or in *Alien* where that penis-like Martian explodes out of John Hurt's stomach and shoots what looks like Kermit the Frog's love juice everywhere. Even before I set up my own fortress of solitude in the English office by spending a quarter of the department's budget on a mini fridge, water cooler, kneel-sit chair, and personal computer, I stayed far away from that electric farting leper colony.

Back when Stephen roamed the halls like Pigpen, Jan, the longtime librarian, let me keep my lunch in her small fridge in the AV room off the library. I consider Jan the smartest colleague at our school, even though she doesn't teach Latin or precalculus. Most of her intelligence comes from having to (wo)man the library (read: holding pen) for kids during their free periods.

f removing photocopied porn from encyclopedias and
kids out for playing tongue hockey in the stacks has
made her an expert on aberrant human behavior.

One day I went to retrieve my lunch from the AV room and it
wasn't there. I thought maybe I'd forgotten the paper sack at
home since I'd been out late the night before, listening to a punk
band and drinking liquid Prozac. When I called home, Lala said
I'd left nothing but dishes in the sink and hair in the shower. I
thanked her for her sympathy and went to Jan.

"That's funny," she said, leaning back in her chair. "Some of
my lunch has been missing lately too."

"Some?"

"A cookie, some cheese. They left the fruit and chopped vegetables."

I thought of a thief who would specifically avoid such healthy
choices. "Seventh-graders?"

Jan gritted her teeth and spat out: "Students never, ever, go
into the AV room. Get that, mister?"

"Easy, killer," I said, patting her clenched fist. "I'm on your
side, right?"

She sighed. "Sorry."

"What kind of twisted fuck-knocker would steal our lunches?"
I asked, searching the pimply teen hordes in the library for a
likely culprit. Then Stephen walked by. His lips were covered
with a gooey lipstick the shade and texture of cherry pie filling.

It turned out that my lunch wasn't the only one being pilfered.
Stephen had swiped Tina's Tupperware, Bill's brown paper bag,
and Wanda's Weight Watchers. In our own dysfunctional way of
dealing with conflict, the faculty and staff started hiding their
lunches in file cabinets and bookshelves like they were the answer keys to final exams. This cowardly solution isn't that sur-

prising coming from a group that accepts "work avoidance disorder" as a reason for a senior slacker not to fulfill graduation requirements. Some victims of the vittles crime said that they didn't want to hurt Stephen's feelings, seeing how he had such a serious neurosis involving food. Others called it diplomacy in an overly cramped working environment. I called it fucked up.

At the end of the year, the school said it no longer had work for Mr. Messy Man, even though there were a slew of nutty part-timers who showed up on parole the next August. Right before the year of the slovenly ended, Lala and I were driving to Albuquerque with Poppy to buy a new stroller we couldn't get in Santa Fe. Descending down La Bojada hill, we approached a blue Yugo puttering slowly in the right lane. The driver had owl glasses, unkempt gray hair, and a jacket that looked like the one Michael Jackson stroked in "Beat It." The driver's face was so close to the windshield that his breath fogged the glass.

"Look at that poor man," Lala said. It was Stephen on his way home to Gallup. In the passenger seat was a sculpture of fast-food wrappers and paper sacks. One of them could have been mine, but I couldn't tell, since my mom stopped writing my name on my lunch in fourth grade. At the speed Stephen was driving, he'd get home just in time to turn around again on Sunday. "Oh, that poor man," Lala repeated.

"Do you think Poppy is old enough to remember any of this?"

Lala looked outside to the sweeping brown landscape just north of Bernalillo and up at a sky the color of unpasteurized milk. "No, she's too young." She shook her head. "Why?"

"That's good," I said, then rolled down my window and let out a string of epithets at the sandwich swindler, nastier than any rotten food ever stuck to another man's outerwear.

II. Maim Course

"What should we do with this?" In the air, Lala waved a bag of crunchy snack food of the healthier variety. "Poppy spit it out. Have you tried it?"

I grew up in a house where we were required to sample all foods, even the ones with organs still quivering, but this specimen had somehow slipped past my Pac-Man mouth. Maybe I had missed it because the packaging was made from recycled grass clippings, and I thought it contained shipping peanuts for Lala's matchbox shrine business. I popped a crisp between my lips. "Oh my sweet Lord," I said, trying to scrape the sandy wood shavings from my tongue with a butter knife. "Get me a beer. This crap is like fiberglass."

She rolled her eyes at my mess hall melodrama. "Should we just toss it?"

"No, that would be wasteful." "Waste not, want not" was the closest my dad got to quoting scripture from the Bible, and I have yet to erase it from my bad memory banks. Besides, I had a receptacle in mind far more interesting than a garbage can. "I'll bring it to school and leave it in the faculty lounge."

"No one with a tongue will eat that," Lala said.

"Wait and see. Those maggots with master's degrees will eat anything."

Just like Mikey with Life cereal, my colleagues devoured items that I thought grown adults wouldn't go near. Any food not secured in a trash bin on campus gets gobbled up faster than a dog can eat his own excrement. It doesn't matter if it's a dairy product with an expiration date from the previous semester or dry pasta used to build a log cabin for a New Mexico history class presentation. The scholastic swarming is so bad that if any legitimate foodstuff needs to be saved for an upcoming board luncheon or class party, it gets double-wrapped in Saran Wrap, taped closed, and covered with a threatening note on top that says "Do Not Eat This!" A few times, the troublemaker in me has replaced the note with "Eat Me!" and left a pair of scissors conveniently nearby. I'm not proud. I just love to watch the carnage unfold.

Back at home, Lala started getting intrigued by this idea of the faculty garbage disposal. With a hearty "They'll never eat this," she sent me to school with stale fruitcake left on our porch for a week or a batch of bananas as gray and soft as gefilte fish. I would position the tray or paper plate in the middle of the faculty table, and if I was feeling especially randy, I'd place a "Please enjoy!" card smack dab on the top.

After first period, I'd check on the progress of our little experiment in gluttony and excitedly call Lala with the gory details. "It's already half gone! Even the curdling custard," I'd whisper conspiratorially into the history department's phone.

"No way," she'd say, breathless.

"Way."

"That's a record." I could hear her stop our kitchen timer and record the results on a notepad on the counter.

By ten or ten-thirty, the tray would be licked clean. I could even see dab marks on the table from where someone had licked his finger to snatch up the remaining crumbs or wipe up the drippings of our little gastronomic gift. With Lala watching in awe, I worked through all parts of the food pyramid, from stale bricks of zucchini bread to cold broccoli smothered in a blanket of hardened Velveeta cheese. Our expired vanilla yogurt went almost as fast as the catfish nuggets in a failed (and congealed) fire-and-ice sauce. The good news was that we had a place to send anything that didn't taste right, and I never again had to feel guilty about tossing a charred roast or raw turkey in the trash. In that respect, my colleagues always had my back. Unwittingly, my young daughter did as well.

As soon as Poppy could stand, she wanted to help in the kitchen. While she was on her tiptoes atop a stool, I'd measure out ingredients into small ramekins and allow her to dump the salt or sugar into the mixing bowl. She felt included in my daily prep for dinner, and it freed up one of my hands for post-work relaxation through the consumption of adult beverages. Everybody was happy. But as Poppy grew older and more confident, she wanted to create dishes on her own. I knew how she felt. When I was a bit older than she was, I'd prepared a soufflé that included liquid smoke, bologna, eggs, and Carnation powdered milk. I thought I was being creative. My dad thought I was trying to poison him.

One day I decided to let Poppy have at it, and spread the contents of our entire spice rack and condiments from the fridge onto the cutting board. I grabbed a Pyrex dish, placed it in front of her, and backed away. Like a mad scientist, she poured, sprinkled, dusted, and squirted everything into a gloopy mess and stirred it with a wooden spoon. Lala came out of her workroom and stood next to me with her arms crossed. My shit-eating grin was impossible to ignore.

"You can't be thinking what I think you're thinking," she whispered in my ear. "No way."

"With a little flour and yeast we just might be able to get that to bake," I said. "And with a little chocolate icing on top . . ."

"Wah-la!" Poppy exclaimed like a mini Julia Child, throwing her goopy hands in the air. Her proud parents eagerly applauded what was before us and what I was about to deliver to the faculty lounge.

III. Desert the Dessert in the Desert

After about five years teaching at Prep, I grew careless with my eating habits. Maybe it was the birth of my second child, London, and the way my life got busier than the lives of those cross-eyed kids in *Spellbound*, but I began to see food more as comfort than as fuel that keeps me from passing out in class the way my students often do. After a sleepless night of walking London in my arms, I became one of those teachers who raced down to be first in line at the faculty appreciation luncheon. I piled my paper plate high with half a chicken, six rolls of sushi, pasta salad, and a few pot stickers and wolfed it all down so I could get back in line to wrestle the remaining deviled eggs from some math sissy's grip. I started to eat as if I was in some contest that awarded points for speed, creative mouthful combinations, and level of disgust. I foolishly believed the lion-sized portions would magically carry me through the rest of the day of meetings that would put a speed freak to sleep. I also felt that I somehow deserved all those good groceries, having had a difficult semester with students who didn't see the true joy of reading and rereading nature poetry from the seventeenth century.

You know why your teachers were so fat when you were a kid? I'll show you. This was my daily diet for almost a year. In the morning there would be doughnuts on the faculty lounge table, so I'd grab two on my way to first-period class. At our midmorning break, the seniors would be raising money for their spring trip by selling breakfast burritos—eggs, cheese, potatoes, bacon—and I just had to support their cause. Lunch was a heart attack on a plate: green chile chicken enchiladas with Spanish rice and sour cream. The sophomores were raising money for the prom by selling pizza after school, so I grabbed a slice on my way to our department meeting, where our head sweetly offered us fresh bagels and cream cheese. Those suckers were free, and I was tired, so I took two and called the bathroom.

Unless you teach PE, the only exercise a paper grader like me gets is walking the twenty-five steps to class and writing on the board, which always throws my shoulder out. In the boys' bathroom mirror, I started noticing that not only did I have more chins than the Chinese phone book, as my dad would say, but even my eyes had little chins of their own. My face was pale, wide, and swelling. I looked like the love child of Mama Cass and Dom DeLuise.

Like my own high school teachers, I purchased larger pants at Sam's Club and started dressing in baggy clothes. I didn't see myself as overweight per se; I was just overworked, underpaid, and dead tired. My bowling-ball head and Goodyear clothing were simply the status quo for pathetic pedagogues like me. I was married and had a steady job where fashion didn't mean shit; what did it matter if I looked like a sheathed pear? I'd learned a lot from the pears of my youth. Then, one day, everything changed. London had just started to talk, and I was in the kitchen fixing dinner for the family. I had my head in the fridge searching for some lost vegetable, and I spotted a can of whipped cream in the door. I figured what the hell. I thought back to teaching Emerson that day and recalled his telling quote: "If I am the Devil's child, I will live then from the Devil." I grabbed the cold metal shaft and rammed its nipple between my teeth, filling my mouth with ever-expanding creamy goodness. Then I shut the door. There was my son, on the kitchen floor, staring up at his old man. He was shocked. To London, I must have looked like some odd hybrid of his father and a chipmunk that freebases dessert toppings.

"Dad, you're fat," London said flatly, and waddled away. I be-lieve the twelve-steppers would call that scene my moment of clarity. The next day, I got through the seven periods by drinking endless cups of coffee and taking a few huffs of Wite-Out. After my last class, I raced to the store, bought the Atkins book, sweated all over it, and committed myself to a new lifestyle of large quantities of meat, no fruit, and tequila instead of beer. Good health, here I come!

Fit

I recently joined a gym. I should say rejoined because I've belonged to this gym before, on and off again for close to fifteen years, my last brief fling with fitness being well before the birth of my son, London, who is four. Like many teachers, in order to avoid looking like an Oompa-Loompa, I alternate between crash diet and exercise, never finding the right balance to what they refer to in the nutrition section of PE as a "healthy lifestyle." Like embarking upon any other exotic adventure, I had to gather up the courage and supplies to relearn how to get into shape. I bought some running shoes on sale (which Lala rightly told me were obnoxiously white), a combination lock, shampoo, conditioner, comb, Q-tips, shaving cream, razor, toothpaste, and brush, because for me to get my money's worth, I need to treat my place of workout as a daily spa.

I needed to gather confidence to join a gym because I've been a teacher for the last decade, not a firefighter, a roofer, or anyone else with a job that requires some remote degree of physical strength. The most strenuous part of my daily grind is putting up the chairs after seventh period. Clapping the erasers is a close second. I'm not especially proud of my body, and places with weights and big exercise balls make me feel a tad inadequate. The only other situations that make me feel so ill at ease are trying to buy concrete at The Home Depot to install a tetherball set for Poppy, or standing next to my close-talking mechanic when he implies that I might want to know something about how the engine in my car needs motor oil in order to run. What I'm saying is that even though I grew up with three brothers and played soccer in college, I've never been much of a man's man. So being viewed by stellar bodies of both genders in a well-lit room filled with weights makes me feel like the scrawny kid in the old Jack LaLanne ads, the one who gets sand kicked in his face by an angry old lady in a wheelchair. Needless to say, it took me a few weeks to step foot inside the hallowed hall of health.

"Hey, buddy" was how the slick guy behind the desk greeted me when I came in with my black gym bag. You could tell from the polished tone of his voice and vacant look in his eyes that he called every man "buddy." Later, as I dawdled near the water fountain, I heard him call a woman with biceps the size of my thighs "sweetie." Every time since then, that's all I hear from behind that desk: "Hey, buddy," "Howyadoin, sweetie?" He sounds a lot like a parrot owned by a bartender at a strip club.

"What can I do for you?" he asked me.

"Um, I'd like to join?" I asked in a slight Valley Girl accent, not unlike some of the teenagers I teach. I was anxious, having considered all the commitment options well ahead of my arrival.

A one-month-membership was too brief and the most cost per workout. Six months was ambitious given the sad history of my fickle bodily commitment. Three months was just right for this gimcrack Goldilocks.

"Sure, buddy, what's your name?"

I told him, and he typed the familiar letters into his computer.

"Oh my God," I said as I saw my fat face pop up and fill his entire screen like a large white clam pizza with extra cheese. I wasn't exactly thin the last time I joined either.

"It's been a while, hasn't it, buddy?" What was worse than staring at my big face with its extended family of jowls was the consoling tone he laid on me. I recalled a time during one of my previous memberships when I had slid off the bench press, having just pushed maybe sixty pounds up and down off my tortilla-thin pectoral muscles, and some guy who was waiting said, "Is that all you can do?" and gave me this coughy laugh like we were still in high school and he had just done a mega-sized bong hit. I felt embarrassed by my sad effort, yet I'm not one to let a comment like that go unreturned, so I said something I'm not very proud of. I squinted my eyes à la Clint Eastwood and whispered, "I just finished my last round of chemo and I'm a little on the weak side." His formerly smug mug collapsed; after apologizing profusely, it seemed he might actually cry into the water fountain.

Back at the registration desk, my face on the computer begged me to run away. The screen didn't even have the decency to flicker. I live in a fairly small town and, this being the most popular gym, I was bound to see a Prep parent or colleague any moment now. They'd ask me what I was doing there, what my fitness goals were, all the topics that make me want to cut out my tongue with a letter opener. I'd rather snort fiberglass than have the history teacher examine my stomach and discuss the battle of my bulge.

"Okay, buddy. You've got a three-month membership with a two-week freeze period. . . ."

"Right. Right," I said, trying to speed him up. My face hadn't gone away yet, but I desperately needed to.

"So let's say you get sick or—"

"I never get sick." I already knew all the benefits of a membership, having called ahead of time (with a phony British accent) so I could avoid being stuck just like this. People started flowing in as we approached the busy lunch-hour period. I saw a few thicknecks I recognized from my previous memberships, including a personal trainer who looked a lot like an orangutan with her painted-on tan, long muscular arms, and hair in a ruffled helmet shape.

"Let's say you want to take a vacation. Do you like to travel, buddy?"

"No!" My bark in the negative sounded crazy, so I backtracked. "Well, yes, in the summer, but could we—"

"See, then you could freeze your membership. How long do you usually . . ."

I kept glancing over my shoulder, watching the wife beaters in wifebeaters stroll in next to the step masters tucked into spandex so tight you could see inside their camel toes. Then I'd look back to the screen and wince at the blubbery face mocking me. Then I saw her—the college counselor at my school. Even though she didn't have a great physique, she told everyone she worked out religiously. Some educators look the same no matter what they do. This humanities teacher I once knew was a huge cyclist, and I mean huge, like Louie Anderson at a buffet. She would take spinning classes five times a week, and I'd see her in full cycling gear on the roads over the weekend, but her speed-bump figure never flattened out. Even her students started teasing her, egging her on in class, asking how many healthy miles she'd logged that week. You can't escape your body issues when you stand in front of a heckling audience for a living.

"Hey," the college counselor said to me, "I didn't know you worked out here."

"Y-yeah, well," I stammered like a student caught cutting class, trying not to look her in the eye, "I did before, you see, and wanted to get back into it."

"Really? When were you last a member?" She put her bag down on the floor, obviously feeling chatty.

Lala thinks it's crazy that I forget someone after meeting them five times or can't recall the last time we drove to Wyoming together, but I can remember all the words to the theme song to *Land of the Lost*, a TV show that went off the air in 1976. I knew I should recall the window of my last membership, but I didn't. I already felt ridiculous enough standing there, bag still in hand, my face unwavering on the monitor, so I made up a number.

"Oh, two years." I shrugged and turned away toward the treadmill section of the floorshow.

"It was five, buddy," the registration guy called over the desk.

"Thanks for the info."

The college counselor was shocked. "You haven't worked out in five years? What have you been doing?"

"Oh, you know, chasing the kids around the house and . . ." I drew a blank. The truth was: nothing. No exercise short of falling off a surfboard in Maui and lifting green chile cheeseburgers and pints of beer at the Cowgirl Hall of Fame.

"Huh?" the counselor asked. I hadn't finished my sentence.

She was in the line of work where fragments meant thin rejection letters in the mailbox.

"I'm going to get changed now," I said, which was obvious given our location and circumstances. I sounded like the self-narrating kids in my classroom who say things like "Can I ask you a question?" when no one else is vying for your attention or raise their hand when the classroom is completely empty.

"Hey, buddy, you forgot your receipt," the front-desk guy called to me.

"I'll get it on my way out." I ran into the men's changing room and after breathing deeply, filling my lungs with sweaty air, I scanned the rows for an empty locker. A lot of men feel okay about leaving their gear unprotected on a bench or in the corner, but I don't. Not after what I'd been through. I opened and closed about six wooden doors before I found an empty one. I tried to get changed as quickly as I could while memorizing the combination of my new lock. Inside my scattered head, I repeated over and over "Seventeen, six, thirty-two" while I stripped off my street clothes. The locker room is not large even by Chinese sweatshop standards, and before I had internally chanted those three numbers ten times, a couple of men in smart casual dress came and placed their gear on either side of mine. I had to change in a cylinder of space barely larger than my body mass. I turned my bag sideways, followed by my torso, so as not to touch the other men, who were also stripping. It was like some homophobic reality show based on the old kids' game *Operation:* don't touch the sides or you are so gay, chained to a lint brush for your entire life. Ha ha ha, don't graze his funny bone! What made it more difficult was that these guys were "gym buddies," a term I would soon come to understand, and they kept talking past me, leaning well into my personal space. It was quite challenging for me to repeat the combination in my head while trying to avoid body-to-body contact with two men leaning like vultures in the vicinity of my naked body of carrion.

Seventeen, six, thirty-two, watch your left, I thought.

The guy on my right leaned in and said, "You know about those new PAC grants, the 1972 act stalled the . . ."

Watch your right foot, nineteen—no, seventeen—no— "Shit!" I barked out loud. They both stared at me: a guy in his boxer briefs wriggling and swearing to himself.

The guy on my left rolled his eyes but kept talking. "Yeah, we worked up some hypotheticals using the 1972 act as text."

I was almost there—had my white sneakers on, iPod plugging my ears—and all I had to do was lock my locker, but for some reason I couldn't open the fucking thing.

"You want some help there, pal?" one of the gym buddies asked me. It's funny, but no one ever says they have a "gym friend." I think because that's too intimate when an army of penises surrounds you in various stages of bloom.

"No, I got it." I was sweating and I hadn't even gotten near a machine. When the shackle finally released, I let out a little victorious "Yes!" which made the two guys stop talking and stare me down.

A lot of the exercise equipment had changed since I last had been on the gym floor, and I probably should have accepted the free tour that came with my membership, but the thought of being led around like the new kid in my new shoes by the orangutan woman while all the regulars gawked made me skip it. Just like my students on the first day at school, I was filled with dread and anxiety. I figured I could do like they do: act casual, scuff up my New Balance sneakers, keep the volume on my iPod high. I'd stick to the familiar: short time on the Lifecycle, do a circuit on machines I recognized, then go home. No one would notice me, and I wouldn't have to discuss my lack of exercise with anyone else, thank you very much.

There was an open bicycle in a bank of occupied ones, so I placed my iPod on the shelf behind the TV screens, the ledge where everyone else kept their portable music devices, water bottles, and urine-colored sports drinks. As I adjusted the seat of my portal into health and wellness and connected the straps to the pedals so my feet wouldn't decide to run away, I looked up and noticed something I had missed only minutes before.

Up until that moment in that gym by those cycles, I'd thought my iPod was pretty hip. I had gotten it for Christmas from Lala's sister Emily and had enjoyed downloading songs from my impeccable music collection, feeling as though I now had an appropriate soundtrack for my so-called life. My shitty car has a shitty radio, but post-iPod such trivialities no longer mattered. But my iPod, as my friend Drew had joked, was an iPod Mini, the kind favored by teenage girls, the kind that came in colors like pink and apple and sky dance. Everyone else's iPod on that shelf was thick, stealth, and sheathed in a hip leather case. Mine was sleek and thin like a razor made by Lady Bic. Maybe it was my own paranoia, but I felt as though the other cyclists were laughing at my missing inches. I slyly swiped my iPod Mini from the shelf and clipped it to the waistband of my shorts, covering the delicate baby with the hem of my T-shirt. The machine caused me some hemorrhaging in my midsection, but it was worth it.

I programmed the Lifecycle for thirty minutes and wanted to quit after seven. My thighs burned, my feet were numb, and I was

short of breath. Pathetic. Especially given that this was the wussi-
est of all the cycles, the one with back support that was low to the
ground so you didn't have to do any climbing to get seated. You
just fell into it like a big ass into a soiled bed. Next to me there
were the tougher bikes, then the treadmills and the stair climbers
and the elliptical machines that mimic cross-country skiing. If I
couldn't survive the pussymobile, how would I ever get to a place
where I was vertical? How could I ever avoid becoming a fat
English teacher? I glanced longingly at the treadmill, and what I
witnessed almost made me leap off. A thin woman dressed in all
black was jerking up and down as if the belt was moving too fast
for her matchstick legs. Her hands gripped the rail tightly and
her body moved in fits and starts like David Byrne in the *Stop
Making Sense* video. She seemed to be doing it on purpose to get
into some weird robot shape, or so I supposed. My concern
evolved into fascination, and her near-death spasms ate up at
least ten minutes of my pain.

When I rolled off the machine I couldn't feel my feet, so I
hopped to the water fountain on my shins. My lower back was on
fire, but I was victorious. This was the first day of the rest of my
brief stand with fitness. After a gulp of water that had a light
aroma of ass crack, I was ready now to push some air.

The weight machines I had planned to use had just been installed five years previously. They employ air pressure for resistance, and you can easily adjust the weight by pushing these little
white knobs. They were the perfect machines for me to start on:
easy to use, and I wouldn't have to carry a clipboard around to recall my poundage since I could adjust as I went. The best part was
that no one could look on and see how much I was actually lifting.
No metal plates to gauge, no numbers viewed by buff passersby.
And I could push the button to increase the pressure just before I

stepped off, fooling the next user into believing the guy with the seventies hairdo and double chin was far stronger than he looked. I sat on the machine that worked your abdominal muscles and after ripping my headphones out of my ringing ears, I readjusted my iPod so I could bend over easily. On the down bend, I saw my new New Balance sneakers; bending up, I saw the college counselor huffing contentedly on the treadmill. I was humming along, happy I had no one to share my machines, no one to interrupt my circuit. Oddly, even though the club was crowded, no other member wanted to use my machines. I could do my routine without interruption, hit the shower, do a bit of manscaping, then leave. It seemed so easy. I invited the burn at my midsection, increasing the pressure more and more. I'd have a six-pack in no time. Then, on an up bend, I was shocked to see a group of geriatrics hobbling over toward me.

Oh no, I thought. *Please don't come this way. Don't use my machines.* Like the Night of the Nearly Dead, they crutched, hobbled, farted, and limped over to the air apparatuses. One woman had a black eye and a patch of hair missing near her temple, and she used a two-handed walker. The man escorting her had his arm in a sling and shiny blue dress pants draped over wingtip shoes. They swarmed the machines, occupying every last one. The college counselor smiled at me as if to say *Look, your new friends are here.* I was using the old folks' machines and listening to Hilary Duff's iPod in my fresh-out-of-the-box sneakers. I wanted to quit or die, whichever came first.

It took the grandparents so long to enter, use, and exit each machine that I almost fell asleep. I tried to look on the bright side: at least I didn't have to add weight before I got off in order to impress them. Most of them couldn't read the numbers anyhow, and they left the seats dusty rather than sweaty.

Why didn't I leave? Because I wanted to get my money's worth, damn it. Exercise is extravagance where I come from. Why didn't I use another machine? Like my students with OCD, I'd built up the scenario for so long that bailing before I'd done my circuit, albeit slowly now, would have felt like the kind of failure you don't recover from. Besides, the embarrassment of not knowing how to use the other equipment coupled with the fit folks viewing my few stacks of metal would have been a far worse fitness fate.

Instead of taking one hour to work out, it took two, so when I ended up back in the locker room, I was ready for a decent steam. I peeled off my clothes, threw them into my locker, and grabbed my little manscape artist bag and towel. I hung the bag on a hook and threw my towel over it. I had chosen a peach-colored towel before I left home because of an altercation I'd had here previously. Years before, I'd come out of the shower and my white towel was missing. A similar-looking model was dripping a few hooks away, and a little farther down I spotted a cut yet effeminate male drying his hard ass with my towel. I was naked and wet. He was naked too, as was the gaggle of men surrounding him in a Socratic semicircle. In the old days of the gym, before renovation, the clientele consisted mostly of gay men who had discovered that fitness was good for you before the rest of us fat boys did. The towel stealer was holding court, relaying a story that the bevy of nudies found simply delightful. I'm not a good fighter fully clothed, so fighting naked was not an option. I would employ reason instead of barbaric fisticuffs.

"Um, excuse me," I said.

The guy turned, annoyed at my interruption, and did what I'd never do in a room brimming with naked men: he scanned me up and down. Slowly. He was obviously underimpressed with my flesh mini.

"Um, I think you have my towel." I cocked my head in what I believed was a nonthreatening manner.

"No, I don't." He narrowed his eyes.

"You do, actually. Mine has that thin blue piping and was dry. The one on the hook over there does look similar, but it's really not."

"I told you. This is not your towel. End of story."

Who says "end of story"? But there we were, or there I was, because he had put his leg up on the bench and resumed telling his story with his johnny-ride-the-pony swinging proudly. He not only outnumbered me with his Brazilian-manicured pals but outmuscled me as well. I stood there angry, wet, and helpless. What does a well-adjusted man do at a time like this? I couldn't walk out naked and tell the guy at the front desk that somebody had swiped my towel. It was a "he said, he said" crime anyway. So, like a puss, I ended up drying myself off with my undershirt, throwing it away, and leaving in a huff, vowing to bring only pastel-colored drying devices from then on.

One of the parts of my new regimen I looked forward to was the steam room, a place where I could relax and not feel the need to get something done—no essays to grade, reading to catch up on, balanced meals to prepare. I could just do what men were meant to do: sit and sweat. Maybe fart. Yet when I opened the glass door, I rediscovered that I never get what I want in places like these. In this ten-by-ten-foot tiled room, one guy was lying on the top level, taking up over half of the sitting area. I couldn't even sit below him because he was sprawled out with his arm dangling toward the floor like he was drifting along lazily in a canoe. The other guy in there was in the center of the other half, doing some sort of nasty-ass yoga stretches that put parts of his body far too close to the openings on his face.

Their sense of ownership didn't encourage them to say "Excuse me" or curtail their activities to move over a smidgen. Instead, what was available to me was a corner of the lower bench next to the spigot where the steam passionately blasted out. I sat down and started to fry my face off. Clouds of scalding steam surrounded my body, making my session far closer to torture than relaxation, but once again, I wanted to stick to my plan and take advantage of the full spectrum of my membership. As I fried, I had another flashback, one I had managed to successfully suppress until now. Back in the day, I had just finished a decent workout, one where I had actually run for forty minutes on a grown-up treadmill. I was playing soccer then, still in my twenties, pre-marriage, pre-children, pre-teaching. I entered the locker room whistling, something I rarely do, and was ready to hit the steam. I walked up to the glass and through the mist I could just make it out: a man reclining on his side on the lower bench and "pulling his pork," as Lala would say. An adult male was jerking himself off in a room frequented by other men. Almost open to the public. I freaked. The gall of this guy. I ripped open the door, grabbed the hose, and turned it on the twisted fuck. Well, that's what I wanted to do, but instead I put on my sweater and sneakers like Mr. Rogers and went to see the buddy guy at the front desk.

"Excuse me?" I was panting with excitement.

"Hey, buddy."

"A guy in there is, well . . ." I placed my palms on the counter to steady myself.

"Yes?" He smiled, showing off recently capped teeth. Could a place this small have a dental plan?

I settled my nerves. "I'm just gonna say it: he's jerking off in the steam room."

All the buddiness drained from his face. He gave me the cold stare that I'm sure lay forever dormant behind his eight-buck-an-hour glazed gaze.

"I'll take care of it."

"Because that's sick and I don't deserve to—"

"I said I'd take care of it."

But I knew he wouldn't. Would I go looking for something that nasty if I were him? No way in any version of steam room hell.

After I showered and got dressed, I thought about what I'd tell Lala when I got home and she asked me how it went. Would this notion of physical fitness endure for more time than a seasonal allergy? Would my relationship with my body last longer than the time it takes for unrefrigerated milk to go sour? Would I ever see a muscle develop in a place that had been previously fallow or fatty? Like my students after a sweet summer break, could I learn to relearn?

I wanted to see myself with the trim and buff physiques of a few of my colleagues in the athletic department, the ones who skip lunch and run five miles uphill, the ones who keep checking their Nike Triax watches during class to see how long they have until they can pump themselves again, the ones who claim that a carb never touches their lips a week before their Arctic triathlon. But I think the only Olympics I'll ever win is the one that gives medals for marinating a decent pork loin, choosing a drinkable wine, and being a smartass in faculty meetings while still maintaining a full head of hair.

Fear Factor

Just before Halloween, the U.S. history instructor and I combine forces and concurrently teach about the Salem witch trials. He gives the students packets and lectures on the emergence of a colonial government and Salem village history, while I have them read and discuss Arthur Miller's *The Crucible*. If the reading gets too dry and my students need a dose of sexy bad acting, I'll screen a few choice scenes from the 1996 movie, starring Winona Ryder in a push-up bra as a horny Abigail trying desperately to take off her waistcoat and shift so that Daniel Day-Lewis will drop his breeches and garters to do the nasty in the type of woods you'd find if Tim Burton did naturalist porn. The film may not be classified by many as art, or educational for that matter, yet the combination of zit-free bare skin and heavy breathing works well for the kids who have to pine until college to find a date.

Even though the students get Dutch-oven-loads of information on seventeenth-century commerce, trade, and how those
tight-ass Puritans created the FCC, what they really love talking
about is drugs and sex. They come into class drunk on a few shots
of collusion served by Howard Zinn and Amy Goodman and feel
compelled to act like Mel Gibson in *Conspiracy Theory* twitching
to buy another copy of *The Catcher in the Rye*. They jones the same
way earlier in the year when they find out that the poet Walt
Whitman might have been gay. They ask me about the degree of
his homosexuality as if we're in some taboo math class where
such a thing could be measured in calories or Scoville units. Did
he wear gay clothes, eat gay food, or decorate his Long Island
home with a nineteenth-century queer eye? Whoever said a little
information can be a dangerous thing wasn't thinking of post-
goth teenagers discussing tripping witches and a bearded man
singing a kinky little song to himself.

"They were so wasted," one of my students says, referring to
the cause of the Salem teenagers' fits in 1692. Danny's the kind of
boy who loves to inject drugs into all our discussions, his otherwise inappropriate comments protected by the safety net of a free
and open seminar-style education. The influence of illegal sub-
stances or massive quantities of alcohol can easily explain any
type of aberrant behavior by the characters we read in novels,
stories, or plays. According to Danny, Romeo and Juliet were just
whorebag winos; Tom Joad got so baked, dude, on Humboldt
County stickybud; Jay Gatsby was as drunk as Christian Slater on
bootleg liquor; and all signs point to Holden Caulfield being a
heavy glue huffer. It's right there in the text. Discussion over.
Case closed.

"No, it was that, um, you know, yeast thingy, on the bread,"
his classmate Heather corrects him, inarticulately citing a theory

that says a yeast spore found on wheat may have been the cause of the hallucinations that rivaled Hunter Thompson at his best.

"Same as wasted." Danny rolls his eyes at such petty technicalities. You say yeast spores, I say blotter acid. Let's call the whole thing off.

"Shut up, dumbass." Heather flips him off when she thinks I'm not looking, and I let her, since what I really want to teach in my class is social and gender justice.

"I heard they were all part of this lesbian cult," a blond boy named Devon offers softly. He's a sex-starved guy who, when asked during our poetry section to name his favorite word in all the English language, happily said, "Tits."

"Where'd you hear that?"

"Oh, on the Internet," he says. For my students, the Internet is like an electronic version of my childhood friend Dart, who misinformed me that babies came from eating too much shellfish and that a reliable form of birth control included a grapefruit spoon and 7-Up.

"Your mom's on the Internet," someone whispers, and we all laugh because this discussion so far is about as educational as Carmen Electra reciting lines from Chaucer out of her coochie.

My perhaps overly lofty goal in this unit is to try to connect the fear-based hysteria in Salem with what's happening in America today, but my students have a tough time relating. Even if they think *The Crucible* has merit, they tell me each year how hard it is for them to apply these ideas gussied up in doublets and petticoats to their own lives of drive-in fast food, MP3s, and trips to the mall. Even after I link the current terrorist scare and fascist Patriot Act to Joe McCarthy's blacklists and then back to the witch trials, they still look at me, their glazed eyes like two dozen Krispy Kremes.

"But twenty-five people died in Salem!" I shout, banging on the desk hard enough for effect but not enough to bruise my dainty chalking hand. "McCarthy ruined whole family's lives!"

Yawn. Drool. Stretch.

"Japanese internment camps? Wen Ho Lee? Bosnia? *Hotel Rwanda?*"

Blink blink blink. Fart.

Okay, I think. *What if I apply these themes to school-related issues? That might grab them.* "How about lockdowns and invasive searches for weapons or drugs in hallways and lockers?"

"But that goes on at big public high schools," they say flatly. "We don't go to those." Collectively, they glance at the bored atomic clock hanging itself over the doorway.

Instead of getting angry and calling them overprivileged zombies whose biggest scare is their cell phone batteries running low, I breathe deeply, think of the Dalai Lama in a Pilgrim hat, then query kindly, "Well, what exactly are you creatures interested in?"

"I dunno," Tiffany says, looking up past her side ponytail at the ceiling for answers. She lifts one padded shoulder. "Relationships?"

Well, I do know about those. In my house, the roles are reversed. I'm the skeptical (read: dumb) student and my wife is the impassioned teacher, pounding on the table (or my head), wanting me to pay attention to what she considers some seriously deadly issue.

I arrive home exhausted after pleading my case in front of the teenage tribunal, hoping for some family normalcy after my role as the hysteria whore. Poppy is at the dining room table busily working on narrative math homework that has sent both her parents to tutoring. London is squatting on the floor in the living room, tying up his Rescue Heroes, macho civil servants with aberrantly large feet who do not object openly to bondage. Lala io out of my line of sight, sequestered in her studio filling another order of matchbox shrines for some New Age store in Cleveland. An ominous storm has moved in over downtown Santa Fe, and thunder claps overhead like a giant courtroom gavel.

"Get the kids away from the windows!" Before I have a chance to place my weary ass on our juice-stained couch, Lala bursts into the room. The apron she's wearing is splattered with shiny glitter like she's some fairy butcher after a particularly successful sylph slaughter session.

"Why?" I sigh, like one of my own jaded students.

"I saw another thing today on TV that said that lightning can strike you through windows."

I roll my eyes. "Come on." She's tempting me to put a tack on her chair.

"I'm not kidding." She points at our son, in the middle of the bound cluster of randy rescuers. "London, move closer to the center of the room."

"Lightning is not going to seek out London like some infrared missile," I say.

"Tell that to the poor woman who died in Wal-Mart." She crosses her arms.

"Huh?"

Her eyes widen. "You didn't even watch the news, so you wouldn't know about it, would you?"

I do know better than to compare the human-interest story she saw on television to the lack of interest in my dusty classroom that day. In America, a land where celebrity has-beens with names like Screech and Horshack get paid to mix it up in a boxing ring, TV will kick a book's sorry paper ass any time. Instead, I pace around the house, avoiding windows and warnings, wondering what Cotton Mather or Edward R. Murrow would do in my place. "How many people has this happened to, exactly?" I ask calmly.

"Enough for us to be concerned about the safety of our children."

"Nice answer," I say. Lala must have studied history to know that invisible enemies like witches, communists, and acts of God are mostly unheard of until it's too late and everyone's already too dead to object.

As I stand dumbfounded, Lala searches our house for nooks and crannies vulnerable to tricky thunderbolt attacks. "I wonder if skylights count as windows," she says to herself, looking skyward. "Better be on the safe side. Poppy, go do your math homework in the bathtub."

I may sound like the typical callous husband, but after years of hearing about bear attacks, West Nile virus, Africanized killer bees, and Lala's aunt's cousin's friend getting mad cow disease in Dubuque, I feel sick from my hysteria hangover. Lala's frequent fear-induced frenzies really cramp my style. I can no longer use my cell phone within two miles of a gas station since a video of a woman spontaneously combusting made its rounds on late-night slow-news programs. London is now forbidden to visit Mickey or Minnie in the rodent section of PetSmart because of hantavirus, the southwestern version of Asian bird flu. Poppy will never get a cat because of the plague even though more people die each year from splinters than from the feline version of a disease that can trace its origins like some fucked-up version of evolution—flea, rat, rabbit, cat, dog, human. The only solution I see to this domestic delirium is similar to the sentence rendered by Reverend Samuel Parris, Salem's version of Donald Rumsfeld, only with Fabio's hairstyle. I can't decide whether I want to burn or hang our television, though. Hanging is so painfully slow, and burning, well, it's just plain messy.

Right around the time of our Salem block, a low-level administrator calls an emergency faculty meeting right after school. Not many people show on such short notice since most teachers are already off to yoga and Pilates classes before the final bell rings. Those, like me, who shun physical fitness race to the library, secretly hoping their least favorite colleague or student has been required to withdraw, or "disappeared," as we whisper in the hallways.

"Someone is leaving threatening notes in the middle school lockers," the portly administrator says with a degree of earnestness that would rival Alan Greenspan during a ten-year recession. He pinches a scrap of paper by the corner as if CSI needed to dust for fingerprints right after we adjourn for doughnuts.

"What did it say?" someone calls out.

"Because of confidentiality, I don't want to reveal too much, but since we want the faculty on full alert, I'll read this one." He lifts the square like it was a dead rat and examines it closely. "It reads, 'Not nearly frightened enough. I know what hunts you.'"

"That's bullying!" someone cries. Bullying on the playground (and in cyberspace) has been a hot-button topic in education lately, and like good dogs, our school begins chasing its tail like the rest of the pedagogical pack. This ruffian rhetoric gets so hot that we invite the FBI to storm the campus, armed with laptops and laser pointers, to make us all feel safer as we download funny pictures of George Bush dancing like a gay marionette.

"Let's have a lockdown," a math teacher suggests.

"School's over. Everyone is gone. Who would we lock down?" the global studies teacher asks.

"I bet whoever did this is wasted." The media literacy guy sits back in his chair and crosses his arms.

"We should at least search the middle-schoolers and their lockers." The math teacher needs something, a solution or answer key to our problem set, before she leaves for the day.

"For what? Paper and pens?" The global studies teacher isn't buying it.

The math matron glares at her partner. "Are you endorsing this type of behavior?"

"Do we have hidden cameras on campus?" a new faculty member chirps, then peers around the library in a magical-thinking moment. Sadly, all she sees are torn copies of *Rolling Stone* and two stained armchairs.

Luckily, the headmaster arrives late from a meeting and calms everyone down, not wanting to turn the school into a police state unless it helps with fund-raising in some way. Instead, for the next few days, we are told to monitor the middle school like starving hawks, hoping to find the culprit in a trench coat and fedora tiptoeing to a locker to slip in the menacing message, proving to us humanities sissies that the pen could be as mighty as the sword.

Back at home, it seems each week Lala has a new pressing issue to warn me about. I can't say I respond in a patient, caring manner. Over the course of my ten-hour day, I come into contact with over a hundred people, most of them needy adolescents, some in one sort of emotional crisis or another, a few carrying viruses of the more fluid variety—head colds, stomach flu, severe

conjunctivitis. The last thing I need, even after all my hand sanitizing, is another dose of the old drama and trauma. Since she is
self-employed, Lala lives a more isolated lifestyle, completely the
opposite from mine, so by the time I fall into the door, she's been
waiting all day to unload on her captive adult audience of one.
She's an amazing wife and mother, but working all day with the
television on gets her, well, a little worked up.

When I pull up, she's in the driveway, putting the trash can on
the curb for pickup the next day. "Did you hear about those shark
attacks?" she asks before I get out of my car.

"How would I hear about shark attacks," I answer, trying to
extricate myself from my seat belt, "when I've been in a classroom talking to myself all day?"

She continues on without pause. My glaring ignorance of vital
current events is not her problem. "Pretty scary. Florida and
Hawaii. That one girl lost an arm. I'd think twice before going in
the water now." She presses her lips together and nods in what I
refer to as a "mourning warning."

We live in the high desert. I remind her that the closest body
of water for us is the public pool, which has enough chlorine in it
to choke a pod of blue whales. I point down the street, since we're
still outside, and I hope this unnecessary gesture will redirect her
thoughts. I think to ask her about the kids but figure they're
probably safely ensconced in bubble wrap under her worktable.

"We still need to be concerned," she tells me.

"Why?"

"I can't believe you're a teacher and a parent. With your attitude, I wouldn't be surprised if you got hit by lightning, or attacked by a bobcat, or got food poisoning. None of the people on
the news saw it coming."

"What about getting hit by lightning while being attacked by a bobcat with food poisoning?" I grin like a boy about to be sent to in-house suspension.

"Shut up," she says, turning her back on me. I believe she'll stomp away, but then Lala halts and pivots. "And you know, Mr. Smartass, they really did see bobcat tracks by your school a few days ago. I'd watch out if I were you, going up there so early in the morning carrying whatever the hell it is you eat for lunch."

I laugh at her warning, but then a few days later, something remarkable happens. London wakes one morning with these small red spots around his mouth. He shows no other signs of ill-ness—no sore throat or fever—and he still has the spastic energy to hit me on the back of the legs with his light saber, though he refers to the pulsating phallus as his "light saver," as if *Star Wars* had some sort of underlying energy conservation message.

"I bet it's impetigo," Lala says boldly, naming a disease that sounds like you'd contract it on a rusty African frigate ferrying lepers.

"Now you're a doctor? Come on, it's probably just a minor ir-ritation."

When I drag London to the pediatrician the next morning, his words echo those of my spousal sawbones at home. "Yup," Dr. Kleiner says, nodding over his glasses. "Impetigo with a case of strep too. Poor little guy." Poor little guy? Even with his myriad infections, London won't suffer the same pain as his father after calling home and telling Lala she was right. In fact, London gets a coloring book and Oreos for his behavior. I, on the other hand, deserve to endure the biggest shit storm this side of Salem.

Lala's spot-on diagnosis and subsequent (and rather de-served) verbal castration force me to wonder if I'm taking all these supposed real-life issues too lightly. Maybe I should be worried about cleaning up mouse crap under the kitchen sink without a mask since I do live in the hantavirus home state. And given Columbine and all the other school shootings, maybe I should have asked more questions about the notes left in those lockers. After all, isn't that what I want from my students? To pay closer attention and wake up to the issues that surround them?

In the faculty mail room the next morning, I spy the note-waving administrator looking rather sullen as he fishes some memos out of his box. His appearance and demeanor mirror the room we are in: disheveled, a bit too small, and smelling of burnt coffee and toner cartridges. I rush over to him, desperate to shed my apathetic ways and become more involved in the criminal investigation. Maybe I could offer to head a committee to interview suspects expertly culled from my lengthy detention lists.

"Are those notes still circulating? Because I'd really like to help." I speak too quickly and too close to his face, so he steps back and braces himself against the copy machine.

"We figured it out," he says, sounding like Eeyore with a load of shit weighing down his pants.

"Who was it? Do I know him?" I ask excitedly. I quickly scan through the entire student facebook in my mind. My mouth drips with anticipatory saliva. "Did you have to expel the bully?"

He looks at his shoes. "No, it was all a hoax." He seems saddened by the lack of an evil scapegoat or a decent public hanging on the middle school quad. "Those notes were just harmless pieces of dialogue from *The Lord of the Rings*."

Methinks I misheard. "Huh?"

"The movie, not the book. One of the notes mentioned 'the throne of Gondor,' which kind of clued us in."

"Shit. Sorry," I call after him as he is leaving, wondering what Roy Cohn said as he watched a drunk and beaten Joe McCarthy pack his handbag, put on his high heels, and wobble away from Washington. Now that my one new cause has evaporated I have nothing left to do but go home, put on my doublet, breeches, and stockings, and choose among the bilbo, pillory, or stocks that Lala is bound to offer this forever doubting Thomas.

Oh, Behave!

The term *appropriate* has been haunting me lately. I hear it used daily, mostly in the negative sense: "Jack was acting inappropriately in class today when he imitated a flatulent monkey" or "*Fight Club* is not appropriate reading material for easily influenced middle-schoolers who just need an excuse to throw some haymakers." Teachers and administrators bandy the term about with authority as if there is a Goofus-and-Gallant-style reference book hidden somewhere in the teachers' lounge that lists the right and wrong ways for a thirteen-year-old boy to adjust his junk in class or if it's better to teach sexist Hemingway than racist Twain in a freshman literature course. The truth of the matter is that the A-word is both reflexive and relative in nature. The dictionary definition flatly states that something's appropriate if it's suitable or compatible. It doesn't say to whom

and under which set of circumstances. Talking about female ejac-
ulation in health class with a lesbian teacher is fair game (and an
easy A); doing the same with a mysteriously celibate math teacher
is not. That's why in 7:00 A.M. detention this week I monitored a
set of still-confused boys who hadn't seen anything wrong with
throwing wet toilet paper at a window or drawing gigantic boobs
on the chalkboard with a bean burrito. They weren't hurting anybody (compatible), and everyone in their small audience seemed
pleased with the outcome (suitable).

Yesterday, in our beloved auditorium, in front of the set for
Romeo and Juliet, a play you could argue promotes teen suicide, a
visiting writer named Steve Almond spoke in front of two hundred boys and girls ranging in ages from fourteen to eighteen. In
the back sat visitors to the school, administrators, and any faculty
who decided not to cut to check e-mail or go down the street to
gulp coffee and read the paper. Steve is an old college buddy of
mine, and he read from *Candyfreak*, his best-selling book on his
obsession with candy, and how he channeled this freakish fetish
to learn more about the declining state of the privately owned
confection industry in America today. The school was worked up
about his visit, since half the students had read the book and the
other half expected to see candy in some state of undress during
the talk. Even the faculty wanted to know what happened to
their favorite candy bars, which had disappeared with their youth,
good looks (if they had them), and senses of humor and self-
awareness. Needless to say, the Candy Man's (as the kids called
him) presentation was as well received as an all-you-can-eat
buffet by a pack of ravenous truck drivers. During the Q&A por-
tion of the show, Steve told them he'd give away chocolate bars to
the first five students who asked questions. Hands shot into the
air like fans vying for a home run ball during the World Series.

Steve spoke to them in a wide variety of ways about a wide variety of subjects, including:

1. Playfully calling our constituency a bunch of fucknuts
2. Impelling them to reintroduce the word *dickweed* into their vernacular
3. Mentioning that he masturbated on a regular basis
4. Admitting freely that he'd gotten high at his bar mitzvah and binged on candy because, after all, "he was a man"

I should say in full disclosure (even though no one ever fully discloses when they accuse something of being inappropriate) that he also spoke eloquently on the nature of beauty and art, self-awareness, writing, and the state of American manufacturing. As you might expect, all the kids and some of the faculty adored the Candy Man. He offered the correct blend of candor, wit, politics, and showmanship that they craved from a mandatory event where you are required to sit silently for just under an hour. A mob followed him out of the auditorium, shaking both his tainted hands, shouting various forms of slang thank-yous at his back, and begging him to sign their candy bars as well as books. In fact, one student told me later when asked to describe the Candy Man's style that it was, I kid you not, "appropriate."

The other reaction I received, although indirectly, was that Steve's use of profanity and glorified mention of drug use was, in fact, the opposite. It was inappropriate for a formal presentation at a school. Even though I knew where that kind of reaction would come from, it bummed me out. I started thinking of my most closed-minded, tight-assed, out-of-touch, lame-o colleagues, and what kind of karate moves I'd employ if they confronted me with such blather. Then I realized that trying to convince someone to change their opinion about language and the profane was like my brother trying to persuade my father at the dinner table that pot slowed the world down and made him a better driver.

The messy idea of behavior suitable to the circumstance isn't limited to students in the educational clusterfuck. The week before Steve showed up at our school bearing his GooGoo Clusters for all to see (and touch), the faculty had been bused down like a junior varsity basketball team to Albuquerque to attend a conference. I basically slept through the keynote speaker, who carried the radical message of taking computers out of education until the high school years because, like text messaging, they were just a time-wasting distraction. His appeal was diluted by a distinct lack of preparation, a most anemic presence onstage, and the fact that he performed mime part time on the side. The only ones who seemed to care about his ideas were a group of computer geeks who had heightened (and disconcerting) emotional reactions in the manner of a child being forcibly weaned from a sugar tit.

After the talk we were shepherded across the street in so-called affinity groups. I lingered, checking my cell phone for messages from Lala, who was picking me up (read: saving me) in a packed minivan after my brief tour of dull duty. We planned on spending a weekend in southern New Mexico, where it was warmer and where more of my alcoholic friends lived. The English teachers' klatch was held in the basement of the Albuquerque Convention Center, an artificial corridor that the sun's rays had never penetrated. We met in a small room with an overabundance of fluorescent lights and peach chairs stolen from some Italian wedding reception. About a dozen English teachers sat in a circle atop hideous floor covering, nervously fondling their name tags. Oh, what a motley crew we were! Two of the men looked as though they were in a contest to see who could grow Walt Whitman's beard the fastest. Most of the women had bad dye jobs—metallic rinses that made their mousy brown hair look like the color of old candy wrappers. I wasn't any better with my *James at 15* haircut and two-day-old stubble, highlighting my extended family of chins. It was a sad sight indeed. To make it worse, none of us could even remotely dress. Bad polyester suits, white socks with black shoes over pants far too short for an adult male who could still walk on his own. Even our discussion leader had on a rumpled V-neck sweater lost in the forgotten land between argyle and plaid. Seeing his fabric hangover next to such a hideous carpet made me want to hurl my overpriced Starbucks.

We pathetic pedagogues went around confessing our names, schools, and classes taught. Bad Sweater Guy had typed up some questions based on a presentation none of us had witnessed the day before. We held the paper in our hand and studied the Courier type, but we were all just stalling, like our best bullshitting students faking their way through the unread opening of *Heart of Darkness*. The hour ahead of me felt depressingly unmoored, overeducated boats drifting out to sea, so I was surprised when one of the women lifted her arm even though no one else was fighting to speak. Seeing an adult raise her hand in a silent conference room made me even sadder than watching a boy with scabby acne and greasy hair eat his sandwich alone in a crowded cafeteria. Sweater Guy called on her.

"We've just finished teaching *Julius Caesar*," the woman said, not really having anywhere to go with the story.

"That's funny, we just killed Caesar too!" a chirpy lady in glasses answered far too excitedly given the tenuous though rather bloody connection.

The first woman mentioned a Web site about checking essays for plagiarism. A few people wrote the URL down. We all looked at each other. After a pause, another woman talked about her love for the theorist Peter Elbow and his "voyage out" and "voyage back." Everyone nodded. That sounded fine. Voyages were fine. Out or back. Didn't matter which. It was clear that our hour together would be fine, nice, okay, appropriate, and totally uninteresting. Maybe it was the sheets of fluorescent light too close above my scalp, but I felt transported somehow, watching the group from a distance—my voyage out, if you will. What an odd meeting this was, thirteen complete strangers in a basement talking about Web sites that probably wouldn't help anyone catch cheaters (and *everyone* cheats, I was reminded in this meeting). The gathering was absolutely humorless and without a cuticle of human connection. During my voyage back, my disconnection turned into aggravated irritability.

"Any more questions?" Sweater Guy asked with a watered-down smile. In my boredom-induced delusion, the V-neck became a giant mouth for this man.

I wanted to yell *Yes, I have a question. What blind person designed this awful carpet and what exactly was the bastard thinking?*

When the V-mouth belched, "What else, as teachers, do we need?" I wanted to go *Liar Liar* on their asses and shout, *Look around! We all need someone to teach us how to fucking dress! Even my worst nerd knows not to wear white socks with black shoes. Who will teach us to groom ourselves? Have you guys ever heard of a beard trimmer? Can't we go get some goddamn exercise? We should all be at fat camp right now rolling on balls or sweating on stationary bikes so we don't up and die in class like my geometry teacher did on me!*

After my interior rant, with my department head beside me (who wears only purple, I might add), I felt horrible. I'm sure all these teachers were deeply dedicated to their students and the profession, and I was a terrible man for thinking these things even though I included myself fully in my own misguided rage. I shouldn't be a high school teacher, I thought, if I can't care about TurnItIn.com or finding new rubrics to assess spatial-visual learning projects for someone with a nonverbal learning disorder and chronic dandruff.

The chirpy woman to my right raised her hand even though again no one was vying for the floor. On her nose perched small spectacles with frames as round as Necco wafers, and her Dorothy Hamill haircut showed flecks of silver that flickered in the glare of artificial light.

She nodded as if in prayer. "I feel I need to share something with the group." I hoped it was something confessional, like she was a damn convincing pre-op tranny or was prone to farting if she felt claustrophobic. Anything to save the day.

"I created something I call Junior Poet, and oh God . . ." She was getting worked up now. "This is so exciting. Wait until you hear this." Her hands accordioned in front of her face like she was manically trying to decide the size of a fish she once caught in Lake Killmyself. Her breathing quickened and became more audible. I couldn't stop staring at her ass, not because it was particularly shapely, but because it kept lifting ever so slightly off the banquet chair. This woman desperately wanted to stand and deliver.

"I tell them, 'Fall in love! Fall in love with a poet! Keep reading and reading until you fall in love.' " She had the habit of adding an additional modifier or noun in her sentences, even though her point was quite clear without the extra sauce. Given our pulseless meeting of strangers with a limited amount of time, I could tell that (a) this woman would go on way too long even for gassy windbags, (b) everyone thought her level of emotion and ramble was inappropriate, and (c) I loved this woman for saving me from jamming my Pilot Precise V7 fine-line pen into my right tear duct.

"One boy—oh, he's a good one—he chose Carl Sandburg's 'Chicago' poem, you all know the one that goes 'City of the big shoulders'?" I don't know if it's a cliquey thing or we lonely English teachers need to feel validated in what we teach, but we all assume the other pencil pusher has read what we have. I knew as much about Sandburg as I did about photomultiplier tubes, and I bet I wasn't alone, but I nodded like a goddamn bobblehead anyway.

"What this boy did with the poem was . . ." Here's where the happy lady lost her shit. She didn't stand up per se (though I desperately wanted to invite her to) but leaned forward in such a way that she looked as though she was taking a dump in a nasty outhouse and didn't want her ass to graze the diseased seat. In this weird diving position, she reenacted her student's entire project, including other classmates recruited to play the roles of characters in the poem.

"Shovel shovel shovel," she said dramatically, pantomiming a character in the poem holding an oversized spade. "Shovel shovel shovel."

The gawking group relaxed a bit after the tidying ended, thinking she'd wrap it up, but then the toolmaker came out with his own particular set of sound effects: "Chink chink chink," she sang. "Chink chink chink." It was like a one-woman show of *Nicholas Nickleby* as we sat through the sounds of the hog butcher, wheat stacker, and player with railroads. I knew the next week I would hear my colleagues complain how this nutball wasted all our time but for now I tried to enjoy the show as I waited for my getaway van, complete with dual DVD players to hypnotize the kids, to come and rescue me.

Arrested Development

Some administrators believe that professional development is an essential part of a teacher's growth and might prevent guys like me from turning into the dead batteries and dust piles I had putting me to sleep in junior high. Besides the in-services held on campus where an overpaid facilitator is flown in to introduce the faculty to a new method of disciplining without the use of duct tape, teachers are encouraged to conquer their xenophobia and venture outside the safe confines of campus to learn something new elsewhere. Science teachers routinely attend conferences with sexy titles like "Waiting Time and Seed Selection for Homology Search" and "Why Our Students Are So Obsessed with Hermaphrodites." You can tell the lab rat has been away from school by the fresh sadistic look in his eye, a new tie-dyed lab coat, or a recently purchased necktie with the chemical formula of sheep semen printed boldly on the front. History teachers annually present papers on whether Columbus spread more syphilis than Al Capone, and at their conferences I imagine math geeks reenact scenes from *Star Wars* using protractors for light sabers. After nine years at Prep, I figured it was time for me to sit quietly in the back of a class instead of shouting in front of one. My friend Nancy, who teaches adult writing seminars, wanted to do the same, so we found a workshop in a locale that offered seaside air for her and a slew of microbrewed beers for me. Since there was money available for professional development, I swiped the school's credit card when the business manager wasn't looking and off we went.

The goal of the workshop, according to the brochure, was to "push your writing to a more perilous level." Most of what I do in my class is work around the idea that writing isn't masturbation and someone has to read the damn thing, so it might want to make some sense. I try to explain to my teenagers that stories that end with "and then I woke up" or "suddenly I turned gay" aren't very satisfying to the reader, nor are stories where everything gets slaughtered by a guy who looks a lot like Quentin Tarantino in a trench coat. I thought the idea of taking more risks in their work was a good one for my students and might remind me what it's like to be a student again.

Nancy and I checked in to our hotel, which was rubber-tipped pointer distance from the beach. Unlike arid New Mexico, where urine evaporates before it hits the bowl, the air in the Pacific Northwest was rather moist and chilly enough to make my nipples stand up and salute. Since this was going to be a period of professional and personal renewal for me, I decided to adopt a ritual like the ones I taught in books, most notably *Walden*, where Thoreau dragged his hairy ass into a murky pond every day to forget about never getting laid. I too would plunge myself into the water each afternoon to "Renew thyself completely each day; do it again, and again, and forever again." I told Nancy all about my plan.

"Thoreau was a fatty and nuts," she said. "Besides, that water looks cold." We watched the waves roll in.

"No big deal," I boasted. "I grew up on the water. I could swim before I could walk." As kids, my brothers and I were never afraid to go into the ocean. That was until I slipped on an errant clam and fell off a dock. My friend Andrew's father, who worked for the fire department, had to pull me out by my hair like a drowned troll doll. Later that year, he got promoted to fire chief, while around my house my older brother promoted me to Pussy of the Year.

Still, even with my ostraconophobia, I was ready for something to wake me up from close to a decade of teaching teenagers. "Don't you want to go?" I asked Nancy, who was reading a glossy brochure on picturesque hikes in the area. "It will renew you!"

She didn't even bother to glance up. "I'll be renewed enough watching."

"Suit yourself," I said, and scampered up the stairs to my hotel room to slip on some shorts and grab a towel. The beach was littered with people starting bonfires and riding rented bicycles that allowed you to recline while you pedaled. Huge rocks infested with wildlife framed the long beach, and I couldn't contain my excitement at being in such a lovely setting after nine months in a dusty classroom under lights that hummed louder than a plague of locusts.

"Maybe we could rent some of those bicycles when we get a break during our workshop," I told Nancy as we walked to the water's edge.

"Do you feel okay?" She pressed the back of her hand against my forehead.

"Yes, why?"

"I'd rather die than get caught riding around on bikes that are for people who are too fat to walk the beach. Look over there." She pointed to a rotund family of four who pedaled frantically in circles, trying to steer their squat-cycles. "The mom still has fudge stains on her shirt."

Nancy sat with her back up against a beached log and crossed her legs. Behind her loomed what appeared to be a small white oil derrick with a huge clown nose at one end. Because the beach was so long, these contraptions, when pulled, alerted lifeguards to emergencies like a possible drowning or a fudge eater who couldn't extricate himself from his smelly bike seat.

"No one over thirteen is even near the water, you know." She placed her hand over her eyes and scanned the shoreline for anything resembling a sane adult.

"Don't be such a wuss," I said, but she had a point. The only ones swimming were young kids in jeans who had enough blubber on them to live with seals in the Antarctic. I removed my shirt and sunglasses and sprinted across the wet sand. In that brief moment, I made a mental note to call my father to tell him how I was proudly carrying on the Wilder tradition of swimming in any body of water in any season. His second son was the only adult brave enough to even try to tackle the piercing Pacific. My profession hadn't made me soft, content to sit on a couch with an out-of-print book sipping tepid coffee in a music teacher's mug that reads "Out Chopin." Then my feet went numb and I fell headfirst into a wave. I've had mini nightmares of cardiac arrest before—my arm going dead after throwing a football with London, or chest pains after a very spicy chimichanga—but this water let me know I wasn't even close to experiencing the real thing before. My frank and beans recoiled into my chest cavity, my heart stopped, and my scalp felt as though I had been struck by lightning. Panicked, I could see Nancy on the shore staring up at the sky instead of watching her friend die. My legs were like two frozen salmon, and I could hardly get out of the water. I made two long strides toward the shore, then flopped onto the hard sand. "Did you see me out there?" I asked before spitting up a pint glass worth of seawater.

"I thought about pulling the emergency flag, but I'm feeling a bit jetlagged." She yawned and scratched her back on the log.

"Thanks a lot."

"Well, if you want to get your blood moving, why don't you rent one of your special-ed bikes?"

The next morning we attended orientation in the local elementary school gymnasium. Our workshop was made up of mostly other English teachers who were either developing professionally or trying to fool themselves into believing they'd write the great American novel instead of teaching it. In addition, there were some locals who had been through the workshop before, including a punk rocker, two massage therapists, and a guy who tried to sell us green algae wholesale out of the trunk of his car. Our first assignment given to us by our ex-hippie instructors was to compose two pages of writing that was so honest and true that just reading them would stop someone from jumping off a ledge. We would each read our work aloud the next day, and our instructors would teach us how to approach the manuscript using their patented technique. The whole thing seemed straightforward enough, but something didn't sit right with Nancy.

"Did the energy seem okay to you?" she asked me during a coffee break.

"Energy?" I thought that outside of our New Age hometown of Santa Fe, she wasn't allowed to use such psychobabble.

"Something didn't feel right about those instructors. Even the students seemed a bit off. Why would someone on a ledge need two pages of writing? Wouldn't they need a ladder or a decent shrink?"

"I'm sure it will be fine," I said, patting her back.

"You felt the same way yesterday about swimming, but you ended up looking like a comatose manatee."

I didn't care what she said; I needed this workshop. After a decade of reading three-to-five-page essays, I was burning out. It wasn't that my interest was waning on the role of roadkill in *The Grapes of Wrath*; I was just dog-tired. These benevolent instructors would help me rekindle my energy for the fall semester. I saw myself coming to class on essay day and grabbing those fresh pages like a patient happily reaching for his meds.

Our group met in the kindergarten classroom, where we squeezed into small chairs with desks attached. You could tell by the orange blinds and wood paneling that the building was erected when Gerald Ford was still falling down the presidential stairs. There was a lot of nervous energy in the room. The punk rocker was sticking a pen in and out of an aperture in his earlobe the size of a dog's asshole. Nancy had been up all night working on her piece and was a bit edgy, running her hands through her hair and squirming in her little seat like a speed freak.

"Welcome," our instructor, Chi, said. He was tall with thinning hair and wore sandals made from nautical rope. "I hope you all had a chance to familiarize yourself with the index of terms in your packet, since we will be using those as we work through each page."

"Index?" I asked Nancy.

"First I heard of it."

We thumbed through our packet of readings and found what they were talking about: three single-spaced pages of terms, definitions, and symbols. It read more like the Rosetta stone than the *Dummies' Guide to Teaching Writing*. The urban massage therapist volunteered to go first and read her story about a woman who liked to shout at men she saw on TV.

"Wow," Chi started. "You honor us with your voice. What I notice right away is how you Jacob's ladder your way into the piece, embedding the bodyness before you employ the scaffolding move. Very nice."

"What's a Jacob's ladder?" Nancy asked.

"It's in the index," the female teacher answered from inside her tent of a dress. She had two names that ran together when she said them. I heard Tigerlily, but Nancy later said it sounded more like Piccadilly. We never bothered to clarify. "It's an emotional hook for the reader," she told us.

"Another way to look at it is a barrel roll reversed," Chi added, nodding.

"Barrel roll?"

"It's in your index." Tigerlily pointed to the paper in front of her.

"Right." Nancy rolled her eyes.

It seemed that except for a few other English teachers and a nicely groomed guy from New York, everyone else was well versed in this cryptic language. Even the punk rocker, with his love/hate/death tattoos wrapping around his wrists, knew the score. "I'm always wrong and I kinda hate myself so you shouldn't listen to me," he said, "but I really like how you keep your words in a straight line. Mine always end up crooked. But that's me and I basically suck."

"Crooked?" Nancy asked, but was met with a chorus of disapproving looks. "I know." She nodded fatefully. "In the index."

My head was spinning. While I tried to make sense of the cryptic glossary, Nancy had quietly slipped her packet and sixteen copies of her story into her backpack and waited with her hands folded on the kidney-shaped desk.

"Mmmm," Tigerlily moaned. "I love the violet symmetry you achieve in the bed scene, but I'm not sure about the exactitude of your prescription bottle description."

"Yeah. I hear your music, but is the essence of the bottle truly orange?" Chi peered closer.

"More brownish," someone said.

"Sienna," the rural masseuse suggested.

"Native American sunburn," an Asian woman from San Francisco chanted.

Then we heard a rattling from the punk rocker's desk. He was holding up what had to be painkillers. He shook them over his head like a flamenco dancer trapped in the Betty Ford Center.

Nancy stood up. "I'm using a Jacob's ladder to get the hell out of here. I've had enough of this Jim Jones shit."

Either they were accustomed to folks bailing on the first day or they didn't notice because their noses were too deep up the story's ass, but no one said a word as Nancy exited by the picture of George Washington, the caption underneath him reading "Do you know who this is?"

I cannot tell a lie: I was there to help my teenage students write better, but I was caught in a bizarre world where people spoke fairy language about a subject I thought I knew something about. I have never had the balls to walk out of a Michael Bay movie, let alone a class. A round English teacher in a maroon turtleneck who regrettably resembled an eggplant placed her piece facedown on all our desks. When Punk Rock Guy turned it over and started reading, she shouted, "Don't! We all have to turn it over at the same time!" When she realized what she must have sounded like to a group of adults who weren't in her therapy group, she clamped on a smile and said, "Is that okay? I just need it that way."

"It's totally fine," Tigerlily whispered. "We call that requesting the requested."

I should have taken the woman's outburst as a sign to run away, because after we turned her pages over and she started reading, it became quite clear that these two sheets of type were the most unintelligible things I had ever seen. I could understand the words—*contraction, fluid, canal,* even *undulate*—but the way they were put together made Charles Manson appear logical. My daughter's fourth-grade classmate fresh off the boat from Russia could write more coherent sentences using just his feet. The room was as silent as old George scowling at us from the wall. The students looked to the instructors to save them using their fog machine language, but even the hippie pair was perplexed, their red pens frozen above the page.

"Wow," Tigerlily said, as I'm sure she'd said so many times, but this *wow* sounded the way a stoner might have said it if he'd accidentally killed and eaten his girlfriend during a particularly bad mushroom trip.

The English teacher jumped into the middle of our circle, shaking her pages. "Did everyone get it? I mean, you all know it was written from the point of view of a fetus being born. Right? Right?"

"But a fetus can't talk or even think, really." Chi clasped his hands together in prayer.

"I know." She arched her back. "That's why I'm excited about this piece. It's so fresh."

Punk Rock Guy fiddled with the string of bullet casings around his neck. "I'm probably wrong and fetuses are definitely cool, but it is kinda confusing."

"I wanted it to be that way." She crossed her arms defiantly.

Tigerlily nodded dauntingly. "What you've done here is brave and risky, but I have to what we call sear your heart." She turned to Nancy's empty chair. "It's not in the index yet." Then she turned back to the sad eggplant. "What you are trying to do here is nearly impossible. It will be a real battle to make something like this work."

While she was talking, you could see a slight tremor ripple in the English teacher's face. She had tried to hold it together, but when Tigerlily said that last line, everything above the maroon turtleneck broke open like a giant infected zit.

"I'm tired of battling!" she yelled. "I'm tired of people telling me I'm impossible!"

"If you'd let me help you . . . ," Chi said, holding his hennaed palms open.

"Everyone is always trying to silence my inner writer."

"Think of what you are attempting to do. You're trying to tell the story from the perspective of something that has no language, no thoughts. We need more from a story."

The English teacher threw herself to the floor. "How can I do more? I only have a fetus to work with!"

I don't know if this is human nature, but the rest of the class came to her defense in some rally-round-the-lunatic moment.

"That is true, she does only have a fetus," the rural masseuse admitted, running her fingers through the hair on her legs.

The metrosexual from New York thumbed desperately through the index trying to find the right term to offer. "Maybe she could use a humming engine to drive this story."

"My inner writer doesn't agree with you!" the eggplant shrieked.

"That lady dude is really messed," the punk rocker said, and started having intercourse with his ear using a ballpoint pen.

Nothing we said seemed to comfort her. What I realized was that I had left my family in order to reinvigorate my career but ended up in a *Cuckoo's Nest*–meets–*Christmas Carol* version of my own classroom back at home.

When I hauled myself back to my hotel room, I called Nancy and told her to meet me on the beach, stat. I needed a decent heart attack after all that cultish insanity.

"So tell me, how did it go?" she asked, reclaiming her position against the log. Her face looked refreshed from the sea air while mine was as pinched as newborn monkey's ass.

"You won't believe me if I told you." I sighed.

"Did you learn something to help your students?"

"Yeah, don't drink the Kool-Aid."

Nancy told me about an amazing hike she'd taken that afternoon in a scenic national park. We had both seen wildlife that day, but hers was far less frightening than mine was. She would spend the rest of her week trekking woody trails, watching surfers on a nearby beach, or sipping espresso in little cafés along the coast. Since Prep was paying, I would be forced to spend four more days trapped in a workshop haunted by the ghost of Timothy Leary on a very bad acid trip.

"Now you know how your students feel," Nancy joked.

"Very funny."

Not even the baby seal kids dared to go in the frigid water that afternoon. I had to redeem my day and this trip, so I summoned up the courage to swim again. I took a running start and raced into the water, feeling the familiar shock and awe in my genital junk drawer. When I resurfaced, I realized the water was actually colder than before, just below fifty degrees. My body went numb, and I lapsed into shock. On the shore, Nancy was chatting away with a bearded man dressed in a red flannel shirt and a yellow raincoat. I tried to signal to her that this was the big one, but she was far too busy ignoring me. Starting to panic, I dragged my frozen body to shore using my elbows and knees. Just before I hit land, a huge wave rocked me from behind, tumbling me like a frozen drink and spitting me onto shore in a twisted heap.

"Oh fuck," I yelled, trying to untie my limbs.

"That was a sneaker wave," the Morton's fisherman said to Nancy. "Your friend should never turn his back on the ocean."

Sneaker wave? I knew Nike was big in this area, but could they buy actually rights to a goddamn force of nature?

"These rogue waves can be pretty fierce," the salty dog continued. "Probably how this here log ended up on shore." He waved a crooked finger at Nancy's Appalachian La-Z-Boy. "Them sneakers can run as much as a hundred yards up the beach. In water this cold, they could probably kill you."

"Did you hear that, Rob?" Nancy shouted to me. "You got your ass kicked by a sneaker wave."

As I sat there in a crumpled mess, I thought this was how my students must feel after a rigorous year of chemistry, precalc, American history, PSATs, SATs, APs, sports, and community service, not to mention my own Jacob's ladder assignments of reading and writing. I'd come a long way to help my pupils write better, but instead it took a near-drowning experience after a class full of wackos to realize what it was like to be a student again. I vowed to take it a little easier on my classes next fall and keep an eye out for stories about the unborn.

Gradufection

My British friend Harry says that graduation at Prep reminds him of a proper bloody English garden party. He had dropped someone off at our most recent ceremony and witnessed what I have grown to consider usual, even for southwestern-casual Santa Fe: hordes of women in white dresses and wide-brimmed straw hats walking arm in arm with men in the formal outfits usually donned by undertakers and members of the Secret Service. "I thought in America you all wore those stupid mortarboards and blue polyester gowns," he added in his thick Oxbridge accent. I think what struck him as strange was that with our recent drought, you can't find a green garden within miles. To him, the sight of two hundred people in white and blue trudging across the brown background of New Mexican landscape made him wonder if the Mormons had left Utah to find an imported beer and edible enchilada.

At Prep, it's been a long-standing tradition that the girls in the graduating class wear cream-colored dresses and carry flowers while the boys wear jackets and ties. Even though no one says it outright, this code of arms and legs feels classier than the plastic tablecloths the kids at the large public high school drape over themselves come graduation day. People don't actually say "classier" or "more elegant," however; they whisper "Isn't that a nice idea?" or "I think they look nicer than caps and gowns, don't you?" as if prep school fashion was somehow connected to extreme acts of kindness, and the Dalai Lama was just waiting on his delivery of a midnight-blue legacy blazer from J. Crew. But as with any degree of class or snobbery of distinction, a level of one-upmanship always occurs, and this year I noticed it first-hand.

The week before graduation, the maintenance men wheel the pressure washer out of the closet and hose down everything, erasing any evidence of child, adult, or animal that ever scurried down our hallowed halls. Every nonessential item is obliterated: the colored chalk on the cement celebrating Tina's sixteenth birthday; limp ribbons tied to the handrails left over from the middle school dance; dog-eared copies of Cliff's Notes littering the quad; inhalers, acne cream, and the prescription drugs of the young and unhealthy; even a few copies of *Walden* that were sadly untouched (not unlike Thoreau himself). After the educational enema, mothers on the graduation committee drive in and unload racks of flowers from the backs of air-conditioned SUVs. This year's arrangements were even more spectacular than the last, shoots and buds exploding from pots like floral fireworks frozen in midair. Yellow and white blossoms erupted at the ends of long green stems, which were then hung around the upper school quad like shrunken heads at a cannibal cabal.

During the procession, every girl's dress seemed fancier than the one before, each creamier in color, lighter in fabric, draped like the smallest European curtain or laced like a sailor's silky guide to tying the most elaborate knots. Some wore shiny silk bodices over skirts waving with scalloped edges; others dared to go strapless, hoping their newfound twins would hold up fine during the ceremony.

Even the flowers the girls customarily hold seemed to be vying for some botanical prize. The first girl, last name beginning with *A*, carried the standard fare of a half dozen white roses, at which the crowd let out an audible yawn. "So last year," you could hear someone whispering under the portal in the back. "And the year before that," someone else added. The next girl in the line went for volume, sporting a dozen white roses tangled in a bondage of greenery. Due to its girth, she cradled it in her arms like a newborn baby weaned on Crisco. In the middle of the procession, one girl switched her point of attack and went not for volume, creativity, or freshness but exoticism, pulling out a single bird of paradise. Photographers rushed to the grassy runway, trying to capture the revolutionary change in mood, but quickly stopped shooting as the shampoo ginger, and heliconia platystachys also sprang into view.

I took Poppy along this year, not because our babysitters had all quit or as a unique form of discipline, but because the kid actually wanted to attend. Her horseback riding teacher had been named valedictorian, and Poppy wished to support her, but with my daughter, it runs deeper than that. She loves drama and performance of any sort. She can sit through two and a half hours of sentimental baccalaureate speeches and dramatic readings from

Dr. Seuss' *Oh, the Places You'll Go* and barely wrinkles her program. Last year, Lala and I brought London to the ceremonies, thinking he had inherited the same über-focus gene, but we were dead wrong. Instead, we spent 150 minutes taking turns watching our son spit into the ornamental fountain outside the auditorium.

After the lineup of awards, presentations, commendations, remarks, reflections, choral exercises, benedictions, handshaking, backslapping, and ceremonial ringing of bells, I retrieved Poppy from her seat with the horseback family and headed toward the reception held at the school commons building. I do not consider myself a bitter man, yet after ten years of graduation ceremonies (not counting three of my own) and the gassy garnishes that accompany them, I find the reception fare as difficult to swallow as stale popcorn with a light sprinkling of asbestos. It's a lot like speed dating when you are severely hung over—you are surrounded by, and expected to speak to, current graduates, their extended families and friends, postgraduates who come to show off their facial hair, and parents who are still recovering from last year's empty-nest syndrome and are not ready to leave the Prep cult just yet. A teacher in June has just finished grading essays and blue books, calculating grades, writing narrative reports for each and every student, inventorying books, making space in the office for the new hire, and attending meetings, committees, final sports events, and all the painful sideshows leading up to graduation. You're spent. By June, you're not only exhausted but fully unprepared for the "Hello, how are you?" and "Where ya from?" and "You must be proud!" small talk of the reception. What you are prepared for is a frontal body massage, big-screen TV, and a long bath filled with imported vodka.

Luckily for me, my date was raring to go. Lala had dressed Poppy in a blue floral top, a skirt with ruffles, and a snow-white skullcap stolen from the artist formerly known as Cat Stevens. My feeling of dread was balanced by my daughter's optimism that yo, she was gonna party up in here. Without London to demand we ride the handicapped elevator at least six times, we descended the stairs to the dining hall with all the other well-dressed marchers. At the landing below, next to the PE teacher's postings on rampant eating disorders, there was a logjam of people in varying shapes and sizes all trying to get inside to shovel the food into their mouths. I placed Poppy in front of me to shield her from the well-loofahed hips and elbows, and when she took her place, two metal shanks clipped the back of my heels, sending shooting bolts of pain that buckled my knees. "What the fuh . . . ?" I asked, barely cutting the profanity off at half-mast. I turned around, expecting to see two students playing some sort of revengeful joke on me for receiving bad grades. What I viewed instead was a lady as old as *The Odyssey* in a wheelchair pushed by a member of the board.

"Sorry," the pusher said, and if it hadn't been so packed I would have bent over to massage the last shreds of my Achilles tendons. Turned out that my lack of mobility or personal space was a blessing of sorts. Because I couldn't move, I didn't have to make small talk to those around me. It is impossible to turn and visit with your neighbor if you cannot pivot your head without kissing the person next to you. If this were my graduation in the 1980s, I would have made a joke about a Who concert set in Cincinnati. Instead, I listened as the middle-schoolers started mooing loudly like cattle with microphones.

"What's going on?" a current parent asked no one in particular.

When parents visit schools that cost over $15,000 a year, they expect immediate answers even if they don't know who exactly they're asking.

"I'm not sure," the pusher said, shrugging. "It's usually crowded, but never like this."

One of my more crisis-driven colleagues spoke up just as he did in faculty meetings, in-services, and any pancake breakfast within one hundred miles. Some people live for emergencies, and this was the type of guy who wanted to call the ambulance for a nosebleed. "We need a bigger venue," he demanded, holding a finger high in the air. "I told the admin that last year, but they never listen. They never listen!"

"I say we put a tent on the field next time!" a chirpy member of the fund-raising committee offered, always trying to put a positive spin on any unfortunate event ranging from overloaded detention rosters to prisoner abuse in Iraq. Bad news meant a failed capital campaign, so sadness was mostly unacceptable.

"It's the chocolate bar," a graduation mom whispered from behind her program. Like her daughter, commencement was a great occasion to show the world she had breasts, and her dress helped us all understand the sum of her assets.

"The what?"

"It's supposed to be a surprise. They have a fountain of chocolate. You can dip stuff in it." She giggled conspiratorially, then peered around the crowd as if she just let slip the identity of Deep Throat.

At the mention of chocolate, Poppy's face lit up like a Roman candle in a gunpowder factory, and it stayed frozen in that shape as we shuffled along, past the locked networked classroom with its computer screens newly purged of porn and violent role-playing games. Then, as we turned the corner, we saw it. Towering

over the fancy mob was a three-tiered chocolate tower, straight
out of Willy Wonka's phallic wet dream. The liquid chocolate was
pumped from a deep well, spurted in bursts, and then cascaded
over three cliffs in sheets like a Hawaiian waterfall. At the pool's
edge lay various items to dip into the cocoa lagoon—strawberries,
small cakes, and cookies in shapes and sizes as varied as the
dresses and flowers we had seen hours earlier. Poppy started
jumping up and down like a skinny Oompa-Loompa ready to eat
Veruca Salt with a dash of pepper. I sent her to stand in line with a
dreadlocked student of mine who was really annoyed by war while
I waited on the perimeter with all the sweaty claustrophobics. In
years past, the spread at the reception had offered everything
from stale Vienna fingers and anemic punch to healthy wraps
stuffed with bean sprouts and tofu brined in clam urine. The
chocolate fountain was hands-down (and fingers-in) the most
extravagant show so far and everyone realized it, crowding the
area like, as my father would say, "it was going outta style." One
man walked by with a plastic plate piled high with a mound of
chocolate-covered business; by the windows looking onto the
soccer field a woman showed no fear, nibbling corn-on-the-cob
style on four dripping strawberries skewered in a row.

The parents on the graduation committee were hauling strawberries in by the crate, sweating like cross-dressing Teamsters
and having to butt people with their heads in order to restock fast
enough. The chocolate goo spread like the sweetest Ebola virus
you ever saw—on lips, cheeks, chins, and fingertips—into the
milling masses. The terra-cotta-colored sauce spilled onto the
tablecloths and lined the edge of the skirting near the fountain.
As people pushed through the throng, the chocolate on the exiting plates smeared across the shoulders of pressed white shirts
waiting to indulge. The infected tip of a long bamboo skewer

raked across the lapel of a seersucker jacket. The girls in the graduating class turned from the bar with hands full, smiles on their faces, and jagged lines of chocolate waist high on the dresses where their exotic bouquets had once rested. I couldn't help but look beyond the obvious and deserved elation of the day toward all the chocolate smears no one else seemed to notice. I knew from the gossip mill how much these dresses cost and could only imagine how much it would take for these stains to be removed. Was this some great cosmic joke on the nouveau riche or did one of the members of the graduation committee have a stake in a local dry-cleaning chain?

Deep into my candy-coated daydream, I lost track of Poppy but found her vertically challenged body in front of the gurgling urn. Horrified by what might occur, I frantically called her name, but it was too loud in the low-ceilinged room, and I was too late. She turned to face me with two smears across her face: the first in the shape of an oversized prison tattoo teardrop just below her left eye, and on her right cheek a dark smudge lingering like a dead man's fingerprint. There were drops and splatters on her top and skirt as if she was a living Jackson Pollock painting. I could hear Lala's voice echo through my sorry and damaged skull: *How could you let this happen? Do you know how hard it is to get chocolate out of these fabrics? Do you have any idea how much clothes cost? Why didn't you bring me any chocolate home, you thoughtless bastard?*

I had to push away Lala's future finger wagging because of the pure joy spread across my darling daughter's face. In fact, even though their expensive clothes were ruined and their teeth looked like they belonged on exiled hoboes from Candy Land, everyone else was still very happy. Maybe I was a bit too sour to taste the saccharinity of graduation day after all. Poppy scurried up to me, balancing a plate full of what would most likely come out of the Easter Bunny's ass. "Oh, Dada," she cried, "I can't wait to graduate from Prep. It will be so sweet."

I figured if I lasted that long, my daughter just might be right.

Acknowledgments

I am deeply grateful to Christopher Schelling for being a full service consejero, and all the fine folks at Ralph Vicinanza, Ltd. At Bantam Dell, I'd like to thank my dedicated editor Danielle Perez as well as Barb Burg, Chris Artis, and the rest of the crew that help champion a book. In addition, I'm thankful to Julia Goldberg, Andy Dudzik, and the *Santa Fe Reporter* staff for their ongoing encouragement.

Deep thanks and love to the following people and their families: the Wilder brothers, the Carroll sisters, Eva Wilder-Kramer, Natalie, Chris Gray, Boz and Toni, Kath and Tony, Andy and Sue, Tom and Katie G-Funk, Shireen and Jay, Jim and Mary, Lynne and Margaux, Todd and Sylvie, Annie and Jean, and all the occupants of Pinon Farm.

My deepest love and thanks to my holy trinity: Lala, Poppy, and London.

Finally, I'd like to thank the entire Santa Fe Prep community for their great sense of humor and years of support, not only for me but also for every person who steps foot on that idyllic campus.

About the Author

ROBERT WILDER is the author of *Daddy Needs a Drink*, an acclaimed collection of essays on parenting. A writer and teacher living with his wife and two children in Santa Fe, New Mexico, he has published fiction and nonfiction widely, has been a commentator for NPR's *Morning Edition*, and writes a monthly column for the *Santa Fe Reporter* called "Daddy Needs a Drink."